34.50
70u

D1525834

WITHDRAWN

"This Popular Engine"

"This Popular Engine"

New England Newspapers during the American Revolution, 1775–1789

Carol Sue Humphrey

DELAWARE

Newark: University of Delaware Press
London and Toronto: Associated University Presses

Associated University Presses
440 Forsgate Drive
Cranbury, NJ 08512

Associated University Presses
25 Sicilian Avenue
London WC1A 2QH, England

Associated University Presses
P.O. Box 39, Clarkson Pstl. Stn.
Mississauga, Ontario,
L5J 3X9 Canada

The paper used in this publication meets the requirements of the American National Standard for Permanence of Paper for Printed Library Materials Z39.48-1984.

Library of Congress Cataloging-in-Publication Data

Humphrey, Carol Sue.
   "This popular engine" : New England newspapers during the American Revolution, 1775–1789 / Carol Sue Humphrey.
      p. cm.
   Includes bibliographical references and index.
   ISBN 0-87413-430-7 (alk. paper)
   1. American newspapers—New England—History—18th century.
2. Press and politics—New England—History—18th century.
3. Newspaper publishing—New England—History—18th century.   4. New England—History—Revolution, 1775–1783.   5. New England—Politics and government—1775-1865.   I. Title.
PN4891.H86   1992
071'.4—dc20   90-50938
                                                                  CIP

PRINTED IN THE UNITED STATES OF AMERICA

To Mom and Dad

Contents

Contents

Acknowledgments

I am indebted to many people who have encouraged my work over the years. I am particularly grateful to Dr. Alan D. Watson, University of North Carolina at Wilmington; Dr J. Edwin Hendricks, Wake Forest University; and Dr. R. Don Higginbotham, University of North Carolina at Chapel Hill for their advice and support.

Many people aided in the development of this book. The staffs of the following libraries helped immensely in the research: American Antiquarian Society, Worcester, Massachusetts; The Connecticut Historical Society, Hartford, Connecticut; Essex Institute, Salem, Massachusetts; Maine Historical Society, Portland, Maine; Massachusetts Historical Society, Boston, Massachusetts; The New-York Historical Society, New York, New York; and Yale University Library, New Haven, Connecticut.

Several chapters in this book have been published previously. Chapter 3 appeared as "Producers of the 'Popular Engine': New England's Revolutionary Printers," *American Journalism* 4 (1987): 97–117. Part of chapter 5 appeared as "'That Bulwark of Our Liberties': Massachusetts Printers and the Issue of a Free Press, 1783–1788," *Journalism History* 14 (1987): 34–38. Both appear here with the permission of the editors of these two journals.

I owe thanks to Rachel Applegate for proofreading the original version of this book and to Rilda Smith for proofreading the final version. As nonhistorians, both of them asked questions that forced me to rethink parts of the manuscript. The final product is better as a result of their efforts.

Finally, and most important, my deepest love and thanks go to my family for their prayers, support, and encouragement through the good and bad times. Their faith in me and my abilities has kept me going when I wanted to give up and quit.

Introduction

Residents of Great Britain's American colonies generally viewed printing as a disseminator of information. Presses were in operation in some colonies soon after initial settlement. By mid–eighteenth century, a large portion of all printed information reached the people through the medium of newspapers. Indeed, prior to the twentieth century, most reading material consisted of the Bible, almanacs, and newspapers. Described by one Tory as "this popular engine," newspapers in the Revolutionary era constituted the most important source of information concerning public affairs.

This work studies newspapers during the American Revolution. How did they function? What role did they play? What were newspapers actually doing during the years of war and political consolidation?

For over two hundred years, historians and journalists alike have asserted that newspapers played an important role in the history of eighteenth-century America. Historians have particularly emphasized the importance of the press in rallying opinion against the British in the years before the Revolution and the function of newspapers as political party organs in the early years of the new government established by the Constitution. The years in between, however, have remained a virtual blank. Numerous essays and articles have been written, but there are no existing general works on the newspapers between 1775 and 1789. Arthur Schlesinger's *Prelude to Independence: The Newspaper War on Britain, 1764–1776* (1965) considers the years prior to the war itself and ends with the Declaration of Independence. Philip Davidson's *Propaganda of the American Revolution, 1763–1783* (1941) looks at the war years, but considers a much broader area than the newspaper press alone. Most secondary material concerning the press in this period can be found in general histories of American journalism, but even here, there is very little of real substance. Some discussion is made about changes in journalism in the period, but little effort is made to deal with the general function of the press in America at the time. Most authors quickly survey the war years

and then jump to the Constitutional Convention, apparently assuming that little of interest or importance happened during the
years of actual fighting and that the 1780s were only a time of total
chaos that finally ended with the adoption of a new form of
government. This study fills this gap through a consideration of
the Revolutionary newspaper press in New England.

In order to understand Revolutionary newspapers, one must
know something of the American press prior to the outbreak of
fighting. Chapter 1 deals with this subject. Chapter 2 discusses
printing as a business, concentrating on the problems involved in
publishing newspapers and the financial success (if any) of their
printers. Chapter 3 concerns printing as a trade, focusing on how
someone became a printer and paying particular attention to the
ninety men and three women who published the newspapers
under consideration. Chapter 4 considers the overall nature of the
newspapers at the time—what kinds of materials they contained,
how much space was devoted to what types of items, and how
widely newspapers circulated. Chapter 5 focuses on the relationship between the press and government, dealing with such
issues as government use of the press, interactions between the
government and the press, and, of course, freedom of the press.
Chapters 6, 7, and 8 consider the involvement of newspapers in
politics, not so much as a party press per se, but rather with how
the press dealt with political issues of the period. Chapter 6 looks
at how newspapers covered various problems during the war;
chapter 7 considers how the press viewed the politics of economic
concerns during the 1780s; and chapter 8 deals with how the
public prints covered the move for and adoption of a new form of
government for the nation. The final chapter contains a summary
description of what the press was like during the period under
consideration and the conclusions reached from a study of it.

The scope of the project has been limited geographically to
New England in order to examine a concise and manageable
group of newspapers. If this limitation reduces the overall ap-
plicability of some of the study's conclusions, it is balanced by the
fact that presses in New England produced more influential and
long-lived papers than those in any other section of the country.
In all, seventy-one different New England newspapers appeared
between 1775 and 1789. Of these, eleven operated for most or all
of the period.

Although restricted geographically, this study still provides an
indication of what broader role the American newspaper fulfilled
in the 1770s and 1780s. In order to better understand eighteenth-

century America, historians need to comprehend more fully this informative institution that reached so many people in an age of limited communication. By providing an in-depth examination of all the above, I hope to provide a scholarly bridge between the propaganda sheets of the 1760s–early 1770s and the political party organs of the 1790s.

"This Popular Engine"

1

Growth and Development of New England Newspapers prior to 1775

It is impossible to understand the Revolutionary press in New England without some knowledge of the beginnings of the printing industry in this area. In reviewing the development of the press prior to the Revolution, it becomes clear that the spread of presses throughout New England was a slow but steady process. The first printing press was set up in Massachusetts in 1638, but all of the New England colonies/states did not acquire their own presses until 1785. The spread of newspapers proved somewhat slower in the beginning for the first successful newssheet did not appear until 1704 (in Boston). Newspapers spread more quickly through New England, with all the colonies/states having a viable newspaper by 1785.

Stephen Daye established the first New England printing office in Cambridge in 1638. Daye and his successor, Samuel Green, published government materials and pamphlets from their shop across the river from the capital in Boston. They were joined in the business in 1665 by another shop in Cambridge and in 1675 by a Boston firm. For many years all of the printing for New England came out of the Boston area, but each colony eventually moved to gain a local printer in order to ease production of necessary government materials and as a sign of prestige for a growing area.[1]

For most eighteenth-century printers, prestige for the business came from the production of a newspaper. Benjamin Harris attempted such a publication in Boston in 1690, but was shut down for failure to acquire government permission. The first successful British American newspaper, the *Boston News-Letter,* appeared in 1704. In 1721, a second Boston sheet, the *New England Courant,* appeared. For thirty years, these two papers were the only locally produced newssheets in New England. However the establishment of printing firms throughout New England encouraged the

founding of newspapers in each of the colonies as well. By the end
of the Revolutionary era, all the states in New England had at least
one successful printer producing a newspaper, and most areas
had more than one.[2]

These facts indicate that printing spread slowly but steadily
during the first one hundred and fifty years of New England
history. Several essential elements were needed in order for the
printing business, newspapers in particular, to grow. One of these
elements was a high literacy rate. According to one study, New
England society went from being 50 percent literate in the mid–
seventeenth century to nearly universal male literacy by 1800. In
1660, the male literacy rate stood at approximately 60 percent. By
1710, it had risen to 70 percent. By 1760, approximately 85 percent
of the men residing in New England were literate.[3]

In general, the growth and spread of the press closely followed
population expansion and settlement patterns. Massachusetts's
population in 1640, two years after the arrival of the first press,
stood at close to nine thousand, with at least one thousand people
living in Boston. In the rest of New England, however, the pattern
called for a larger population. When Thomas Short moved to the
small port of New London, with a population of approximately
one thousand, Connecticut had nearly forty thousand people.
James Franklin was one of four thousand colonials in Newport
when he arrived from Boston in 1727, but these four thousand
people constituted only one-fourth of Rhode Island's total population of more than fifteen thousand. Daniel Fowle entered a
province of about thirty-three thousand New Hampshirites in
1756—about four thousand of whom lived in Portsmouth. Vermont's population stood at between forty-five and fifty thousand
when its first successful press began operation in 1780, while
Maine's had topped the fifty thousand mark before Thomas B.
Wait and Benjamin Titcomb opened their business in 1785. From
these figures, a minimum number of ten to fifteen thousand
people in a colony, with at least one thousand in the printer's
hometown, could be considered necessary for launching a printing business. Massachusetts differs slightly from this estimate,
but the press there had solid financial support from the government and the college. Furthermore, the Cambridge press produced materials for all the other New England colonies until they
acquired local printers. These two factors considered together
explain the relatively low population figures for Massachusetts at
the time of its first press.[4]

As the printing trade grew, more newspapers appeared. In
1735, four newspapers operated in New England, all in Boston

Boston — 1704
1719
1734
1735

Map 1-1

New England Newspapers, Dec. 1735 (with years of initial publication)

Portsmouth – { 1756
                1765

Boston – { 1704
            1719
            1734
            1735

Providence –
1762

Hartford – 1764

New Haven – 1755   New London –
                    1763

Newport – 1758

Map 1–2

New England Newspapers, Dec. 1765 (with years of initial publication)

(see map 1–1). By the time of the Stamp Act in 1765, there were eleven, with the same four still in Boston (see map 1–2). New sheets had been founded in Portsmouth, New Hampshire; Providence and Newport, Rhode Island; and New London, New Haven, and Hartford, Connecticut. All of these prints began publication in port cities, indicating that not only were people necessary, but also a certain level of commercial activity was essential if the paper was to get enough advertising to survive. The ports also provided access to foreign news that arrived on ships from abroad. This coastal commercial trend remained dominant until after the Revolution. Even so, the war itself brought some changes in the geographic distribution of newspaper publishing; public prints appeared in towns other than ports, beginning with the forced move of Isaiah Thomas's *Massachusetts Spy* from Boston to Worcester in 1775. For the most part, however, newspapers and port cities continued to go hand in hand, with additional papers appearing in cities that previously had sheets and others beginning in new localities such as Salem and Newburyport in Massachusetts.

Surprisingly, the quarrel with Great Britain, which began in the mid–1760s, had little, if any, clear impact on the physical growth of newspapers in New England. Some new sheets did issue forth in response to the disputes. The *Portsmouth Mercury* began publication in 1765 because some patriot leaders felt that Daniel Fowle, printer of the *New Hampshire Gazette* in Portsmouth, had not spoken out strongly enough against the Stamp Act. In Boston, in 1767 and 1771, progovernment papers appeared in an attempt to overcome the damage done by the Whig sheets led by the *Boston Gazette*. The overall number of newspapers in New England, however, did not change very much during the period. In 1765, eleven public prints appeared in seven cities. At the end of 1774, the number stood at fifteen in ten cities (see map 1–3). Rather than enlarging in spurts, the newspaper press had continued a slow, steady growth that accompanied the expansion of New England's population and economy.[5]

The press in New England, both newspapers and printing in general, experienced a gradual but consistent growth from its inception in 1638 to the Revolution in 1775. The war interrupted this expansion and public prints stagnated. Papers came and went, but the total number each year still averaged fifteen to eighteen. Only with the end of the fighting would newspapers once more be able to expand, and then their numbers would skyrocket as the country turned to face the years ahead.

Portsmouth – 1756

Newburyport – 1773

Salem – { 1768
          1774

Boston – { 1704
           1719
           1734
           1735
           1770

Providence –
1762

Hartford – 1764

Norwich – 1773   Newport – 1758

New Haven – 1755

New London –
1763

Map 1–3

New England Newspapers, Dec. 1774 (with years of initial publication)

2
Printing as a Business: One Problem after Another

During the eighteenth century, a printer's life could be vexatious: a host of problems confronted participants in the trade. Acquisition of the necessary equipment and materials usually proved difficult either through the lack of enough capital or simply through lack of availability. The usual British sources disappeared after 1775, and attempts to make local equivalents did not always succeed. During the war, newspapers often experienced interruptions in production because of military activities. Other problems, such as the procurement of news and the collection of subscription payments, abounded.

Life very seldom proved simple for those who made their living with paper, ink, and printing press. Still, most who entered the business managed to succeed, and the years following the war witnessed a phenomenal growth in the number of newspapers in New England as printers began to set up shop in towns other than the larger coastal cities.

During the Revolutionary era, a newspaper printer confronted many problems, but many still entered the profession. This proved particularly true after the war ended. The number of New England newspapers at the beginning of 1775 stood at fifteen (see map 2–1). During the war years, new sheets appeared. However, others failed and the total dropped to fourteen by the time Cornwallis surrendered at Yorktown (see map 2–2). In the next eight years, more than seventy different newspapers were published at one time or another in New England. By 1789, the total number of newspapers had reached thirty-two, more than twice as many as had appeared in 1775 (see map 2–3).

More important than the growth in numbers was the location of the new sheets. No longer limited to the larger port towns, newspapers sprouted in inland towns such as Springfield, Massachusetts; Middletown, Connecticut; Exeter, New Hampshire; and

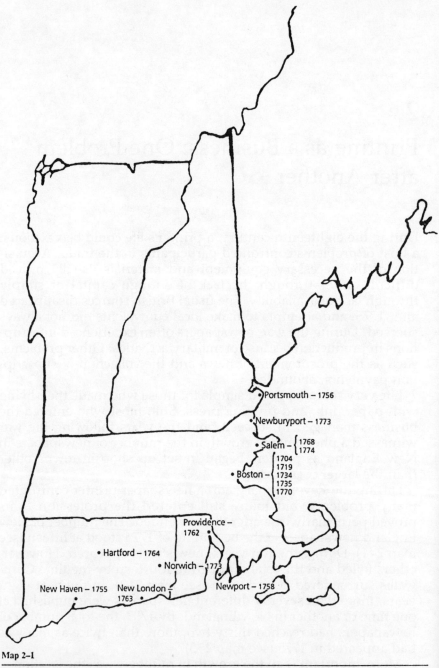

Portsmouth – 1756

Newburyport – 1773

Salem – { 1768
           1774

Boston – { 1704
           1719
           1734
           1735
           1770

Providence –
1762

Hartford – 1764

Norwich – 1773

New Haven – 1755

New London –
1763

Newport – 1758

Map 2–1

New England Newspapers, Apr. 1775 (with years of initial publication)

Portsmouth – 1756

Salem – 1781

Boston –
1719
1776
1776
1778
1781

Worcester –1775 (1770)

Providence –
1762

Hartford – 1764

Norwich – 1773

New Haven – 1755

New London –
1763

Newport –
1780 (1758)

Map 2–2

New England Newspapers, Oct. 1781 (with years of initial publication)

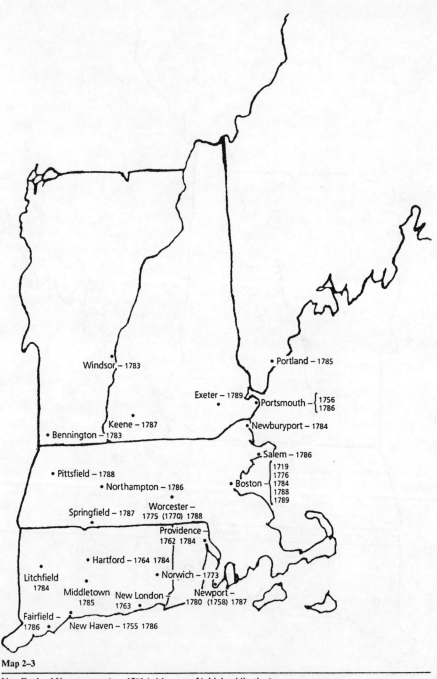

Map 2–3

New England Newspapers, Apr. 1789 (with years of initial publication)

Bennington, Vermont. The public prints, spreading westward with the population, no longer depended totally on a commercial oriented environment for survival. The coastal commercial trend, which was dominant prior to 1775, had weakened. Although trade and advertising remained important to the success of a newspaper, population and subscribers rose in importance after the war.

At the beginning of the Revolution, printing as a trade had existed for more than three hundred years, yet it had changed very little since the days of Gutenberg. In order to produce one page, thirteen separate processes had to be performed by two men operating a press. Type had to be set by hand and then locked into place in the press. After the form was positioned, one man would ink the type using two large deerskin balls. He would next place a piece of paper on top of the type and ensure that everything was in its proper place. Then his co-worker would pull twice on an iron lever that would press the paper onto the inked type, producing one printed page. The sheet would then be hung up to dry, and the process would be repeated with the next page. The hourly output from this procedure averaged two hundred to two hundred fifty sheets, resulting in a total of two thousand to twenty-five hundred pages for a ten-hour day, that is, if nothing interfered with the routine.[1]

Establishment of a printing business during the eighteenth century was a risky venture. Costs varied depending on the shop size one desired and on whether the equipment was new or used. Printshops were generally described as either one-press, two-press, or three-press operations. The one-press shop, a small establishment run by the printer and his family and one or two apprentices, proved the most common. The two-press shop was a more successful operation, and was commonly found in large urban areas, while the three-press shop was extremely rare and indicated a very successful business, such as that of Benjamin Franklin and David Hall in Philadelphia in the 1750s, or that of Isaiah Thomas and Ebenezer T. Andrews in Boston and Worcester in the 1790s. One estimate placed the cost of establishing a one-press shop with new equipment at £85 sterling while the same equipment used would run about £50 sterling. Second-hand equipment for a two-press shop would come to about £83 sterling while outfitting a three-press shop cost from £175 to £250 sterling, depending on how well the place was equipped. One study estimated a printer's average yearly income at £247. If this figure is correct, a person could spend from one-fifth to one-third of his expected income just to acquire the needed equipment for a small shop, and his earnings might be less for several years while the business became firmly established. Clearly it took capital to set up a printing business in the eighteenth century.[2]

During the colonial period, the American printer imported almost all of his equipment and supplies from England. However, the adoption of nonimportation measures in the mid–1760s broke the printer's normal supply lines and forced him to search for new ways to acquire the materials and equipment needed to carry on his business. The outbreak of fighting in 1775 only worsened the situation and intensified printers' efforts to find American sources for presses, types, ink, and paper, resulting in a growth of American manufacturers of all these items.

Home production of printing equipment did not reach full development until the early nineteenth century. Prior to then, printers called on a variety of craftsmen to produce the tools of the trade. One of the few detailed accounts of how a printer kept his office equipped is in the records of Mathew Carey of Philadelphia between 1785 and 1817: stone masons carved press stones; a turner produced ballstocks; wooden items came from cabinet-makers; while a house carpenter constructed type cases. These same artisans also repaired the equipment when it broke.[3]

The most important piece of equipment in a printing office was the printing press. Throughout the eighteenth century, presses proved difficult to obtain. Because they generally had to be imported, presses were expensive, and it cost a sizable amount just to have them shipped. Consequently, a press was used a long time and repaired over and over again. Many printers acquired a press from another printer who possessed an extra one, had one to dispose of after retirement, or left one as part of an estate, while others tried to get presses built. As early as 1750, Christopher Sower of Germantown, Pennsylvania constructed his own press, but it was not until 1769 that the first American press was produced to be sold when Isaac Doolittle, a New Haven watchmaker, built a press for William Goddard of Philadelphia. The manufacture of American-made presses slowly increased over the years. By 1776, they were being produced in both Philadelphia and Hartford, and by 1789, presses had been made in Charleston, South Carolina, and Fayetteville, North Carolina. Several men, especially Benjamin Dearborn of New Hampshire, also attempted to improve the mechanical operation of the press, but with very little success. By 1800, American printers had practically ceased

importing presses because they were able to purchase them locally.[4]

Although the printing press usually constituted the most important part of a printer's equipment, the type faces were the
costliest to maintain. Unlike a press, a printer's type had to be
replenished on a fairly regular basis in order to maintain the
quality of his work. Type broke or wore out and had to be
replaced. Type faces proved to be very expensive, primarily because they had to be imported. A printer often found that the
value of his type faces equalled or exceeded the total value of the
rest of his equipment. In 1786, Isaiah Thomas spent £106:11:5 for
new type for his Worcester shop.[5]

Imported types came from foundries in England, Scotland,
France, and Holland, but acquisition of types from overseas
ceased with the outbreak of the Revolution. In 1778, Isaiah
Thomas complained in the *Massachusetts Spy* that "printing uten-
sils are no where to be procured in this country at present, types
in particular, are not made in America." Throughout the period of
trouble with Great Britain, American printers tried a variety of
methods to replace their worn-out types. For instance, in October
1770, Thomas agreed to pay Zechariah Fowle £6:13:4 to rent his
printing types. In 1780, he bought additional types from Hudson
and Goodwin of Hartford, Connecticut. Later, in 1785, Thomas
sold some of his extra type to printers who were in need of it. In
general, printers depended on each other for types when none
could be had from foundries—they either bought extra type or
borrowed some for a short period of time in order to complete a
special project. With the end of the war, printers once more
acquired most of their types from overseas. As early as November
1786, Bennett Wheeler of Providence, Rhode Island, imported
new types from London, and in 1786 the *American Herald* of
Boston advertised that it had acquired new types from William
Caston of London, the type founder of George III.[6]

Although the best types still came from Europe, several people
attempted—with limited success—to produce American-made
type fonts. The type-making process was a slow, one-man job that
required a great deal of patience and dexterity. Typefounding
proved to be a demanding occupation, with scarcely a handful of
men good enough to make a living at it. In 1768, David
Mitchelson from Scotland tried unsuccessfully to establish a
foundry. In 1769, Abel Buell of Killingworth, Connecticut, after
setting up a makeshift foundry, moved to New Haven upon

receipt of £100 and a promise of more from the Connecticut assembly if the business succeeded. He made several fonts of type, but his business failed to prosper. Buell tried again in 1781, this time producing types that were actually used by several Connecticut printers, although his business once more failed to thrive.[7] Finally, in 1787, the first successful type foundry in America was launched in Philadelphia by John Baine and his grandson. The senior Baine learned the craft of making type in Scotland, and his desire to carry on his trade in America brought praise from printers everywhere. On 8 August 1787, the *Newport Mercury* reprinted a piece from a New York paper announcing the opening of the Baines's foundry and stating that the Baines intended to sell their types "much cheaper than can be imported, should they be encouraged by the printers in this country, which it is believed they will be from patriotic as well as convenient motives." Even though the Baines succeeded in their type-making business, it was not until 1796, with the creation of the large firm of Binny and Ronaldson in Philadelphia, that American type founding could effectively compete with the foundries of Europe.[8]

Along with presses and types, American printers also imported a great deal of another essential of their business—ink. Most imported ink came from England, but, even prior to the implementation of nonimportation in 1765, some printers used other sources for their ink. The ingredients needed for ink were lampblack and linseed or flaxseed. Since linseed and flaxseed were readily available in the colonies, many printers purchased the necessary components separately and then mixed their own ink. This method of acquiring ink had two advantages: first, the printer had an emergency supply of ink readily available if needed; and second, the quality of the product could be improved if a printer mixed it himself. Finally, it proved an easy way to save money, something the printers always considered. Still, many printers did not want to go to all the trouble to make their own ink, and they continued to look overseas for their supply. It was after the end of the Revolutionary era before the American manufacture of ink became anything more than a cottage industry for one's personal use.[9]

While printers generally made some ink in their own shops, the same proved impossible with the other major material they needed—paper. To make paper, ideally one needed clean white linen rags and a good deal of clear flowing water. This meant that paper had to be manufactured in a mill if one desired to produce large quantities. All the work involved in making paper had to be done by hand and each sheet was made separately, requiring a period spanning several days for the production of a sheet of dry perfected paper. Although American-made paper appeared fairly early, printers continued to import voluminous quantities from England because as the demand for paper continued to grow, the infant American papermaking industry proved unable to fill the total need. The process required skilled workmen, who were difficult to find, and large numbers of rags, which were always scarce. Even acquisition of the tools needed for actually making paper proved a continual vexation. In addition, imported paper was of a better quality, and printers desired to use it over the local product any time they embarked on a major project. Newspapers and pamphlets could be printed on American paper when necessary, but book publishing required the importation of quality paper from Europe.[10]

Although printers continued to import paper throughout the colonial period, some entrepreneurs tried to establish American paper mills. Paper costs often accounted for one of the largest segments of a printer's monthly budget, second only to labor costs, and many printers hoped to cut these costs when the papermaking industry became firmly established in America. In 1729, Daniel Henchman opened his paper mill at Milton, Massachusetts, the first mill to begin operation in New England.[11] Prior to 1775, three other mills began operation at Milton while two others also opened in New England—one at Falmouth, Maine, and one in Norwich, Connecticut. These mills turned out only about 20 percent of the total paper required in New England, so that this deficiency had to be remedied through British imports.[12]

The Stamp Act Crisis in 1765 ended the importation of paper from England. Shortages became widespread, sparking efforts to increase American paper production, which were strengthened by the inclusion of imported paper among the Townshend taxes. The advent of the Revolution in 1775 made the local production of paper essential if the presses were to remain in operation. Consequently, many printers began to take an active interest in papermaking ventures in order to secure a steady supply. In December 1775, Ebenezer Watson had to suspend publication of the *Connecticut Courant* for lack of paper. To prevent a recurrence, Watson built a paper mill in 1776 in partnership with Austin Ledyard. The year 1777 witnessed the construction of a mill at New Haven, the papermakers hoping "to prevent these inconveniences, and as far as they are able to promote the public good, consistently with their own private advantage." Other entrepreneurs launched paper mills in Sutton, Massachusetts, in 1777; in Exeter, New Hampshire, in 1778; in Watertown, Massachusetts, in 1780; and in Providence, Rhode Island, in 1780. Vermont's first paper mill opened for business in 1784, resulting in the following praise in the *Vermont Gazette:*

> The State of Vermont in the seventh year of her independence, and the town of Bennington in the 23rd year of its settlement, may boast of enjoying privileges, unknown to any State in the Union, at a similar age, in the enjoyment of the arts of Printing and Paper Making. May we be wise to improve these and all other advantages.[13]

Colonial and state assemblies also clearly considered printing and papermaking to be "advantages" that deserved encouragement. In order to help in the establishment of the first New England mill, the Massachusetts assembly passed an act in 1728 granting the proprietors of the Milton mill the exclusive right of making paper in Massachusetts for ten years. Other encouragements included granting bounties and authorizing lotteries to pay for construction. In January 1778, the Connecticut assembly approved a lottery to raise money to reconstruct the Hartford paper mill, which had burned in December 1777, because "rebuilding the said paper-mill is of public necessity and utility." Another important way in which public officials supported the papermaking industry was by encouraging people to save the rags needed for production. In 1776, the Massachusetts House of Representatives urged saving rags as a patriotic duty: "the inhabitants of this Colony are hereby desired to be very careful in saving even the smallest Quantity of Rags proper for making Paper, which will be a further evidence of their Disposition to promote the public good." George Washington recognized the need for the production of paper—he gave one publisher a supply of tent cloth for making paper so that his soldiers could have access to a newspaper. Furthermore, he agreed to exempt papermakers from military service so that they might continue to ply their invaluable trade. Encouragement of the infant papermaking industry apparently succeeded for in 1787 printer Josiah Meigs wrote that "our paper makers can vastly undersell the importer."[14]

Although the industry received great encouragement during the Revolutionary period, it still failed to manufacture enough paper to furnish America's needs. Difficulties encountered in acquiring paper became a major problem and a source of great embarrassment for the American printer. Newspapers continually urged people to save rags for the paper manufacturers. In several towns, printers sent wagons around collecting rags so that people would not have to go to the trouble of bringing scraps to the printing office. Generally, individuals received cash for their rags. During the 1780s, Isaiah Thomas wrote frequently in his diary about his purchases of rags, but he also regularly inserted advertisements in his newspaper that trumpeted the great need for more. Fueled by heavy demand and inflation, the price given for good clean rags in central Massachusetts leaped from three pence per pound to ten shillings per pound between 1777 and 1781. If cash proved undesirable, printers offered books, writing paper, ink, tea, materials, needles, pins, razors, ribbons, and combs. Several enterprising printers even suggested rags be exchanged for subscriptions to their newspapers.[15]

In order to further encourage the saving of rags, printers resorted to stronger appeals, appealing to patriotism as a reason for helping the paper industry: "the inducement therefore must arise from the love of our country, and the benefit that individuals will receive, in a full enjoyment of freedom and property in common with the whole community in general." One advertisement urged people to save rags because "encouraging useful arts and manufactures of every kind, is the surest way of supporting the dignity of the State." Another printer put it another way: "Save your Rags and Save your Country."[16]

In their ongoing efforts to urge the public to retain their old rags, the printers particularly appealed to women, describing their saving of rags as a necessary expedient for the education of their children. Furthermore, saving rags was an easy way for women, as noncombatants, to contribute to the war effort. Several studies of American women during the Revolution referred to patriot efforts to encourage women to aid American manufacturing by wearing homespun and increasing the amount of spinning they did.[17] Very little research has been done, however, concerning attempts to get women to succor paper manufactories by saving old material. In a recurring ad in the *Massachusetts Spy*, Isaiah Thomas

earnestly requested that the fair Daughters of Liberty in this extensive Country, would not neglect to serve their country, by saving for the Paper-Mill at Sutton, all Linen and Cotton and Linen Rags, be they ever so small, as they are equally good for the purpose of making paper, as those that are larger. A bag hung at one corner of a room would be the means of saving many which would be otherwise lost. If

the Ladies should not make a fortune by this piece of economy, they
will at least have the satisfaction of knowing they are doing an essential service to the community.[18]

Another type of appeal, more common after the war, was ably
summarized by a piece appearing in several New England newspapers: "It . . . behooves every friend to his country, to contribute
his endeavours to promote the paper manufactory. It not only
retains money in the country, but employs great numbers of its
inhabitants." Printing was considered an important trade, paper
was essential for printing, and rags were essential for making
paper. Therefore, saving rags was an essential pastime of all good
citizens.[19]

Although the scarcity of scrap cloth constituted the most troublesome cause of paper shortages, there were many other problems as well. Paper shipments were delayed for a variety of
reasons. Common excuses for failure to meet publication sched-
ules included no water to run the mill, illness of the papermaker,
bad weather, and distance from the mill. During the winter
months, printers often cut the size of their newspaper for weeks
at a time because bad weather prevented paper mill deliveries.[20]
On occasion, the reasons proved much more serious, as in the
case of the paper mill owned by the proprietors of the *Connecticut
Courant.* When it burned in 1777, George Goodwin, suspecting
sabotage, urged future precautions: "Thronged as this town is
with British and tory prisoners rambling with impunity at all
hours of the night, and open to the secret malice of every hard-
ened villain, Would it not be proper that a suitable guard should
nightly patrol the streets not only for the security of private
property, but for the safe keeping of what nearly and deeply
concerns the public." In 1788, another paper mill near Hartford
burned, and this time the *Middlesex Gazette* appeared in a reduced
size because its printers depended on the Hartford mill for paper.
On one occasion, the paper shortage in Connecticut became so
acute that Ebenezer Watson issued the *Connecticut Courant* on
wrapping paper. Frequent reductions in newspaper size because
of paper shortages produced printers' apologies and promises of
future improvement. Most, however, declared that any newspaper was better than none at all because of the importance of
events during the period. In 1775, the printer of the *New
Hampshire Gazette* defended the smallness of the paper, declaring
that "brown Bread with Liberty, will please more, than white with
Slavery."[21]

Acquiring the items to print in their newspapers could also be a headache. Many stories came from the columns of other newspapers, which the printers acquired through an extensive exchange system that stretched from Maine to Georgia. Printers used the mails to exchange the newspapers, so a late mail delivery meant delayed news. During the winter when the roads became heavily snow-covered, the printers found themselves having to postpone or cancel publication because of the failure of the mails to arrive on time or even at all. On several different occasions, the New England area went for weeks without news from the south or west. During Shays's Rebellion in 1786–1787, the southern posts were cut off completely from those areas north of Massachusetts until the disturbances ended.[22]

Because of the problems involved in depending on the exchange system, many printers increased their use of alternate sources of information. These alternatives consisted primarily of items given by individuals in the community who had received letters or newspapers from channels other than the usual ones open to the printers. These sources proved particularly important in the area of foreign news because many letters from overseas were hand-delivered by sea captains who also had information that could be passed on for publication. On occasion the printers publicly requested such assistance in the pages of their newspapers. In October 1775, the *Boston News-Letter* carried the following notice: "The Publisher would be extremely obliged to Gentlemen, into whose Hands Papers or Articles of Intelligence may accidentally fall, if they would be so kind as to favor him with them: They would thereby not only oblige the Printer, but afford the greatest Satisfaction to the Public." The printers considered these alternative news sources extremely important and urged their own friends and acquaintances to pass on anything of interest. Early in 1776, for instance, John Carter asked Joseph Trumbull to write about what was going on at Washington's camp because "our Accounts here are generally very imperfect." Thomas Wait of Portland, Maine, considered such items from personal letters "the heart and soul" of his paper and also the reason for the popularity of his newspaper throughout Maine and even parts of Massachusetts.[23]

Sources for news remained a recurring problem through the entire Revolutionary period. The fighting often severed the usual mail routes, delaying and sometimes destroying the printer's usual news channels. Even when the mails ran on time and local individuals submitted pieces for publication, printers complained of a lack of materials to print. The problem became worse after the end of the war in 1783. For example, in 1786, the *Falmouth Gazette* declared that "papers from the westward are this week barren as the desert. It is true they contain accounts of births, marriages, deaths, &c. but these are of no consequence to any but the parties concerned; and ofttimes, if we may judge by appearance, of but very little to them." Although the lack of news to print was a big concern, it was also one of the few problems that produced humor in the columns of the newspaper as the printer poked fun at the tastes of the public in news and how he acquired materials for his weekly sheet. In 1785, the *Independent Ledger* of Boston declared that printers should put the following advertisement on their windows:

> Wanted, a war between the Emperor and the Dutch—a bloody battle on the Musquito Shore—a tumult among the Congressional gentry at New-York—the death of some eminent man—a horse race—bullbait— bear-fight—a comet—a meteor—an eclipse—a perturbed apparition— a recent crime, con—a run-away match between a pair of fond lovers, or any other kind of intrigue—a balloon—a duel—a paper war— original witticisms—poetry—nervous paragraphs, &c. &c. To compleat the allurement, it should be added, with a 'seven pence halfpenny a piece will be given for well-turned paragraphs, upon any of the above-mentioned subjects, and no enquiry made into the authenticity.'[24]

Obviously, excitement sold newspapers. In 1788, the printer of the *United States Chronicle* vowed that the people would "no Doubt be gratified in the Events of the War between the Russians and the Turks.—We anticipate with Grief, the Rivers of Blood which will flow—the dying Groans which will ascend—the War of Russian and Austrian ambition! In what dreadful Calamities of the Passions of the Great involve Mankind!" A piece in the *Falmouth Gazette* in February 1786, praised the coming spring because it meant the return of news and urged everyone to take advantage of the approaching "news-thaw" by subscribing to the *Falmouth Gazette*, "the channel through which this freshet of News, Truth, &c. will flow." He concluded with the hope that "here and there an Advertisement will be found floating on the surface." Even while concerned with how to fill the pages of his sheet with news, a printer could enjoy the amusing aspects of his profession.[25]

Interference resulting from military activities constituted another set of problems that dogged newspaper printers. Publishers had to delay or cancel their issues because of nearby British forces.

Printers dealt with these disruptions as best as possible, resuming their publications whenever practicable so that "the Course of Intelligence may not be wholly stopped, & the Public deprived of that invaluable Privilege, among others, we are constitutionally contending for." In New England, the British occupied only Boston and Newport for any length of time. In Boston, all newspapers, except the two Tory sheets published by Margaret Draper and the partnership of John Mills and Nathaniel Hicks, shut down following the skirmishes at Lexington and Concord. The Fleet brothers' *Boston Evening Post* promised to resume publication as soon as "Matters are in a more settled State," but they never revived their paper. Benjamin Edes and John Gill parted company. Edes fled to Watertown where he soon reestablished the *Boston Gazette*, while John Gill remained in Boston, only to be imprisoned by the British in August 1775. Isaiah Thomas also fled Boston, moving his operation to Worcester, where it remained thereafter. Edes returned to Boston after the British evacuation, but he and Gill never resumed their partnership. In Newport, Solomon Southwick buried his press and type just before the British landed. He did not return to Newport until 1780. In general, however, these interruptions proved temporary and short-lived.[26]

Another problem resulting from the war came in the form of accusations of Toryism against Whig printers. Generally proven to be of little substance, charges and insinuations of Loyalism usually appeared in response to an unpopular newspaper piece. Some of the accusations had repercussions that did the printer a disservice. During 1775 and 1776, Ezekiel Russell attempted to start two different newspapers in Salem, but both failed because Russell was a suspected Tory sympathizer. In 1781, Ezra Stiles, president of Yale College, accused Thomas and Samuel Green of New Haven of running a Tory press and then sent the commencement theses to Hartford to be printed rather than having the job done locally. The Greens were supporters of the patriot cause, but their lack of extreme enthusiasm for the war effort cost them business. Because of their failure to restart their paper after the departure of the British forces from Boston, Thomas and John Fleet likewise faced charges of Loyalism. It seems clear, however, that they did not resume publication because the times prevented them from producing the nonpartisan paper they wished to publish and also because the Fleets did not desire to undertake the financial risks involved in reestablishing their newspaper.[27]

Daniel Fowle, printer of the *New Hampshire Gazette*, also had to fend off occasional accusations of Toryism, or at least a lack of ardent support for the Revolution. In 1765, a rival newspaper sprang up in Portsmouth because some patriot leaders considered Fowle's stance against the Stamp Act weak. In January 1776, Fowle suspended publication of the *Gazette* after being strongly reprimanded by the state legislature for printing an essay by "Junius" against American independence. Neither incident lasted long and Fowle resumed his normal practices. In many ways, Daniel Fowle represented the mainstream of older printers in this period. Remaining in one town for most of his career, he ran a quiet business that did not stir up much controversy. Fowle learned the trade from Samuel Kneeland of Boston. He set up shop in Boston for a while, but moved to Portsmouth in 1756, where he stayed until his death in 1787. Fowle backed independence during the war, though less ardently than some of his fellow printers from Boston. A conscientious printer, he concentrated most of his efforts on the newspaper because he considered it the lynchpin of his business. He produced some pamphlets and a few books while in Portsmouth—none of major importance.[28]

If Daniel Fowle typified the norm of printers in the Revolutionary era, then Benjamin Edes typified the ardent Whig publisher. Trained by Samuel Kneeland, Edes and his partner, John Gill, carved out a reputation as strong defenders of American liberties during the Stamp Act crisis. Throughout the prewar crisis, the *Boston Gazette* inundated its readers with pieces that praised the Americans and portrayed the British as villains and oppressors. While both Edes and Gill upheld the Whig position, Edes took a more prominent role in patriot activities than his partner. Edes, an active member of the Sons of Liberty, participated in the Boston Tea Party. Forced to flee the city in April 1775, Edes set up shop in Watertown and continued to trumpet the patriot cause in the pages of the *Boston Gazette*. Returning to Boston in 1776, Edes continued to publish there until his death in 1803, always using the pages of his sheet to support issues he favored. In 1785, he spoke out against the Massachusetts Stamp Act as an infringement of the liberty of the press, but the impact of the *Gazette* had waned in the late 1780s and the 1790s, primarily because Edes spoke out against the Constitution and the Federalist administrations of Washington and Adams. Both prior to, during, and after the war, the *Gazette* constituted the major portion of all printing done by Edes. As was the case of Daniel Fowle in New Hampshire, Edes produced pamphlets and books as a secondary business.[29]

In addition to the interference produced by the fighting, numerous other difficulties confronted the printer. Illness or death in the printer's family could result in a publication delay, a size reduction, or cancellation of an issue altogether. Labor scarcity proved an almost unsurmountable problem. Even when enough help existed, it was not always qualified or capable. On two different occasions, the *Vermont Gazette* had to be reduced in size because the types had been accidentally knocked down after being set up for printing. Apparently this was not an isolated incident for Isaiah Thomas posted the following poem in all of his printing establishments in order to prevent such mishaps: "All you that come this curious Art to see, / To handle anything must cautious be, / Lest, by a slight touch, as <?> you are aware, / That mischief may be done you can't repair: / Lo! this advice me give to every stranger, / Look on, and welcome; but to touch there's danger."[30]

Many other troubles confronted the printer in the execution of his business. During the 1780s, problems over copyrights became common as every state (except Delaware) passed a copyright law. Even though efforts to acquire a national regulation failed, printers became more concerned with the issue of copyrights and the possible repercussions for failure to honor them.[31] On many occasions, the printer delayed publication of a newspaper in order to do some work for the government or because of a public fast day or day of thanksgiving. In 1787, the town of Northampton fined William Butler for working on the Sabbath—he had gone to Springfield for the mail. Also in 1787, the printers of the *Essex Journal* experienced a frustrating but humorous example of an out-of-the-ordinary misfortune that might confront a printer. On 12 September 1787, the *Essex Journal* contained the following advertisement: "A Boy having last week stolen a considerable number of Types from the Printing-Office, and disposed of many of them to other Boys—the parents of those children who may have any in possession, are requested to be so obliging as to give orders for them to be immediately returned."[32]

The problem that proved the most troublesome, because it apparently never went away, concerned the failure of customers to pay subscriptions promptly. Most printers established quarterly rates that could be paid annually or at the end of each quarter. Time and again, particularly during the winter months when times were hard and people would temporarily stop their subscriptions, the printers had to urge their customers to pay up.[33] The printer of the *Norwich Packet* declared that those who subscribe for News-Papers, ought to consider, that the Printing of them is attended with great expense—that Types, Paper and Ink cannot be had without ready Cash—that Printers have to pay away money in large sums—that their debts for News-Papers are small, and in many hands—that the trouble of collecting is great and perplexing—and finally they should consider that unless they Punctually discharge their small accounts, Printers and Post Riders cannot possibly continue their business.[34]

Many printers willingly accepted the paper money of the various states while others offered to accept provisions, wood, or "any of the Necessaries of Life" in lieu of money. Threats to cease publication often accompanied the pleas for some form of payment. Finally, some printers resorted to the courts against certain delinquent customers. The publishers of the *Boston Gazette,* exhorting their customers to follow the Golden Rule, concluded that "sorry we are to say it is not regarded by a great number of our Customers, who are becoming indebted for Papers 6, 8, or 10 Years." In announcing a general day of Thanksgiving in 1787, Thomas Wait of the *Cumberland Gazette* requested that his customers pass on some of their bounty so that he might have something to be thankful for. His conclusion to this request might have been that of many a New England printer who had had trouble collecting monies due him: "And, should the Printer by this means be blessed with one day of feasting, it will be, at most, but a slender compensation for a year or two of fasting in your service."[35]

The financial woes of the printer worsened because of inflation. The price of everything went up, including newspapers. Subscription prices in Boston shot from three shillings a year in 1776 to over one hundred shillings a year in 1779 in inflated currency—produce was accepted in the amount of the old prices. If the end of the fighting in 1781 brought some financial relief, newspaper prices never returned to their prewar levels. By the mid-1780s, the average yearly price stood at six to eight shillings. Official efforts at price regulation proved unsuccessful, and the printers had to raise their prices when the prices of other goods went up. The Boston printers spoke for all printers when they defended their 1779 price rise to thirty-six shillings per quarter: "when News Papers cease to bring in a Price in proportion to Bread and Beef, we must quit printing them."[36]

Printers discovered that publishing a newspaper required a regular cash flow in order to keep the paper solvent, and many colonial printers found this difficult to maintain. Isaiah Thomas's personal papers, some of the few such records to survive, provide an excellent example of the trouble in keeping an adequate amount of cash available. By the early 1780s, Thomas managed to stabilize his business in Worcester to the point of being able to buy a few luxuries, such as chocolates and silk, as well as building a new house. Still, Thomas proved unable to keep enough liquid capital on hand for the operation of his business in the manner he preferred. In 1784, he attempted to acquire copies of Noah Webster's books, but could not pay the asking price all at one time. Webster refused to lower the price and would not arrange a trade or time-payment, so Thomas failed to get the hoped-for materials. Thomas conducted most of his business dealings on a barter-type system, trading books and writing supplies for the goods he needed. He once told George Goodwin that his "interest is much in other people's hands." Apparently, affairs remained in this state throughout the Revolutionary era and beyond. In 1791, Thomas faced attachment of his property for failure to pay an overdue debt.[37]

Most printers, including Isaiah Thomas, realized that they could not support themselves and their families on the income derived from their newspapers' subscriptions and advertisements, so they turned to other enterprises to make the needed money. The eighteenth-century American newspaper printer was, above all else, an entrepreneur who attempted to use his knowledge and skills to make a living in whatever manner possible. Those men who remained printers directed most of their efforts to the printing trade or closely related areas.[38]

Printing ventures other than the newspaper varied. Most eighteenth-century newspaper printers did job printing. They produced, upon request of an individual or a group of people or the government, a variety of broadsides, pamphlets, and books. Materials published during this era included such titles as "The Management of the Tongue," Webster's *American Spelling Book,* "The Character and Conduct of the Female Sex," "General Gage's Instructions," "The Narrative of Colonel Ethan Allen," and the "Fables of Pilpay." The variety was almost endless. Printers also regularly undertook certain printing projects on their own whenever they considered the product obviously marketable. The major items in this category were all kinds of forms needed for various legal arrangements and, more importantly, almanacs. Every printer either produced his own almanac or sold a well-liked version published by a competitor. Some printers even did both. Almanacs proved very popular during the eighteenth century primarily because they were inexpensive and full of a variety of informative and entertaining materials.[39]

In addition to his almanacs and other printed materials, the printer generally sold additional items in his shop, ranging from paper and ink to cloth and buttons to household goods such as pewter ware. The printing office often fulfilled the role of general store as well, so varied were the items offered for sale. The type of customers in the area influenced the materials carried in the shop. For example, the printers of the *Newport Gazette* sold knives, orderly books, and epaulets during the British occupation of Newport from 1777 to 1779. Still, the primary merchandise in a printing office remained books, whether or not they were published by the resident printer. Printers usually advertised their wares in their newspapers. In 1784, Benjamin Edes of Boston regularly ran a full one-column ad in the *Boston Gazette* listing the books available in his shop. Content ranged from Bibles to history books to books for children to books of advice and instruction. Most books were shipped either from overseas or from another part of the United States. Printers also held various government jobs, such as town clerk or postmaster.[40]

Even with the variety of efforts to make money, many printers had trouble remaining solvent. Several printers lost their equipment because they were unable to keep up the payments. On one occasion, Isaiah Thomas had to sell practically brand new types in order to raise cash. Numerous appeals for overdue payments emphasized the general feeling among printers that they made little profit. Financial success proved illusive for many.[41]

Wartime popularity was no guarantee of success. Benjamin Edes, probably the best-known printer in New England during the Revolution, had to cease publication of the *Boston Gazette* in 1798. In bidding adieu to his readers, Edes declared that "the cause of Liberty is not always the channel of preferment or pecuniary award." Many another printer probably shared the same opinion as he attempted to get paid for the work already done.[42]

Problems for printers abounded, but the postwar growth in newssheets indicated some success on the part of printers. Still, the newspaper publishing business did not hold any guarantees of an easy or successful life. Acquiring and maintaining the necessary equipment and supplies constituted a full-time headache for most printers. Other hazards, such as getting enough help or receiving payments when due, hounded the printers' steps. The advent of the Revolutionary War only exacerbated the troubles. Although some individuals attempted to find new and different solutions to the age-old problems, few prevailed. As shown by the increase in the number of public prints in New England, the profession experienced growth during the Revolutionary era, but being an eighteenth-century newspaperman was not easy. Genuine improvement in the mechanics of American printing came only after the dawn of the nineteenth century, while finances remained unsteady and unpredictable well into the 1790s. The Revolutionary printer, much to his dismay, had to depend on Europe for most of his materials and on unpredictable customers for money.

3
Producers of the "Popular Engine": New England's Revolutionary Newspaper Printers

Given the publishing difficulties that a newspaper printer could encounter during the Revolutionary era, one might assume that printing was a troublesome way to earn money and that those who chose it as a profession formed a special group of hardy souls. Although records from the period are scattered and incomplete, some conclusions can be reached about the people who printed newspapers between 1775 and 1789.

In reality, printers differed little from other artisans of the time. American craftsmen of the eighteenth century, although practicing a wide variety of trades, had certain things in common. Most learned their profession through a formal apprenticeship system that passed the "art and mystery" of the craft from one generation to the next, even though the system, such as it was, lacked the formality or structure connected with printing in Europe. In New England, skilled artisans lived in urban areas where there were enough people with money to pay for their specialized goods. Printers, particularly those who produced newspapers, fitted into this category of urban craftsmen, for their trade depended on population and commercial activity. Printing establishments tended to be small, family-run affairs, with a few apprentices to help out. Journeymen worked only in the larger shops. Most master craftsmen, including printers, maintained a firm position among the "middling sorts" of the population. The possession of a marketable skill enabled them to make a secure living for themselves and their families. Although few eighteenth-century craftsmen advanced into the upper class, most managed to keep from slipping down into the class of hired laborers.[1]

While sharing many common experiences with other craftsmen, printers differed in some respects. It has been asserted that most eighteenth-century artisans could read and write, but literacy was essential to the printer if he hoped to be truly successful. Most artisans lived in cities; still, some managed to survive in rural areas by broadening the scope of their trade. Printers, however, could not function well outside urban areas because of their need for advertisements. Through newspapers, printers provided an advertising medium for all their fellow craftsmen, a service that could never be truly reciprocated. Finally, printers had the potential of greater impact because they did more than provide goods and services for the public: they informed and educated, with the possibility of swaying anyone who read what they published on behalf of one cause or another. No other craft could make this claim.[2]

Most printers began as apprentices to a master printer. Prior to 1800, the apprenticeship system provided the major means for learning a trade and acquiring an education. An apprenticeship, for all practical purposes, consisted of a contract between the master craftsman and those responsible for the well-being of the youth involved, be they parents or other civil or religious authorities. The master agreed to instruct the apprentice in the "secrets" of his craft in exchange for work. In general, the master also provided food, lodging, clothing, and other essentials.[3] On occasion, a regular education would also be provided, as was the case with Benjamin Titcomb, who wrote home from Newburyport in September 1776 that he had a tutor who was an excellent musician.[4] In return for such provisions, the apprentice promised to serve the master craftsman faithfully and to do whatever was required of him for a specified period of time.[5]

The contract drawn up for Isaiah Thomas's apprenticeship in 1756 indicated what was generally expected of the two parties involved in such an agreement. Thomas's master, Zechariah Fowle, promised to train Isaiah in the printing trade and to teach him to "Read write & Cypher." He also agreed to provide food, lodging, and clothes for the length of the indenture and to give Thomas two full suits of clothes upon completion of the contract. Thomas's obligations consisted of the following long list of instructions:

the said Apprentice his said Master and Mistress well and faithfully shall Serve; their Secrets he shall keep close; their Commandments lawful and honest every where he shall gladly obey; he shall do no Damage to his said Master, nor suffer it to be done by others, without letting or giving seasonable Notice thereof to his said Master; he shall

not waste the Goods of his said Master; nor lend them unlawfully to
any; At Cards, Dice, or any other unlawful Game or Games he shall
not play; Fornication he shall not commit; Matrimony during the said
Term he shall not contract; Taverns, Ale-Houses, or Places of Gaming
he shall not haunt or frequent; From the Service of his said Master by
Day or Night he shall not absent himself; but in all Things and at all
Times, he shall carry and behave himself towards his said Master and
all theirs as a good and faithful Apprentice ought to do to his utmost
ability during all the Time or Term aforesaid.[6]

Clearly, on paper at least, an apprenticeship was an agreement
that should not be taken lightly.

Most printing apprentices served a term of five to seven years,
being bound over in their early teens and serving until the age of
twenty-one.[7] There were, however, numerous exceptions, including Thomas. The Overseers of the Poor of Boston bound Thomas
to Zechariah Fowle at the age of eight.[8] Apprentices also ended
their term of service earlier than originally scheduled for a variety
of reasons. Some became proficient in working at the press and
would establish their own shop after acquiring an early release. In
other instances, the contract would be abrogated because one of
the parties involved had failed to carry out his share of the
agreement. On some occasions, the apprenticeship ended
abruptly when the youth ran away in order to escape what he
considered an intolerable position.[9]

Although all printing apprentices did not suffer from intolerable conditions, the hours were long, and the work hard. The day
began at six o'clock and continued until dark, with only two short
breaks for breakfast and dinner. During the early years of service,
the apprentice functioned primarily as an errand boy and office
cleaner. He ran errands all over town, cleaned type, swept floors,
stoked the fires, and fetched water. With age and experience, the
apprentice began to set and ink the type and run the press. If all
went well, by the end of his service, the apprentice would be
knowledgeable enough in the printing business to sell his services
as a journeyman for whatever wages he could negotiate.[10]

Most journeymen worked for a master printer for several years
in preparation for amassing enough capital to set themselves up
in their own shop. Although not always successful, most tried at
one time or another to establish themselves as master craftsmen in
their trade by launching their own businesses. To indicate their
final arrival at the pinnacle of their profession, many began the
publication of a newspaper.[11] In fact, ninety-three printers in New
England did just that between 1775 and 1789.

Although an apprenticeship constituted the usual method for entry into the printing trade, it was not the only way in which a person acquired enough knowledge to be a printer. One could just be taught by someone in the trade (rather than going through a long period of formalized training). Of the ninety-three printers in this study, forty-nine definitely served an apprenticeship to a master printer while twenty-four others were probably trained by a relative or a business partner. That leaves twenty unaccounted for, and many of these may have served apprenticeships. There is simply too little information available to make an educated guess as to where or how the twenty learned printing. Clearly, however, one needed the "blessing" of a person knowledgeable in the field before embarking on a printing career.[12]

In the case of most of the New England newspaper printers, this "blessing" can be traced to the Boston area, the place where American printing began. Of the forty-nine printers known to have served an apprenticeship, thirty-seven either served their apprenticeship in Boston or under printers who themselves came from there. All thirty-seven, in a figurative sense, can be traced back to Samuel Green of Cambridge, who apparently learned the trade from Stephen Daye, the original printer in New England in 1630 (see charts 3–1, 3–2, and 3–3). The Green family constituted a printing dynasty that flourished for almost two hundred years, reaching from Vermont to Maryland. Most of the printers in Connecticut and Vermont during the Revolutionary era learned their trade from a member of the Green family. Daniel Fowle of New Hampshire also proved prolific in training others. He tutored almost single-handedly all of the Revolutionary New Hampshire newspaper printers.[13]

The networks that resulted from the apprentice system were useful in providing a support system for printers. Information and needed materials flowed through these networks. Isaiah Thomas's records contain numerous references to a variety of dealings with other printers, including Barzillai Hudson and George Goodwin of Hartford, Hugh Gaine of New York, and James Rivington of New York. Thomas counted John Carter of Providence and John Mycall of Newburyport among his personal friends.[14] All of the ninety-three newspaper publishers examined here expressed a kind of kinship for one another because of the business they all participated in, and these ties had many of their roots in the interconnections produced by the apprentice system. The networks developing out of the apprenticeship system fell into two categories: business partnership ties and familial ties.

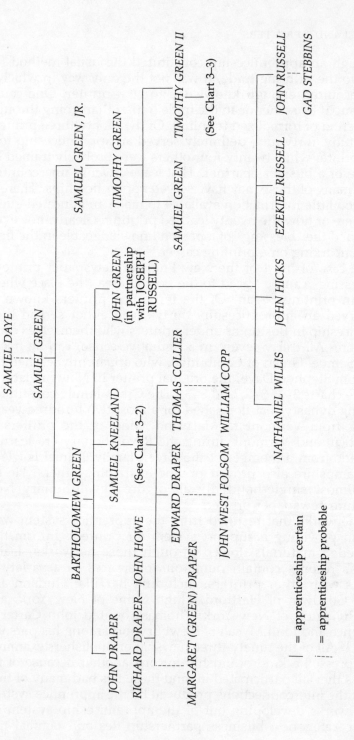

Chart 3-1

| = apprenticeship certain

--- = apprenticeship probable

Chart 3-2

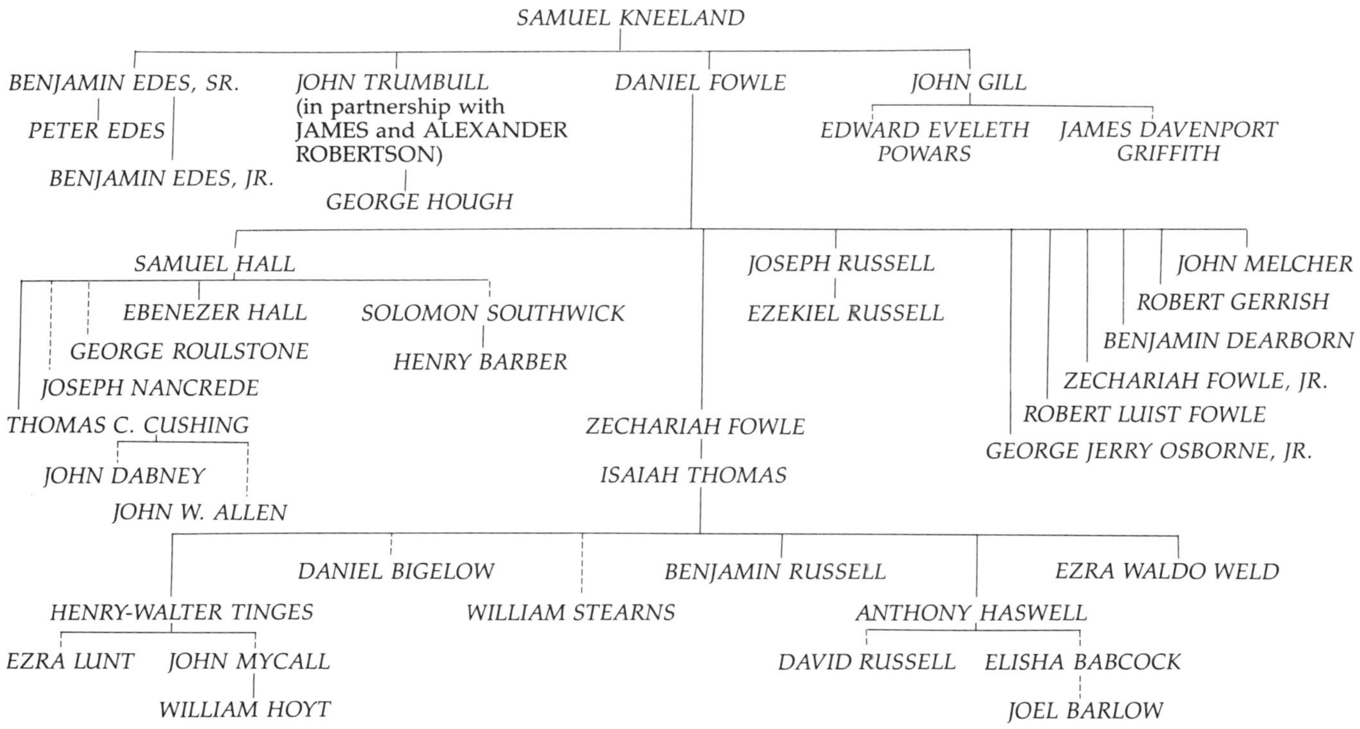

SAMUEL KNEELAND

BENJAMIN EDES, SR.
PETER EDES
BENJAMIN EDES, JR.

JOHN TRUMBULL (in partnership with JAMES and ALEXANDER ROBERTSON)
GEORGE HOUGH

DANIEL FOWLE

JOHN GILL

EDWARD EVELETH POWARS
JAMES DAVENPORT GRIFFITH

SAMUEL HALL
EBENEZER HALL
GEORGE ROULSTONE
JOSEPH NANCREDE
THOMAS C. CUSHING
JOHN DABNEY
JOHN W. ALLEN

SOLOMON SOUTHWICK
HENRY BARBER

JOSEPH RUSSELL
EZEKIEL RUSSELL

JOHN MELCHER
ROBERT GERRISH
BENJAMIN DEARBORN
ZECHARIAH FOWLE, JR.
ROBERT LUIST FOWLE
GEORGE JERRY OSBORNE, JR.

ZECHARIAH FOWLE
ISAIAH THOMAS

DANIEL BIGELOW
WILLIAM STEARNS

HENRY-WALTER TINGES
EZRA LUNT
JOHN MYCALL
WILLIAM HOYT

BENJAMIN RUSSELL

ANTHONY HASWELL
DAVID RUSSELL
ELISHA BABCOCK
JOEL BARLOW

EZRA WALDO WELD

| = apprenticeship certain

---- = apprenticeship probable

Chart 3-3

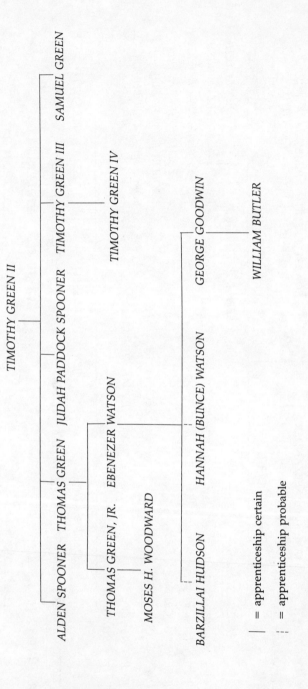

TIMOTHY GREEN II

ALDEN SPOONER   THOMAS GREEN   JUDAH PADDOCK SPOONER   TIMOTHY GREEN III   SAMUEL GREEN

THOMAS GREEN, JR.   EBENEZER WATSON   TIMOTHY GREEN IV

MOSES H. WOODWARD

BARZILLAI HUDSON   HANNAH (BUNCE) WATSON   GEORGE GOODWIN

WILLIAM BUTLER

| = apprenticeship certain

|= apprenticeship probable

Although the two often overlapped, they generally constituted separate groups. The outstanding example of partnership ties was between Isaiah Thomas and his apprentices. On several occasions, Thomas joined with a former apprentice in establishing a press in a new area—with, among others, Henry-Walter Tinges in Newburyport in 1774 and Ebenezer T. Andrews in Boston in the 1790s, the latter the most profitable of Thomas's partnerships. Even when no official alliance existed, Thomas corresponded with his former apprentices, such as Anthony Haswell in Vermont and Benjamin Russell in Boston, and often had business dealings with them.[15]

Familial ties made up the majority of the New England printing networks. Daniel Fowle, who provides a good example of this type of network, had numerous dealings with his brother and his nephews, both in Boston and in Portsmouth. Upon the death of his nephew Zechariah, Fowle officially adopted one of his own former apprentices, John Melcher.[16] The best example of kinship ties, however, existed in the Green family. The original printer in the Green clan, Samuel, began working in Cambridge in 1649, and his descendants carried on the trade for the next six generations. Connecticut's first printer, Thomas Short, acquired the appointment because the Greens were his in-laws. The Greens received the original job offer, but they decided to remain in Boston and recommended Short as a replacement. During the first half of the eighteenth century, the majority of the Green printers moved to Connecticut, establishing businesses in New London and New Haven. In the 1780s, the fourth generation of Greens and their in-laws, the Spooners, moved to Vermont, bringing that state its first printers. Throughout all of these moves and changes, the Green printers maintained ties with each other that provided a marvelous support network for carrying out their trade.[17]

Development of networks indicated a growth of a sense of professionalism among printers. Several studies have shown that this trend from trade to profession occurred among lawyers and the clergy during the eighteenth and nineteenth centuries.[18] Along with the network system were other signs of a growing consciousness of printing as a vocation with standards and ethics to uphold. They can be most clearly seen in concerns expressed over unknown sources, plagiarism, and copyright.

Increasingly, newspaper printers expressed anxieties over anonymous contributors, often stating they would not publish a piece unless they knew the author's identity. Most of the printers

apparently thought that they would never completely control
their papers until the practice of accepting anonymous submissions ended.[19] John Gill found himself in the unhappy position of
apologizing publicly to a Boston doctor for unsupported allegations in the *Continental Journal*. The unknown contributor had
failed to appear to support the charges, and Gill felt he had no
choice but to correct the error as best he could.[20]

The issue of plagiarism produced problems for Revolutionary
printers. In the world of mid–eighteenth-century newspapers,
the modern concept of plagiarism scarcely existed. Printers freely
republished pieces from other papers without giving credit to the
source. The advent of the War of Independence, however, produced efforts to acquire more accurate news.[21] Several printers,
particularly Solomon Southwick of Newport, Rhode Island, took
this a step further by stating clearly where they obtained their
information. The 1780s brought a gradual increase in the number
of printers who credited their news sources.[22] By 1789, the practice had become normal enough to elicit comment on occasions
when it was not followed, as the owners of the *Herald of Freedom*
discovered:

> Messrs. Printers, Please to give the compliments of a reader to the
> DOERS of a certain big "impartial" paper, and request of them when
> they pilfer paragraphs to give credit for the plagiary. The paragraphs
> republished yesterday on our national birth day, were an entire theft
> from the Salem paper of Tuesday last. The poetry was taken from the
> New Hampshire procession—part from a New York poem—and part
> from a piece published in Boston, during the session of the State
> Convention.[23]

Throughout the eighteenth century, American copyright law
remained a muddle. During the 1780s and 1790s, authors tried to
protect their works through the passage of state and federal
copyright laws. By 1786, all states except Delaware had passed
protection laws, but their strength varied greatly. Printers often
found themselves in trouble when "duped by Authors, especially
when they assume that character, and are only mere Compilers."
Some printers felt torn over this issue. They desired regulation in
order to prevent possible court suits, but they also enjoyed the
freedom to republish anything they desired. Many, however,
agreed with Isaiah Thomas that something had to be done to
clarify copyright regulations: "Confident I am that it is in the
power of the Printers: if they would be honourable to each other

and to their employers, to put business on a much better footing than it now is. A general plan for the good of the whole might easily be draughted and if the Printers would religiously adopt it, it would be greatly to the advantage of all."[24]

Printers' efforts to join together in a common cause also indicated a growing professionalism. Throughout the war years, newspaper publishers, particularly those in Boston, united in hopes of regulating their prices. Following the war, reasons for unity became less obvious until the Massachusetts advertisement tax of 1785 forced Boston printers to become allies in opposing the legislation.[25] On 10 February 1785, twelve Boston newspaper publishers petitioned the General Court on behalf of all the Massachusetts printers, requesting that the advertisement tax be repealed because it damaged their businesses. They also issued an appeal to the public on 27 July 1786, urging their readers to work for the act's repeal since it threatened the survival of the press. These efforts constituted one of the earliest known instances of public cooperation among American printers.[26]

Although ninety-three printers plied their trade in New England at one time or another in the quarter of a century after Lexington and Concord, the number engaged varied from year to year. Twenty-five people published newspapers in 1775. Rising to twenty-seven in 1776, the number dropped to nineteen in 1777 with the exodus of the Loyalist editors. The count of active newspaper printers hovered between eighteen and the mid–twenties until 1784, when it jumped to forty-three from the twenty-seven of 1783. Obviously, the return of peace encouraged many journeymen to set up on their own. The number of newspaper printers leaped to fifty-two in 1785 and fifty-five in 1786. It then dropped back to fifty-two in 1787 and down to forty-six in 1788. Although numerous papers died because of bad management or poor planning, another reason for the large drop was the impact of the Massachusetts advertisement tax, which according to the printers, cut deeply into the profits of some and drove others out of business. In 1789, at the end of the period under consideration, forty-seven different people published newspapers during the year. The leveling off of the number of newspaper printers at a figure one-third higher than those active at the end of the war indicates that the status and stability of the newspaper press had improved.[27]

But who were the ninety-three New England newspaper publishers who thus far, with few exceptions, have been little more than statistics? If our knowledge is sketchy for some and nonexis-

tent for others, we nevertheless have enough information about
these entrepreneurs in the aggregate to make certain observations. First, a newspaper printer (or any printer, for that matter) in
this period would almost certainly have been a man. Yet, there
were three women printers—Margaret Draper, Hannah Watson,
and Mary Crouch; in each case, the woman took over a business
left at the death of her husband, and each immediately took a
male partner who did a great deal of the work. Two of the women
did not maintain their businesses for long after their husbands'
deaths: Margaret Draper left Boston when the British evacuated in
1776, and Mary Crouch, after moving her late husband's business
from Charleston, South Carolina, to Salem, Massachusetts, failed
to produce a successful paper and quit publication within a year
of its establishment.[28] Hannah Watson of Hartford, Connecticut,
remarried several years after her first husband's death, and her
new husband, Barzillai Hudson, replaced her as a partner in the
printing business with George Goodwin.[29]

Knowledge about the printers' ages also can be gleaned from
available materials. These men were fairly young when they entered the trade. In 1775, the average age of a printer was thirty-
four years, and it wavered up and down throughout the period,
falling slightly to thirty-three by 1789. The average age reached its
height in 1782 when it stood at thirty-six. Although older men
always participated in the printing trade, the continual influx of
new young men into the field kept the average age down. Even
so, printers were living longer. One study has discussed the
relatively short lifespan of the colonial printer, adding that eighteenth-century working conditions in all trades tended to shorten
lifespans.[30] By the time of the Revolution, and particularly after
war's end, conditions had improved. A large majority of the
ninety-three printers lived past the turn of the century (1800). Of
those dying prior to 1800, the average age at death was forty-four.
Of those who survived past 1800, the average age at death was
sixty-six.[31] Several lived into their eighties and nineties, including
John Melcher, who died in 1850 at ninety-one, and Daniel Bowen,
who expired in 1856 at ninety-six. In general, a printer's life
improved in the years after the American Revolution, particularly
in the years following the institution of the new government in
1789. In an era of general economic prosperity, a printer's finances
became more stable, enabling him to hire more help and thus,
presumably, reducing the workload for everyone.[32]

If it is obvious that most printers were patriots during the
Revolution, the subject of their wartime loyalties nevertheless

calls for some analysis because of the resulting changes in that profession. Several did openly espouse the British cause early in the struggle before being forced to flee. Four Loyalist printers left Boston when the British evacuated in 1776: Margaret Draper, John Howe, John Hicks, and Nathaniel Mills. James and Alexander Robertson, co-publishers of the *Norwich Packet* (with John Trumbull), also proved to be Loyalists and fled to New York in May 1776. All of these printers, except Margaret Draper, reestablished their presses in areas under the control of the British army. In fact, James Robertson followed the army, establishing gazettes in New York, Philadelphia, and Charleston during the times when these cities were under British occupation. None of these printers, however, were able to reestablish their New England newssheets after the war ended.[33]

Another newspaper publisher accused of Toryism was Robert Luist Fowle of New Hampshire. The nephew of Daniel Fowle of Portsmouth, Robert Fowle published the Exeter edition of the *New Hampshire Gazette* from 22 May 1776 to 15 July 1777. In the spring of 1777, Fowle faced charges of counterfeiting the state currency, which he had originally printed. Though he denied the allegations, he was arrested on 15 July 1777. While out on bail, Fowle fled to Canada, confirming the charges as far as most New Hampshirites were concerned. While it is unclear whether Robert Fowle was a British sympathizer, he did take refuge behind the British lines. He actually had very little choice—there was no where else for him to go. Even though the allegations against Fowle were never proven, he later received a pension from the British government to compensate him for property seized by New Hampshire following his flight. Following the end of the war, Fowle returned to New Hampshire, married his brother's widow, and established a store in Exeter, all apparently with few problems or recriminations.[34]

With the arrival of peace in 1783, a new generation of printers began to make its presence felt in New England. These fresh faces, trained by older printers, would dominate the trade by the 1790s as their predecessors retired or died. In 1784, fifteen new people entered the newspaper publishing field. The following year, they were joined by nine more printers, and each subsequent year saw the addition of two to five more.[35] While all did not succeed in their newspaper enterprises, they brought new blood into the trade. Most successful among this newer group was Benjamin Russell, a Bostonian who had learned his craft from Isaiah Thomas in Worcester. Russell, like several other younger printers, had experienced the Revolution firsthand, serving two short tours of military service in 1777 and 1780. In 1782, Russell received an early release from his apprenticeship, apparently because one of his stints in the army was as a substitute for Isaiah Thomas. Returning to Boston in late 1783, Russell soon established the *Massachusetts Centinel* in partnership with William Warden. Russell's *Centinel* became one of the most important Boston papers in the years to come, particularly in the 1790s under its new title, the *Columbian Centinel.* Russell proved a staunch Federalist and used his paper to support the policies of the Washington administration. He retired in 1828, ending a long and distinguished career devoted almost exclusively to newspaper publishing.[36]

Whereas most of the printers of the postwar era followed quiet publishing careers, still others exhibited a variety of skills and interests that had little to do with printing. Anthony Haswell, a former apprentice of Isaiah Thomas, wrote ballads and poetry.[37] John Mycall of Newburyport conducted a series of experiments with balloons in 1785.[38] The best known in this group was undoubtedly Thomas, the enterprising publisher of Worcester's *Massachusetts Spy,* who became active in preserving the records of the Revolution and the early Republic. With a keen sense for the future, Thomas particularly urged people to save their old newspapers, and in 1812 he founded the American Antiquarian Society to further this mission.[39]

New England's Revolutionary printers included a substantial minority who, failing to remain in the business very long, apparently conceived of printing either as a sideline or as a temporary occupation. Several in this category evidently provided capital for someone else's operation. While receiving credit on a newspaper's masthead and doing some of the work, they were hardly the real printers. Ezra Lunt, who fits this mold, ventured into the printing field only once, working with Henry-Walter Tinges in Newburyport from 1774 to 1775. He later ran a profitable stage route to Boston and managed a tavern in Newburyport.[40] At least three printers left the profession in order to do something else. Benjamin Titcomb of Portland, Maine, became a Baptist minister, while Daniel Bowen of New Haven and elsewhere exhibited wax works in Boston and Philadelphia.[41] Benjamin Dearborn of Portsmouth tried an interesting variety of money-making ventures after he left printing. He ran a store before becoming an auctioneer, opened a school for girls, and established an "intelligence office" or information exchange center. He also invented a set of scales and an engine and made some improvements in the standard printing press.[42]

Although it was an unusual occurrence during the eighteenth-century, a few college graduates became involved in printing enterprises. William Stearns and Daniel Bigelow, both Harvard graduates, managed the *Massachusetts Spy* from June 1776 to August 1777, apparently to ensure its continued existence after Isaiah Thomas left for Salem.[43] Josiah Meigs, with a Yale degree, helped manage the *New Haven Gazette* and the *New Haven Gazette, and Connecticut Magazine* from 1784 to 1789. Meigs continued an illustrious career after his departure from New Haven in 1789, practicing law in Bermuda from 1789 to 1794; teaching mathematics, natural philosophy, and chemistry at Yale from 1794 to 1801; acting as president of the University of Georgia from 1801 to 1810; and serving as United States Surveyor General from 1812 to 1814.[44] Probably the most famous of these college graduates who took a hand in the production of a Revolutionary newspaper was Joel Barlow. Graduating from Yale in 1778, Barlow taught for several years and then served as a chaplain in the Continental Army. During 1784 and 1785, he partnered with Elisha Babcock in publishing the *American Mercury* in Hartford, Connecticut. Barlow, a poet and author of the "Vision of Columbus," worked hard throughout the 1780s to acquire adequate copyright laws. In 1788, he entered government service as an ambassador, serving in France, Great Britain, and Russia.[45]

Other printers besides Barlow filled government posts both at the national and state levels. Some, including John Carter and Isaiah Thomas, served as postmasters under both the British and the new American governments.[46] A few also entered the Continental Army during the Revolution: Benjamin Russell, Joel Barlow, and John Melcher, among others.[47] Judah Paddock Spooner sailed as a privateer in 1777. Captured after several successful voyages, he ended his military career on board the British prison ship *The Old Jersey*.[48] Others, such as Benjamin Edes, Thomas Adams, and Edward E. Powars, paid fines in order to avoid actual military duty.[49] Finally, one New England printer held a major post in the Revolutionary forces during the war: Solomon Southwick served as Rhode Island's commissary general, a post of great importance that brought a good deal of criticism for his handling of the job. Throughout his service, Southwick complained of the problems in acquiring food for the troops. Still, he did manage to keep the Continental Army supplied fairly well whenever it resided within Rhode Island.[50]

Southwick was an unusual printer because he held a higher social position than most newspaper publishers. At the time of his flight from Newport in 1776, Southwick held a seat in the Rhode Island assembly, an unusual position to be occupied by a New England printer.[51] While most printers held some form of public office, they did not acquire anything above the town level. One recent study of Revolutionary Boston concluded that wealthy men continued to monopolize the more important posts, as they had done prior to the war.[52] Printers did not fall into that group. Although the posts filled by these men varied a great deal, they tended to be minor. Their jobs ranged from justice of the peace and town constable to hogreeve and coroner. The most popular appointments for printers were clerk of the market and surveyor of boards, but a few did achieve more prestigious local offices.[53] Barzillai Hudson and Timothy Green III secured seats on the Common Councils of Hartford and New London, respectively.[54] Timothy Green also served one term in the Connecticut assembly, from 1780 to 1781.[55] Josiah Meigs performed as the city clerk for New Haven from 1784 until he left in 1789.[56] All of these posts, while not insignificant on the local level, brought minimal influence beyond the town. Not until the 1790s did printers begin regularly to hold positions on the state level. Still, government leaders did desire their advice and support on occasion. For example, in 1788, Governor John Hancock of Massachusetts asked Isaiah Thomas to recommend someone as a candidate for Worcester County sheriff.[57] Even though printers did not generally hold state office, their opinions carried weight among those in power because government leaders, recognizing the impact of newspapers on the general populace, did not wish to alienate the men who directed them.

The printer was an artisan and a tradesman, a man who worked with his hands. The product of his hands, however, had the potential of influencing everyone and shaping public affairs. Still, many people did not consider printing a fit profession for an educated person. (As stated earlier, few college graduates entered the profession.)[58] In 1781, George Hough wrote of resigning himself to earning a living "by hard labour, among the rest of the mechanical tribes. I once had a prospect of attaining to some other employment; but it is all vanished, and I am left as it were to make the best use of a bad bargain." Clearly, Hough did not have a very high opinion of printing as a profession.[59]

Other indications of confusion over the status of printers appeared in newspaper pages. Because some people had difficulty joining possession of a good character with the job of publishing a newspaper, printers often used eulogies of their fellows to defend their profession. When John Gill died in 1785, his former partner, Benjamin Edes, praised him as "a friend to his country and mankind, whose integrity and industry were equally conspicuous, and not to be unnoticed, though in the vehicle of a newspaper."[60] Daniel Fowle's death in 1787 produced the comment that he had "as good a Character as almost any upon this continent." Moreover, "he confined himself to his own private walk in life, wisely avoiding the dangerous quicksands of politics, and never unnecessarily interested himself in polemic subjects."[61] Even though the printers' actions during the war had shown that the newspapers could be used very effectively in the political arena, many people were still unsure about the role the printer should play in the community.

Still, no one could deny that a printer influenced his readers through the pages of his newspaper. Just the fact that almost everyone in any given community either read the newspaper or had it read to them underscored the potential influence of the printer. This latent power meant that the printer could not be dismissed or ignored. For some printers, this meant a position of some stature in the community, indicated by a certain amount of deference by their fellow citizens. By the middle of the 1780s, a number of printers, including Isaiah Thomas and Timothy Green III, were being referred to as "Esquire," a form of address indicating a high status in the community. Still, printers remained mechanics in the eyes of many, and their social position remained unclear throughout the period, leaving questions that would not be settled until the separation of the functions of printer and editor, a process that began in the 1790s.[62]

Although the recognizable social level of printers cannot easily be determined, generalizations about the overall financial standing of these New Englanders are possible. A previous investigation of the estates of Boston printers affirmed that those who published newspapers proved to be the most prosperous.[63] In general, this conclusion is correct, but estate inventories and wills are scarce; many people died intestate because they did not take time to make a will. However, existing records do provide at least an indication of the overall business success of New England's Revolutionary era printers. The value of the estates examined in this study varied from Roger Storrs's $175.90 to Barzillai Hudson's $115,029.18, but most of the printers who managed to establish their newspapers on a solid footing did well for themselves (see table 3–1).[64]

Estate records provide indications concerning a printer's pros-

Table 3–1
Value of Printers' Estates at Time of Death
(in 1970 dollars)

Name	Year of Death	Personal Estate	Real Estate	Total Estate
Ebenezer Watson	1777	———	———	$ 7,740.02
John Gill	1785	$1,068.01	$ 8,038.15	$ 9,106.16
William Warden	1786	———	———	$ 868.18*
John Nourse	1790	$1,451.31	$ 1,260.12	$ 2,711.43
Timothy Green	1796	———	———	$ 9,824.96
Ezekiel Russell	1796	———	———	$ 519.83
Samuel Green	1799	———	———	$ 2,753.70
Thomas Adams	1799	$9,945.36	$ 9,932.00	$ 19,877.36
Benjamin Edes, Jr.	1801	———	———	$ 203.84
John Trumbull	1802	———	———	$ 7,099.18
Benjamin Edes, Sr.	1803	———	———	$ 8,635.30
John Fleet	1806	$2,955.86	$78,341.32	$ 81,297.18
Thomas Green	1812?	$1,574.78	$ 4,813.20	$ 6,387.98
Roger Storrs	1820?	———	———	$ 175.90*
Barzillai Hudson	1823	———	———	$ 115,029.18
John W. Folsom	1825	$1,304.91	$11,765.60	$ 13,070.51
Thomas B. Wait	1830	———	———	$ 1,187.83*
Isaiah Thomas	1831	$8,790.79	$13,293.60	$ 22,084.39
Benjamin Russell	1845	$3,573.80	$41,599.80	$ 45,173.60

*Died insolvent, with more debts than assets

The original figures for these estate inventories were converted to 1970 dollars using the wholesale price indices of Warren and Pearson for the period 1749–1890 and the Bureau of Labor Statistics table for 1890–1970. Source for these indices: U.S. Bureau of the Census, *Historical Statistics of the United States, Colonial Times to 1970* (Washington, D.C.: United States Department of Commerce, Bureau of the Census, 1975), 1:199–202.

perity, but they can be used only when considering a person's lifetime success. In order to make statements about the Revolutionary era, one must turn to other sources, primarily tax records. Even here, the materials are not always in existence or accessible. Still, the records indicate that the years after the war saw the finances of printers stabilize and slowly take an upward turn. By 1787, Timothy Green III had enough free capital to invest in real estate that cost him £15 in taxes.[65] The real estate valuation lists from Worcester, Massachusetts, for 1778 and 1783 provide a nice portrait of the financial improvements in the lives of several printers because these lists rank taxpayers from highest to lowest.

In 1778, Isaiah Thomas owned personal property worth £14 and was ranked 248 out of 345; William Stearns ranked 217 and owned personal property taxed at £22. By 1783, Stearns, no longer in the printing business, had risen to 58 and was paying £1:15:9½ in taxes. Thomas, on the other hand, now stood at 40 and paid £2:7:10½ in 1783.[66] Five years had made a big difference for Isaiah Thomas. In the years that followed, Thomas's finances continued to improve and his position in the community rose with them. By 1815 he owned $19,720.37 (1970 dollars) in property and had served as a judge of the Court of Sessions for the state of Massachusetts. He owned property in Maine, New Hampshire, and Vermont, as well as in Boston and Worcester in Massachusetts. Thomas had clearly become a man of substance.[67] Thomas, however, is the exception rather than the rule. Few printers of the Revolutionary era achieved either his financial solidarity or his position in the community. One study of Boston estimated the mean assessed wealth of a printer in 1790 as £247, or approximately $2,146.55 (1970 dollars).[68]

The average New England newspaper printer of the Revolutionary era was a hard worker who had learned his profession through an apprenticeship to a master in the trade and then had established his position by opening his own business, more often than not in his early thirties. Through the apprenticeship system, he developed contacts with other printers that formed a useful network for acquiring news, information, supplies, and equipment. These networks demonstrate a growth of a sense of professionalism among printers. As indicated by the development of these networks, as well as concern over anonymous contributors, plagiarism, and copyrights, the eighteenth-century pressman was increasingly conscious that printing was a vocation with standards and ethics to uphold. Politically, the New England printer supported the American side in the quarrel with Great Britain and used his newspaper to further the goals of the American Revolution. He eventually held some sort of political office, mostly on the local level, but maintained some influence on higher levels among leaders who appreciated the influence of his paper with the people. While not financially successful on a grand scale, he did manage to make a comfortable living and died with a fairly sizeable estate to leave his family. Although it seems that much of this success came after 1789, some indications of better things to come appeared in the 1780s as Americans began to rebuild their lives and the institutions disrupted by the war.

4
The Printer and His Public

Ever since the first publication of the *Boston News-Letter* in 1704, the New England colonial newspaper had been a hodgepodge of materials that fulfilled a variety of roles. Both the public and the printers saw the newspapers functioning in several ways. The printer often published pieces written by himself or a reader that discussed the usefulness of a newspaper press and the role(s) it should fill. All agreed that the weekly sheets should provide news, but that instruction and entertainment should also be offered. The pages of New England's Revolutionary newspapers show clearly the conscious efforts of printers to reach this goal through the variety of materials offered in their sheets. One measure of their success is the wide circulation of their newspapers, which often reached three times as many readers as there were subscribers. New England public prints were popular because they gave the average person an inexpensive way to find out about the world around him.

Revolutionary newspapers have been compared to the English provincial sheets of the early eighteenth century. One historian of the British press declared that, at first, the production of the presses outside of London consisted primarily of news items accompanied occasionally by essays and other materials designed to enlighten and amuse readers. By 1740, the provincial newspapers had advanced beyond the role of just a news source to that of providing a variety of items of "intelligence, instruction, and entertainment" intended to expand the knowledge of the paper's readers.[1] This description of the British provincial press could easily be applied to the public prints of New England. By the beginning of the war, printers regularly included a diversity of articles in their sheets, hoping to appeal to a wide audience and to fulfill the different needs and desires of their readers.

Opinions abounded concerning the usefulness of printing and the purpose of newspapers. The colonial sheets themselves teem with a diversity of opinions held by the public concerning printing. In general, the art of printing held a place of high esteem among most learned men. One author, for instance, declared printing to be "the greatest gift that Heaven, in its clemency has bestowed on man." Isaiah Thomas, describing printing as "that art which is the preserver of all arts," urged that it was "worthy of the attention of the learned and the curious." In 1789, one essayist concluded that printing had been "the antidote to the fatal poison that was to enslave us all."[2]

Many essayists, while praising printing as an important trade, issued their highest commendations for newspapers, "the histories of the day." According to one writer in the *Vermont Gazette*, "whatever instruction is reaped from history, may be reaped from a newspaper, which is the history of the world for one day." The public prints should not only keep the people informed of important current events, but they should also educate their readers through "free and liberal enquiries upon points of morality, science and philosophy, government, laws and finance, trade, manufactures, agriculture and commerce." One anonymous essayist praised a father who had his daughter read a newspaper in conjunction with maps and a globe in order to learn geography, all of which was "reading a newspaper to some purpose."[3]

For a number of thoughtful people, newspapers extended the best and easiest means of communicating information to a majority of the people. "Impartialist" affirmed that

> whatever diffuses knowledge to the public ear, whatever informs and animates the soul, whatever is calculated to rectify the judgment and amend the will, whatever tends to rouse, to alarm the stupid and careless, to enliven and prompt the generous and noble, to rise to support and defend the cause of liberty and of human nature, doth answer an invaluable purpose. And that newspapers do in a great measure.[4]

Through the columns of these four-page sheets, New Englanders managed to stay attuned of events in America as well as around the world.

Everyone, however, did not hold such a high opinion of the newspaper press. In the *Boston Gazette*, "Mentor" expressed fears that the public prints "appear to be only calculated to blow up the fuel of discontent." Other writers, while not totally condemning newssheets, fully recognized the possibilities for trouble—"the evils of Pandora's box do not operate more powerfully, or diffuse themselves more extensively, than these paragraphs do over the face of the whole earth." "Quidnunc," the author of the preceding declaration, also complained of the trouble caused by newspapers spreading rumors when accurate information was unavailable.[5]

Still, most stated public opinions praised newspapers for keeping the populace informed and knowledgeable. "Impartialist" concluded that "from news-papers the generality of the good people in this Commonwealth, gain their information of the world at large—from them they learn the conduct of their rulers— what public measures are pursued, and acquire their necessary domestick information." Furthermore, he declared that "a newspaper is the poor man's library—the herald of the times—and the tongue of the people—here alone can the poor honest subject be on a par with the rich oppressor." Newspapers constituted "the imperial tribunal of the public," a forum for handling problems that normally fell outside the reach of the law. Clearly, when seen in this light, the general public afforded a place of importance to the weekly sheets issuing from the printers' presses.[6]

From time to time, a poet would venture his thoughts on newspapers. In attacking the Massachusetts Stamp Act of 1785, one bard declared " 'Tis truth (with def'rence to the college) NEWS-PAPERS are the springs of knowledge." He continued with the thought that "a news-paper is like a feast, some dish there is for ev'ry guest." Another poet expressed this idea even better when he affirmed that "Here you may range the world from pole to pole, Increase your knowledge, and delight your soul; Travel all countries, and inform your sense, With . . . safety, at a small expense."[7]

Throughout the Revolutionary era, thoughtful essayists commended the newspapers for the role they played in the proper functioning of a republican government. "Consideration" stated that "without knowledge among the people, liberty and public happiness cannot exist long in any country; and this necessary knowledge cannot be obtained in any other way than by a general circulation of publick papers. . . . Ignorance is the dark door at which tyranny enters." Newspapers, by providing a cheap and easy method for people to acquire political information, filled an essential role in preserving public liberty. They were "the pulse by which people at a distance generally feel the state of the body politic." Many writers would have agreed wholeheartedly with the author of a widely reprinted piece that appeared in 1788. The writer vowed that "News-Papers are the Guardians of Freedom; by Newspapers only are ye made acquainted with the rise and fall of empires; the mighty revolutions that vary the face of the world; and of the Freedom of Slavery of your own species."[8]

The men who produced the weekly sheets clearly had ideas about what their papers should do and what they could accomplish. Specifically, during the years of the fighting, the printers endeavored to use the pages of their sheets "to keep up a most vigorous opposition to the engines of slavery and bloody oppression." Solomon Southwick, in reply to a verbal attack for supporting the Whig cause, replied with these stirring words:

> I acknowledge I have taken a part in favour of the people; and am determined to employ the small abilities God has given me, in their favor, and in opposing all such tyrants, and traitors to their country, as I look upon you to be, to the last moment of my life. . . . You have my hearty consent to drop my paper. I will never court the favour of those who are enemies to the liberties of mankind, as all the TORIES most certainly are. . . . All enemies to the liberties of the people must be punished, here or hereafter; that all who aiding and abetting the present measures, against this country, are such enemies, and that you, as base tools to others, in hopes of some petty offices, are some of these enemies, is the candid opinion of Yours, &c. S. Southwick[9]

Printers urged people to continue their support for the press because "at a time when our all is at stake; when no less than the fate of the States of America is in agitation, then (of all times) the means of conveying intelligence ought to be encouraged." When Edward E. Powars and Nathanial Willis assumed control of the *New England Chronicle* in 1776, they promised their readers that they would print pieces that would "inspire all orders of men with a true spirit of resolution and heroism in support of our invaluable rights and liberties." They also assured the public that "the character it [the *Chronicle*] has hitherto sustained, in exposing, condemning and execrating the jesuitical and infernal machinations of tories and tyrants, and in rendering due praise and honour to the manly and virtuous supporters of the Glorious Cause of America, we shall, with assiduity and zeal, endeavour to preserve." In 1778, these same two men expressed the general feeling that most newspapermen had concerning the significance of the press in the fight against Great Britain: "If the despotic measures and deep-laid plots of a British court had not been freely canvassed and laid open by means of these publications, we might, before this time, have been fast bound by the chains of tyranny."[10]

Even after the end of the fighting in 1781, printers continued to emphasize the necessity of newspapers for the continued existence of liberty. In urging public support for his paper to prevent its folding, the printer of the *New Hampshire Recorder* declared "our rising generation will doubtless execrate the memory of those, who, by their negligence, have destroyed the greatest bulwark of their freedom, and the only avenue thro' which they might be acquainted with the proceedings of our young but flourishing Empire." At the time of Shays's Rebellion, several editors blamed the disturbance on the lack of regular and accurate information (such as provided by the public prints) in the backcountry.[11] The printers of the *Salem Mercury* presented their paper as an effort "to soothe or heal . . . the publick wounds, made by domestick dissensions, so fatal to the general prosperity of the commonwealth." In establishing the *Hampshire Gazette* in Northampton, Massachusetts, William Butler announced that "in a country like this, where our national character and happiness so entirely depend upon a general diffusion of knowledge among the people, the extensive advantages of such periodical publications cannot be too often explained or too highly estimated." In the first issue of the *Western Star* of Stockbridge, Massachusetts, Loring Andrews affirmed that "if the rulers of a people act uprightly, study the interests of their constituents, and consult the good of the great whole, the people will rest satisfied, if they know it; and the true and only sure channel through which this information can be gained, is a NEWSPAPER."[12]

According to their printers, newspapers fulfilled an important function in Revolutionary New England. Many of them reprinted a piece on the need for newspapers affirming that "every thing that deserves the attention of the public, may, in this channel, be conveyed to their understandings, with more ease and expedition than by any other method hitherto invented." Josiah Meigs concluded that, through a newspaper, a printer could "entertain or instruct, at once, greater Multitudes than those which heard the Orators of Greece or Rome." Many printers also foresaw a long-range use and purpose for their newspapers and urged their readers to preserve them for the future. Isaiah Thomas declared that, by saving one's newspapers, a person would "provide knowledge and entertainment to the rising generations." Benjamin Russell took this one step further, asserting that the newspapers would provide "a just, particular and impartial History of the transactions of the present day."[13]

At the same time, printers envisioned still other roles for their four-page productions. Most printers, desiring that their newspapers be "useful and entertaining," tried to include "useful Speculations, interesting Branches of History, and useful Discoveries, in the Arts and Sciences" as often as possible. They wanted a variety of materials in their papers so that "a man of the most uncommon taste" could "find a something that will tickle his fancy" and encourage "him to proceed hoping that he will find a something more." In fact, many printers considered their role and the role of their newspapers to be to bring to light "whatever may be thought worthy the public eye, whatever may have a tendency to reform public morals, or tend in any sort, to public or private benefit."[14]

Efforts to instruct and educate the people appeared in the form of essays submitted for publication by local readers or pieces clipped from other sheets. The subject matter ranged from scientific discussions of eclipses to agricultural topics such as how to save apple trees from canker worms to strange and unusual stories such as the "account of a girl who subsided on water alone for nearly four years." Many essays, or series of essays, appeared in practically all the public prints. These included items like "Common Sense" and "The Crisis" by Thomas Paine and Dr. Benjamin Price's "Observations on the Importance of the American Revolution." Issues of concern to the general public also received notice. During the winter and spring of 1786, a time when the legal profession was receiving a great deal of criticism in the Massachusetts backcountry, Boston's *Independent Chronicle* carried numerous pieces discussing lawyers, the practice of law, and the judicial system as a whole. Tales of foreign places, such as "Some Particulars of the Russian Peasantry" or "Description of some uncommon Animals, found in the island of Margnam, in Brasil," proved common. Pieces full of advice also abounded. Details on how to grow one's crops or encouragement for the education of one's children appeared regularly. The variety of topics that could be covered almost had no end.[15]

The 1780s brought efforts to appeal more to women who read the papers. Two landmark studies of women during the Revolutionary era found an increased interest in their education.[16] New England's newspapers reflected this interest by including sections designed specifically for the edification of female readers. But even when no designated portion of the paper dealt with female topics, stories about or for women proved popular. Advice or criticism about current fashions appeared frequently. Particularly criticized were the large hats that became popular in the 1780s. Some printers castigated women for wearing them because they prevented others from seeing around them, and they could prove a health hazard. In reporting that a woman wearing such a hat was struck by lightning, John Gill, in the *Continental Journal*, advised that "it was conjectured that the multiplicity of wires and pins used in the construction of those very complicated machines, attracted the lightning, to the great terror and danger of the owner." Furthermore, he urged everyone who wore these hats "to provide themselves with conducting wires which may carry off the electrical fire into a basin of water." A later piece in the *Journal* assailed women who used snuff, for snuff prevented them from appearing "amiable in the eyes of men." John Gill also made a public attack on prostitution, calling on "the public in general to perform their duty in extirpating those nefarious female wretches, who live by the destruction of the morals and manners of our rising generation."[17]

John Gill clearly thought that females had a well-defined role to fulfill, and many of the newspaper pieces dealing with the fair sex were designed to educate women concerning this assigned function. Essays on the differences between the sexes appeared as well as advice on how to be good wives and mothers. One essayist in the *New Haven Gazette, and Connecticut Magazine* complained that Americans overeducated their daughters, preventing early marriages and creating general distress. Many people would have disagreed with this extreme sentiment, but clearly a woman's place was in the home raising a family. A writer in the *Middlesex Gazette* declared that one of "the three greatest Beauties in Nature" was "a young married woman, tidily dressed in her own manufactory, with a babe in her arms." Even tales of interesting occurrences addressed woman's place in society. One of these, originating in New Hampshire, told of a married woman being sold by her husband for a horse and a suit of clothes. The woman did not object to this transaction "because of vows of obedience to her husband." Statements such as this one underscore the fact that eighteenth-century women were sometimes considered the property of their husbands, with few legal means of defending their rights. Society dictated that women fulfill their proper life role in the home as wives and mothers, a concept clearly reflected by New England's newspapers in their coverage of feminine topics.[18]

Medical advice appeared regularly. Most of it dealt with problems that persons might encounter in their day-to-day lives. Advice on how to save a possible drowning victim became very common. Many areas even formed "humane societies" for the purpose of spreading information on how to save someone near death from drowning. Another popular medical topic was what to do if bitten by a mad dog. Essays on how to eat properly and advice on childbirth appeared occasionally. The problem of a toothache produced some novel advice in the *Freeman's Oracle:* "Get a strong artificial magnet; let the patient turn his back to the North, then touch the aching tooth with the magnet, in less than one minute the cure is effected."[19]

Discussions of religion could always be counted on to attract readers, and the printers took advantage of the opportunity as often as possible. The installation of Samuel Seabury as America's first Anglican bishop produced a flurry of comments and essays throughout 1786. The Shaker sect bore the brunt of a great many negative and sneering comments in the New England press in the 1780s. Some editors took great pleasure in reporting that several of the Shakers in Northampton, Massachusetts had been convicted of adultery—"It is said the woman, conceiving her husband to be an unholy man, thought she ought not to cohabit with him, or suffer him to partake of those conjugal pleasures which were his right only to enjoy; but threw herself into the arms and embraces of one of the Brotherhood, who was as she supposed, more righteous; and is said is pregnant by him. It is hoped these disturbers of the peace will all be taken care of." Sarcasm oozed from the printer of the *Cumberland Gazette* when he published that "the Fathers or Elders of the people called Shakers have now, as they say, 'shut up the gates of the kingdom of Heaven forever!' We mention this only to notify those of other denominations, who are travelling thitherward, that they will arrive too late."[20]

The slavery issue also began to rear its head in New England during the Revolutionary era, particularly in Rhode Island. As the years passed, the number of pieces speaking against slavery and the slave trade increased. Because most of the slave ships originated in New England ports, many of the essays attacked Yankee merchants for their role in this blight on America's character. In 1787, a writer in the *Massachusetts Centinel* declared:

> We, as Americans, boast much of our love of FREEDOM—so we ought to do: But we, at the same time, shew to the world, a dastardly spirit, by depriving others of what we ourselves are so fond of. . . . Each of your ships loaded with stolen Negroes, is a hell and you are devils who reign in them, and the prince of the power of the air, the chief of devils, is your master—Humanity bleeds—and it is you who give the wound! Your trade is an affront to reason, and an open violation of all the laws of justice and humanity.[21]

Even as early as 1776, some writers feared the effect of slavery: "What the consequence of our continuing under the dominion of

our vices, Heaven only knows! . . . Is it not an iniquity which
separates between us and our God, that we continue to hold in
bondage the Africans?" This author even verbalized questions
about slavery's overall justification, the inferiority of the Africans,
by asking "Does a difference in colour constitute our right? May
not the same be urged by them against us?" Finally, one essayist
expressed the hopes of many early abolitionists when he requested that "God grant that the spirit of liberty which appears to
be spreading itself over the whole world, may be efficacious in
eradicating that bane to every principle, civil and sacred, SLAV-
ERY."[22]

Even with the large number of essays and letters full of literature, opinions, and advice, most people still turned to newspapers to find out what was going on in the world outside their
own little community. Some of the news items, such as reports of
accidents, crimes, and strange happenings, would often serve the
dual role of information and entertainment. Discussions of violent
crimes would often be sanitized in some manner, such as only
hinting at what actually happened rather than producing a factual
story. This proved particularly true in reports of rape because
societal custom forbade describing these crimes in any great de-
tail. For example, in telling of the conviction of a rapist in 1779,
Isaiah Thomas surmised that "it is supposed that greater instances
of brutality and barbarity, were never exercised in a crime of this
kind, than were exhibited by said Young in the perpetration of
this inhuman deed. The circumstances of which decency forbids
us to publish in a public news paper."[23]

Most news items in eighteenth-century newspapers consisted
of statements clipped from other papers that described events
throughout the rest of America and the world. Happenings such
as the Declaration of Independence, the various battles of the war,
Benedict Arnold's treason, the signing of the peace treaty, Shays's
Rebellion, and the adoption of the Federal Constitution received
due coverage in all of New England's public prints. One study of
the early nineteenth-century country press in New York concluded that while a variety of materials appeared in newspapers
domestic and foreign news contended for the largest amount of
space.[24]

The contents of New England newspapers during the Revolutionary era tended to follow a similar pattern to that found in the
New York study. However, there were some differences (see table
4–1). Domestic and foreign news vied for a large share of the
available space, but domestic items generally prevailed. Adver-

Table 4-1

New England Newspapers, 1775–1789—Percentage of Total Available Space Allotted to:

Year	Advertisements	Essays and Letters	Poetry	Announcements	British News	Foreign News	Local News	Other Domestic News
1775	19.10	20.61	1.66	7.25	18.51	1.58	7.95	23.34
1776	20.98	15.87	1.22	9.69	13.66	.98	6.38	31.21
1777	25.10	11.40	1.49	11.79	13.77	.84	6.18	29.43
1778	29.00	17.17	1.88	10.79	13.27	1.38	6.09	20.43
1779	25.84	19.30	1.11	8.02	10.38	2.76	6.96	25.66
1780	22.82	19.22	.80	8.22	15.82	3.27	7.25	22.62
1781	28.23	12.23	1.00	7.07	14.28	5.19	4.85	27.15
1782	30.37	15.68	1.37	5.13	16.99	4.77	4.74	20.97
1783	31.12	18.99	1.86	7.56	13.06	4.12	4.72	18.59
1784	32.56	23.27	2.44	4.46	14.45	4.00	4.63	14.20
1785	26.88	31.32	3.47	3.41	10.63	3.10	5.12	16.10
1786	19.30	32.16	3.64	6.75	10.04	2.88	5.87	19.34
1787	20.15	27.13	3.73	8.65	8.57	3.14	7.06	21.60
1788	22.09	24.44	4.01	5.45	10.04	4.34	6.14	23.50
1789	22.35	18.64	3.59	17.08	7.31	6.60	5.86	18.58

See Appendix 1 for explanation of the survey method used to collect data for the above percentages.

tisements always constituted a major portion of each issue, usually taking up one-fifth to one-fourth of the available space and even approaching the one-third mark on occasion. Essays and letters also made up an important part of each newspaper, although the amount of space they covered varied, ranging from just over 10 percent to almost 33 percent. Poetry and public announcements accounted for approximately 10 percent of the available space. Finally, local news took up about one-twentieth of each issue. Local news never proved a major part of a newspaper during the Revolutionary era because people acquired this information by word of mouth. A good example of this appeared in the *Massachusetts Centinel* in 1788 when Benjamin Russell referred to "a late unhappy event" and "accusations" that "have been the cause of so much domestick calamity, and publick speculation." He reported that the accusations had been proved false, but did not actually report what supposedly happened, assuming that his readers had already acquired this information by word of mouth. But, even though local news never took up a great deal of space in any newspaper, it did make up a regular portion of almost every issue, averaging consistently between 4 percent and 7 percent.[25]

Obvious changes over time did not occur in the amount of space allotted to various items. There were, however, differences at specific times that can be attributed to certain events. The increase in domestic news from 23.34 percent in 1775 to 31.21 percent in 1776 resulted from heightened interest in intercolonial happenings because of the war. The drop in the number of advertisements from 26.88 percent in 1785 to 19.30 percent in 1786 can be explained by the passage of an advertisement tax in Massachusetts.[26] The jump in announcements from 5.45 percent in 1788 to 17.08 percent in 1789 is attributable to the inauguration of the new constitutional government and the great curiosity shown concerning its early proceedings. The rise in European news, excluding Great Britain, from 4.34 percent in 1788 to 6.60 percent in 1789 came about because of the French Revolution. Although changes such as these can be seen, no long-term trends can be found.

The contents of a newspaper provided a variety of information and instruction, but it meant very little if the sheets went unread. Valid data on newspaper circulations prior to the nineteenth century is practically nonexistent, but some estimates can be made using the information available. One obvious source is statements by the printers themselves. Prior to the skirmishes at Lexington and Concord, the *Boston Gazette* and the *Massachusetts Spy* claimed weekly runs of two thousand and thirty-five hundred, respectively. Isaiah Thomas's flight to Worcester greatly affected his paper's circulation, which immediately declined to fifteen hundred a week and continued to decrease until it reached a low point of one hundred fifty in the winter of 1779–1780. In 1778, the *Connecticut Courant* laid claim to the largest circulation in New England during the period when it asserted that its weekly output approached eight thousand copies. The *New Haven Gazette, and Connecticut Magazine* contended that they published nearly nine hundred papers a week. The minimum number necessary for a successful operation, according to Isaiah Thomas, was approximately six hundred.[27]

While all of the figures quoted above came from the printers themselves and could be biased, some more recent estimates reach similar totals. Circulations for any New Hampshire paper during the years 1775 to 1789 have been set at a maximum figure of five hundred. A study of the *Connecticut Courant* assessed its wartime subscription list to be seven hundred—total output would be higher because extra copies would always be produced for people who bought papers occasionally. Furthermore, the study figured the average circulation for any New England newspaper at the outbreak of the war to be six hundred. Another scholar estimated that a printer could support a paper with only three hundred to four hundred subscribers *if* he collected 75 percent of his bills and did other types of printing as well, but prompt payments were not common and most printers desired a larger subscription list in order to be somewhat prepared for late payments. From these calculations, a subscription list of approximately five hundred would be necessary in order for a paper to break even.[28]

Even so, subscription lists are not the only sources for clues to newspaper circulations. A possibility for ascertaining how widespread a newspaper circulated is to consider the routes of the postriders. Almost all public prints depended on subscribers both within the town of publication and the surrounding countryside. Those who lived in town generally picked up their papers, while those in outlying areas received theirs from a postrider, a person who contracted with the printer to deliver his papers. The *Hampshire Gazette*, published in Northampton, Massachusetts, circulated throughout the neighboring towns. Eight postriders carried papers to Hadley, Amherst, Williamsburg, Hatfield, Deerfield, and all the other communities within a day's ride of Northampton. The *Hampshire Gazette* was a relatively small paper. The *Connecticut Courant* of Hartford, on the other hand, had a large output and riders carried it throughout Connecticut and into western Massachusetts and New Hampshire.[29]

Although estimates of newspaper circulation during the Revolutionary era are fragmentary and possibly unreliable, there can still be little doubt that the newspapers were read widely. It is generally accepted that newspapers passed from hand to hand until they were dog-eared. Taverns and inns generally subscribed to the various sheets for their customers, who often read aloud for the benefit of those who could not read themselves. One calculation asserted that a minimum of three people read each newspaper issued in a large urban area.[30] A widely reprinted essay, which first appeared in New England in 1783, declared that "the value of them [newspapers] may, in some measure, be determined by the fondness of people to read them.—The moment the paper is published, the office is crowded with readers—the post riders flock from every corner of the state, and must go, let it rain or shine." The Revolution had served as a catalyst, increasing the demand for news and newspapers. Diaries for the Revolutionary era referred to subscriptions to newspapers where none had existed before, attesting to an increased interest in what was going on outside of New England. Most printers would have agreed with a London essayist who stated that "if the merit of a publication is to be judged of by the rapid and general sale it has with the public, and by the number of editions with corrections and improvements, a News-Paper may be ranked among the very first productions of the age, for it is read with avidity by men of all descriptions, from Majesty itself down to the ale-house politician."[31]

New England newspapers during the Revolutionary era provided a majority of the communications that most people received concerning the war and national issues that became important in the early years of peace after Yorktown. Because of their widespread circulation and because there were many more readers than subscribers, the weekly sheets placed an enormous amount of material and information within reach of a large portion of the general populace. The public prints proved able to fulfill the role assigned to them by both the public and the printers, that is, they provided "intelligence, instruction, and entertainment." They were, in truth, "the poor man's library."[32]

5
Newspapers and Government: A Tension-Filled Relationship

Ever since the first periodical publications appeared in Europe, newspaper printers have had a strange love-hate relationship with the government and its officials. This proved particularly true during the newspaper's first century of existence in America. The local or state government proved a good source for printing contracts or public jobs, but it also occasionally attempted to muzzle the press. During the American Revolution, the government continued to provide jobs for printers, both in and outside of their chosen profession. However, the vicissitudes of war disrupted the accustomed practices and produced changes in how the government dealt with printers. The issue of the freedom of the press sparked discussion throughout the era, culminating in the widespread debate that arose in the wake of Massachusetts's passage of a stamp tax and, after its repeal, a duty on advertising.

Because so many people had access to the public prints, newspapers provided an excellent means for the various levels of government to keep their constituents informed. Requests for publication of government actions in the local newspaper abound in surviving public records. While one study asserts that reports about town meetings in the newspapers was not a general policy, announcements of town meetings accompanied by pieces encouraging everyone to attend appeared whenever the printer considered the subject of the meeting important. Newspapers constituted the commonly used medium for the publication of town resolutions, which dealt with a variety of topics of concern to the general populace. During the winter, all papers carried regular warnings about the need to keep chimneys clean in order to prevent fires. Residents were also urged to maintain ladders and firebuckets in case a fire broke out. Other printed public notices focused on the illegality of swine being loose inside the town limits and the dangers of driving sleighs wildly through the streets. Newspaper printers also often took the initiative on local issues by urging the town to action. Two good examples of this appeared in the *Boston Gazette* in 1785. The first, emphasizing the danger of crossing Charlestown Neck in a storm or after dark, advised the town to take some form of action to alleviate the problem. The second called for passage of a tax on transient persons in order to ensure that they helped support the town, which had to maintain them.[1]

New England newspapers frequently carried notices dealing with matters on the state or national level as well. Announcements of meetings of the legislature, copies of state constitutions and laws, and information on elections often took up space in the weekly sheets. Warnings about counterfeiters, pleas for supplies for the army, and ordinances concerning the western territories are some of the subjects the Continental Congress requested that all printers publish in their newspapers. Most printers readily complied because their readers took an avid interest in the actions of the central government. Notices and accounts of public holidays, such as the Fourth of July or a national day of thanksgiving and prayer, appeared regularly and often prompted the printer to call on his readers "to contemplate those blessings, which should cause the warmest effusions of gratitude to ascend in songs of praise to the Great Bestower of every good and perfect gift."[2]

The Continental Congress indicated the importance attached to newspapers as a source of information when it arranged to receive three copies of one publication from every state. Included in this group were the *New Hampshire Gazette* of Portsmouth, New Hampshire; the *Newport Mercury* of Newport, Rhode Island; the *Independent Chronicle* of Boston, Massachusetts; and the *New Haven Gazette* of New Haven, Connecticut. At one time, the Congress hoped to sponsor its own paper, but nothing ever came of the idea. In order to maintain this avenue of communication with the people, various governments often tried to ease the printers' wartime burdens whenever possible. In 1777, the Connecticut Assembly resolved to exempt all individuals involved in the printing business in Hartford from militia duty. Even more helpful were the occasions when state officials managed to acquire paper for the local printer. Twice in 1775 the Provincial Congress of Massachusetts supplied Isaiah Thomas with some paper. Supplies became extremely scarce during the war, and the printers welcomed any and all aid they could get.[3]

Although publication of government notices produced one financial connection between newspaper printers and public officials, the major economic interaction between them concerned the production of records and documents not carried in the weekly newssheet. Printers avidly sought public printing contracts for the prestige they offered as well as for the money they could bring. Prior to the Revolution, most colonial governments had appointed an official printer who did all the government work. The 1760s saw the beginning of a slow breakdown in this process. While public printers still proved to be the rule, oftentimes the assembly had one and the governor and council had another. Some appointments proved short-lived as legislatures began to spread the printing contracts around in attempts to acquire better prices. The need to get things published quickly sometimes induced government officers to turn to the closest printer rather than the officially appointed one. This proved particularly true in Connecticut in the early years of the war. Timothy Green of New London was the official state printer, but the assembly generally gave its contracts to Ebenezer Watson when meeting in Hartford and to Thomas and Samuel Green when in New Haven. Timothy Green still published the journals and laws, but anything needed quickly, such as broadsides about enlistments or proclamations of fast days, generally were done by the person closest to the location of the assembly at the time.[4]

New England legislatures continued to appoint state printers into the nineteenth century. In their efforts to acquire a printer, the legislature of Vermont offered an exclusive printing contract to anyone who would move his operation to Westminster. The Spooner brothers took the state up on the offer and remained the state printers of Vermont into the 1790s. Still, even in Vermont, some government jobs were done by other printers. New Hampshire considered designating a state printer in 1787, but nothing came of the move. Increasingly, state legislatures saw benefits in using the printer whose place of business was close by. In 1785, Connecticut dispensed with a public printer, declaring that, in the future, government work would be "printed in the town or place where said Assembly shall hold their session." Also, government officials realized that money could be saved by encouraging competition and playing printers off against each other. By not guaranteeing any more work beyond the immediate project, government officials forced printers to hold prices down in order to keep their government contracts.[5] Often the government proved to be a bad customer, failing to pay on time. Numerous petitions, noting hard times, requested that public printing accounts be settled promptly.[6]

Printers obviously churned out reams of official documents, ranging from compilations of laws and legislative journals to proclamations and paper money, but historians have disagreed about the importance of government contracts to a printer's income. Some historians of journalism credit government printing with doing more than anything else to encourage the growth of printing in America. Mary Ann Yodelis, on the other hand, concluded in her study of Boston from 1763 to 1775 that official publications constituted only one-fourth to one-third of the total printing done and that they contributed little to the overall success or failure of any given Boston printer. Marylouise Meder, in her biography of Timothy Green III, disagreed, stating that government printing contracts were important to Green during the war because his publishing output at the time consisted primarily of official documents and his newspapers. G. Thomas Tanselle, agreeing with Meder, stated in his compilation of statistics on American printing, 1764–1783, that the number of government publications went up sharply at the beginning of the war. Averages of Tanselle's data for the years 1775–1783 indicate that government printing constituted at least 40 percent of non-newspaper printing done in New England and actually ranged as high as 97.12 percent in New Hampshire (see table 5–1). Although there is conflicting evidence about the financial benefits of government contracts, clearly they did make up a large portion of most printers' total output.[7]

Printing official documents constituted only one form of interaction between printers and government officers. Another involved the post office. One historian asserted that throughout the colonial period publication of a newspaper had often been considered an adjunct of the local post office. Most of the early printers of weekly newssheets were postmasters. The newspaper and the post office grew and developed together, mainly because they shared common goals in the efforts to improve communication throughout the colonies. Most journalism historians support this contention; one even insisted that "the post office may fairly be called the godfather of American journalism."[8]

Further investigation, however, indicates that such assertions are exaggerations. While it is true that some early publishers doubled as postmasters, this did not become commonplace. Well-known printer/postmasters like Benjamin Franklin, William Goddard, and Isaiah Thomas were the exception rather than the rule. By mid-century, very few printers became postmasters. In 1774–1775, Hugh Finlay, Royal Surveyor of Posts, inspected the post offices in New England and the southern colonies. In his

Table 5–1
Government Publications as Percentage of Total Output:
New England, 1775–1783

Year	Connecticut	Massachusetts	New Hampshire	Rhode Island	Vermont
1775	25.00	56.70	100.00	30.60	100.00
1776	66.70	55.10	92.30	63.80	0.00
1777	46.70	62.00	100.00	97.70	100.00
1778	31.30	44.00	100.00	100.00	57.10
1779	50.00	43.40	100.00	61.20	55.50
1780	49.20	44.00	81.80	75.00	83.30
1781	42.40	39.80	100.00	60.30	78.90
1782	38.00	23.50	100.00	52.50	50.00
1783	20.30	23.50	100.00	52.60	61.50
Averages	41.07	43.56	97.12	65.97	73.29

This chart is based on figures in G. Thomas Tanselle, "Some Statistics on American Printing, 1764–1783," in Bernard Bailyn and John B. Hench, eds., *The Press and the American Revolution* (Worcester: American Antiquarian Society, 1980), 315–64. He used two sources for his data: Charles Evans, *American Bibliography*, 13 vols. (vols. 1–12, Chicago, 1903–1934; vol. 13, edited by Clifford K. Shipton, Worcester, 1955); Roger P. Bristol, *Supplement to Charles Evans' American Bibliography* (Charlottesville, 1970). He counts the number of government publications listed, then uses this number to figure the percentage of total output based on the total number of items listed.

journal, he lists thirty postmasters; one, John Carter, is clearly a printer while a second one, Eleazer Russell, may have been. In referring to Carter, Finlay describes him as "a printer, seemingly an active sensible man." Finlay seemed to think that a printer as postmaster was unusual. The possibility of a printer being a postmaster apparently became even less likely during the Revolutionary War. A compilation of those holding postmasterships during 1776 to 1778 contains seventy-three names, but only three were printers. Out of the ninety-three New England newspaper printers under study, only John Carter of Providence, Timothy Green of New London, Solomon Southwick of Newport, and Isaiah Thomas and William Stearns of Worcester doubled as postmasters. New England had twenty-one postmasters in 1788, according to a congressional report from the postmaster general. Of these, only three also printed newspapers (Thomas, Carter, and Green). In fact, out of a total of sixty-nine postmasters, only five were also newspaper printers while two or three others may have been job printers. Clearly, even if possession of a postal appointment was desirable, a printer rarely received one.[9]

Still, existence of a functioning postal system proved essential for the success of a newspaper. The lack of one in Vermont prompted Anthony Haswell and David Russell, newspaper publishers in Bennington, to ask the Governor and Council to establish post offices in Vermont. A good postal setup was necessary because it provided the means for exchanging newspapers, the principal source of information for the public prints. All newssheets generally travelled free throughout the period. So important was this practice that a rumor of its ending cost the postmaster general his job. In 1788, word began to spread that Ebenezer Hazard, an unpopular but very competent postmaster general, intended to stop the free exchange of newspapers through the public mails. What actually happened was that the mails reverted to horseback rather than being carried on stages as had been the custom for several years. Postriders did not want the extra burden and began to refuse to carry newspapers. Reaction from printers, who blamed Hazard for changing mail carriers from stages back to postriders, was swift and vicious. The printer of the *New Hampshire Spy* particularly defended the newspaper exchange system, declaring it to be a "custom of the country" that was "as obligatory as any law of the land." He later affirmed that "the stopping of public newspapers, in a free country, is an outrage upon all mankind, because it interrupts business, and foils the public in general of the only easy and expeditious mode of communicating important events and sentiments." Congress responded to the complaints with a resolution that printers be allowed to exchange papers through the mails at no charge. George Washington, believing the rumor about the postmaster general, feared the impact of stopping the wide circulation of newspapers "at the instant when the momentous question of a general government was to have come before the people." Hazard found himself out of work following Washington's inauguration as president in April 1789.[10]

Printers often worked for the government as publishers of public documents or directors of local post offices, but these jobs did not constitute the only forms of interaction between officialdom and the printing fraternity. In colonial New England printing had been watched over first by the church fathers and then by representatives of the Crown. The royal governor had originally been given the authority to license and censor the press, a right used to control the early newspapers in Massachusetts. By 1730, when the new governor, Jonathan Belcher, arrived in Massachusetts, prior censorship of the press no longer prevailed. Although few legal restrictions on the press even existed, printers still faced the possibility of punishment after publication, if not in the courts then by the selectmen or the legislature. On several occasions in the mid-eighteenth century, the Massachusetts General Assembly arrested a printer for publishing pieces criticizing the government or its actions. By the beginning of the Revolutionary War, printers generally published whatever they desired in the pages of their gazettes, but the possibility of public censure or punishment always existed.[11]

An ongoing debate that grew out of official efforts to control newspapers concerned liberty of the press—the importance of a free press and what one actually constituted. Almost everyone, government officials and printers alike, considered a free press essential for a republic. Nine of the thirteen original states, including Massachusetts and New Hampshire, specifically recognized the freedom of the press in their constitutions. Connecticut, Maine, and Rhode Island all provided for liberty of the press in their original constitutions, adopted in 1818, 1819, and 1842, respectively. The Massachusetts Constitution of 1780 asserted that "the Liberty of the Press is essential to the security of freedom in a State; it ought not, therefore, to be restrained in this Commonwealth." In 1783, New Hampshire copied Massachusetts and concluded that the freedom of the press should "be inviolably preserved." Vermont, not then part of the United States, went even farther than her neighbors, declaring "that the people have a right to freedom of speech, and of writing and publishing their sentiments; therefore, the freedom of the press ought not to be restrained." Furthermore, "the printing presses shall be free to every person who undertakes to examine the proceedings of the legislature, or any part of government." Even the Continental Congress praised a free press as the means of promoting unity among a people "whereby oppressive officials are shamed or intimidated into more honorable and just modes of conducting affairs."[12]

Throughout the Revolutionary era, the public prints carried a variety of pieces addressing the importance of freedom of the press, particularly that of newspapers. A free and open press provided a forum for exchanging ideas and information and for debating issues of importance to the general populace. One writer praised a free press as "a security against errors, for where there is a free Press no false doctrine in religion, policy, or physic, can be broached and remain undetected." "Philoctetes" described a free press as the way by which "every free man can with ease and propriety address the public upon topics which appear to him worthy the attention of his fellow-citizens and countrymen." "Junius" agreed, describing a newspaper as a "vehicle of useful information to the community" through which "every individual has a right to publish his sentiments upon the conduct of the legislative, executive, or judicial departments." A piece from the *Virginia Gazette* appearing in several New England papers asserted that "a free and impartial press will be deemed by every informed American, as the centinel to his rights, his liberties and his honours—that will give the watch-word at the approach of danger, and challenge every alarming evil, while yet at a distance." "The Scourge" affirmed that "without Freedom of Speech and Writing, there can be no such thing as Public Liberty, and Tyrants and Traitors ought to be opposed for the Public Good. . . . Whoever therefore is an enemy to the liberty of the press, and the freedom of public writing, . . . is an enemy to God and man."[13]

By providing a public forum, an unshackled newspaper served the cause of liberty. In 1782, "Plain Dealer" praised a free press for its role in the struggle against Great Britain: "I Exult, I Glory in the Freedom of the Press, that Palladium of Liberty, the Chief Means of Diffusing, through this Wide-Extended Country, Those Generous Sentiments Which Delivered Us From British Tyranny, and Formed the Basis of our Rising Empire." In the same vein, "Junius" declared that "the liberty of the press is the boast of freemen, and essential to the support of a republican government." Furthermore, he equated a free press with liberty of conscience, urging that any encroachment "ought to awaken the resentment of a free and enlightened people." One writer in the *Herald of Freedom* concluded that "the degrees of freedom and safety which any community enjoy, may generally be calculated by the liberality and free state of the press in such community." "Spectator" affirmed that "it is indeed the firm basis on which all our other rights are supported; and, if it should unfortunately fail, the noble edifice of American Liberty, would be necessarily involved in its ruin. . . ." In the same vein of thought, a widely reprinted essay warned that

the key-stone of the arch, whereon this stupendous fabric has been elevated, is cemented by Religious Toleration and the Liberty of the Press. Whether these are torn away by open violence, or consumed by fraud or guile, the result will be nearly the same. . . . The arch will give way—the building crumble to ruin—and involve such a degree of confusion, anarchy, and despotism, as must, even on the most distant prospect, strike daggers to the inmost soul.[14]

Clearly, many New Englanders considered a free press an important part of a republican society. However, what they meant by the term "free press" is not always clear. The issue over what constituted a "free press" was complicated by the lack of laws defining libel. Criminal libel in Britain had been defined over the years by English common law courts rather than Parliamentary statute. Because the basis for an eighteenth-century definition of libel lay in legal precedents rather than laws, it was not always clear what libel meant. In general, libel constituted any printed statement that defamed a person or served to lower their reputation in the public eye. Colonial lawmakers also recognized the legality of "seditious libel," or malicious criticism of the government, but few prosecutions occurred. Even when trials did take place, convictions proved rare because truth was increasingly recognized as an acceptable libel defense. The new state governments passed libel laws in attempts to clarify the issue, but confusion over what constituted libel persisted.[15]

Newspaper essayists clearly thought that printers should not be free to print anything they desired. On numerous occasions, writers criticized newspapers for becoming "licentious" and resorting to "the degrading sphere of reptile slander." One writer declared that "the liberty of the press ought not to be restrained," but "the exercise of that liberty should be confined within the bounds of decency and politeness." An essayist in the *Newport Mercury* urged that the public prints not be used to spread "private slander and defamation" or "in fomenting private quarrels, nor destroying public peace and tranquility." Rather, the liberty of the press "consists in this, in having the privilege in publishing that, which is for the interest and safety of the public to know, and in not being constrained, or rather in not publishing what the public ought not to know." Even poets entered the debate. A poem entitled "On the Continuation of Newspaper Scurrility" gave the following advice:

When nonsense disgraces the papers,
'Tis time to take hold of the pen,
To light the satirical tapers,
And root out the nonsense again.
When music's disciples are jarring,
And write more than folks can endure,

A small dose of feathering and tarring
Would cause an effectual cure.
When ———— and ———— are disputing,
They certainly can't take 't amiss,
If, instead of a solemn refuting,
They meet with a general hiss.[16]

A letter to the *Boston Gazette* from Arthur St. Clair ably summed up the feelings of many people:

> The liberty of the press is a privilege that a free people, and who mean to preserve their freedom, ought to guard with the most watchful jealousy; at the same time they should be careful to prevent the press from becoming licentious. When it is perverted to the circulating falsehood, and thereby raising, and keeping up unreasonable prejudices in the minds of the people, or to the murder of characters, it becomes a nuisance: and when publications which have such tendency, particularly the latter, are generally relished, it is an evidence that the people have lost part at least of that virtue without which liberty cannot long subsist.[17]

Even though many people asserted that a free press could easily be abused, some urged that the benefits always outweighed the evils. "Belisarius" agreed that "this great blessing may be abused," but "in a land of freedom every constitutional member has a right, and it is his duty, modestly to offer his sentiments to the public, when he is of the opinion that his thoughts may be useful to his country." In 1789, "Cato" affirmed that "as long as there are such things as printing and writing, there will be libels! It is an evil arising out of a much greater good. . . . I must own that I would rather libels should escape than the liberty of the press should suffer the least infringment." An anonymous piece agreed: "it must be owned, that the Press is sometimes applied to an ill-use, and is made the channels through which falsehoods and scurrilities flow in too violent a torrent; yet, however injurious the unlimited licence of printing may prove to the feelings of particular persons, the liberty itself is of too great a benefit to the publick in general, to be abolished, or restrained."[18]

The newspaper printers also frequently expressed their ideas concerning the freedom of the press. They all agreed that "the liberty of a free use of the press" was "a matter of very great consequence." Isaiah Thomas described a free press as "the great Palladium of Liberty, every man may express his sentiments— every man may be acquainted with what his rulers are doing—to what use publick property is put, and guard against the encroachments of Tyranny, &c." The *Boston Gazette*'s masthead declared that "A Free Press Maintains the Majesty of the People." Thomas Adams and John Nourse affirmed that "news-papers are centinels placed upon the out-posts of the constitution, and should never be punished, but for sleeping or neglect of duty." In 1776 Benjamin Dearborn of New Hampshire summed up the feelings of newspaper printers concerning the glories of a free press:

> The liberty of the Press has ever been held as one of the most sacred rights of a free people, and when we are abridged of that invaluable priviledge, farewell to Peace, Liberty, and safety, farewell to Learning Knowledge and Truth, farewell all that is dear to us; we must ever after grope in darkness, thick darkness, that may even be felt: may Heaven forbid such a deprivation, and long continue to us this invaluable blessing.[19]

New England printers obviously had some notion of the important role that a free press could play in their country, but even they publicly feared the possibility of abuses. George Roulstone declared that "matters of a personal or private nature" were "improper subjects for a news-paper." The editor of the *New Hampshire Recorder* "conceive[d] it to be his duty, always to distinguish between the sacred Freedom of the PRESS, and the vile licentiousness of it." In 1788 the *Herald of Freedom* bemoaned "the difficulty of supporting the freedom of the press, unalloyed by its licentiousness." On one occasion, Robert Luist Fowle concluded that "sometimes it so happens, that it is thought and may be best, not to allow the full Liberty of the Press, in the strictest Sense of the Words, least some Disaffected Persons might abuse it."[20]

Revolutionary publishers still defined a free press in terms of one that was open to all sides of an issue. Newspapers should present all aspects of any undecided problem so that people could judge for themselves. In publishing both "Massachusettensis" and "Novanglus" in tandem,[21] Daniel Fowle urged: "Let us read both sides with an impartial Mind, without which we must unavoidably grope in a mazy Labyrinth of Error." During the debates over the Constitution, the editor of the *American Herald* declared that he considered "a free press, not as his own, but as public property" that should be "open to all parties, and influenced by none." Throughout the Revolutionary era, newspaper printers fended off accusations of partiality by declaring their goal to be the production of public prints that would contain the ideas of everyone. The printers of the *Vermont Gazette* found this goal to be impossible to attain because "each party finds fault with the Printers in their turn, yet every one eagerly claims his right to the 'freedom of writing and publishing his sentiments.'" John Carter summarized the feelings of most newspaper publishers of the Revolutionary era when he said "that it is exceedingly difficult for the Publisher of a Paper to observe such a Line of Conduct as can fully satisfy the Wishes and exactly coincide with the various Humours and Views of all Parties."[22]

Ever since the first issue of the *Boston News-Letter,* printers had paid some attention to the content of their weekly sheets and had engaged in a form of self-censorship. Often this meant only choosing the best of many available pieces, but failure to publish a volatile essay could also be a sign of prudence in the face of possible recriminations. New England printers regularly announced failure to carry certain pieces either because they had already appeared in another local paper or because the ideas in them were old and did not warrant rehashing. As the printer of the *Cumberland Gazette* put it, some essays "contained old arguments on an old subject; and are therefore omitted.—We had rather have new wine, even should the bottles split."[23]

Generally, however, printers refused to print submissions that they considered inappropriate for a newspaper. The printers of the *Herald of Freedom* declared themselves "unwilling to occupy that part of the *Herald* in strictures injurious to private citizens, which ought to be preserved for political information, and a free discussion of publick measures." The *Boston Gazette* also occasionally refused pieces dealing with specific individuals because the editors were "loath to wound the Feelings of a Family, in pointing at the Misconduct of its Head." Religious essays often caused problems for printers. In 1775, Isaiah Thomas had to face the wrath of the Reverend Ebenezer Chaplin of Sutton when he refused to print several pieces by Chaplin that Thomas considered too poorly written for publication. Chaplin publicly attacked Thomas as an atheist and a Tory, but Thomas managed to survive and remained in business. Essays dealing with Bishop Samuel Seabury, America's first Episcopalian bishop, proved popular, but many produced rejections because, as one editor said, "we wish not to enter into ecclesiastical dispute, which has, almost in every instance, been unfavourable to morals and piety, and would be peculiarly ungraceful among a people who profess to be friendly to Toleration."[24]

Newspaper publishers proved particularly averse to pieces attacking their fellow printers. In 1789, Edmund Freeman refused to accept one essay because "the community can derive no advantage from the publication of what he calls the 'private character and conduct of a venal printer.' " Freeman had earlier rejected a poem that castigated another printer because "such an attack would answer no purpose of publick utility." In 1787, Benjamin Russell defended a printer's right to publish anything presented to him:

> "Castigator" is inadmissable—A Brother Printer cannot be so highly culpable in publishing the Authentick Key to the Door of Free Masonry, as to deserve so severe a "castigation" as is therein given—although the Book may divulge secrets which many persons may wish should be concealed—yet the publishing it, cannot certainly merit the publisher illiberal invective, or abusive threatenings.[25]

Actually, printers failed to publish anything that they feared would endanger their papers. As one editor said, "the newspaper shall contain what the Publisher pleases," and most printers had no intention of alienating a large segment of their readers. The editors of the *Boston Evening Post* expressed the feelings of everyone: "Authors must write with Decency and Truth, or not expect to find Room in this Paper." Even threats from a disappointed author for failure to publish a submitted essay would be "of no avail." In 1785 the *New Haven Gazette* refused several pieces because "many of our customers have expressed their Disapprobation of several pieces lately published in this paper." Daniel Fowle admitted omitting part of an essay because he was "apprehensive it would injure his paper." Isaiah Thomas, in refusing to print two essays, asserted that the authors had "gone far beyond his depth, and he is apprehensive that of the generality of his customers." In sum, printers considered business interests first when deciding whether to publish any questionable essay or letter.[26]

Increasingly, a printer refused to set type for an essay because of the author's anonymity. This represented a change from previous years, indicating a more careful concern in the finished product on the part of newspaper proprietors. The editors of the *Independent Chronicle* asserted that they were not "bound by any tie to assume a responsibility for a publication, which the real author is either afraid or ashamed to acknowledge." John Gill refused to even consider a piece without first knowing who wrote it. The printers particularly invoked their right to know the identity of

authors when the essays involved contained strong invective or
attacks on specific individuals. In considering one article,
Edmund Freeman concluded that "as the author is so bold and
open in his attack, it is necessary that he should make himself
known to the Editors, prior to any publication of such a nature."
In one private dispute that raged in the public prints in 1778,
Benjamin Edes refused to print anything related to the argument
unless the writers signed their real names. The debate over the
merits of the Constitution did not really begin in Boston until
November 1788 because of a Federalist inspired debate over the
use of pen names in discussing the proposed government. A
proposal to stop publishing pieces signed with pseudonyms received serious consideration, but never became common practice
and pen names continued to appear on a majority of the essays
printed about the Constitution.[27]

Clearly, although the printers desired the names of their writers
to protect themselves if called to account for anything they published, custom forbade them revealing their sources unless the
authors gave them permission to do so. According to the editor of
the *Cumberland Gazette*, "it is the right of a Printer to demand the
name of every author; but that Printer is a rascal who exposes the
name of any one author, without leave first obtained." In revealing the identity of one of its correspondents, the firm of Edes &
Son affirmed that it was under no "legal obligation to expose the
author," and it did so only with his prior consent. The problem of
revealing authors' identities haunted printers throughout the
Revolutionary era. Printers affirmed that they could not be held
responsible for essays they published when they did not write
them. They also wished to protect their anonymous authors for
fear that no one would write for the newspapers anymore. In
1777, Adams and Nourse declared that names could not be published because such an action would endanger "the liberty of the
press" and undermine "the valuable purposes of a free press."[28]

Throughout the Revolutionary era, newspapers faced government interference with their operations. Particularly blatant examples involved problems that grew out of the war itself. Prior to
1775, most newspapers became identified with either the American or the British side in the imperial dispute. The outbreak of
fighting spawned efforts on both sides to shut down opposition
journals. Patriot printers in Boston, such as Isaiah Thomas and
Benjamin Edes, fled at the time of the skirmishes at Lexington and
Concord. Both managed to reestablish their newspapers at new
sites within a few months. Edes's partner, John Gill, and Edes's

son Peter did not prove so lucky, both being imprisoned for several months for publishing sedition. Solomon Southwick ceased publication of the *Newport Mercury* because "it was thought impossible for it to Live and Breathe forth that genuine patriotic spirit (for which it was so justly celebrated) after the Enemy took Possession" of Newport.[29]

Other incidents of British interference with the American press took place, but worse censorship occurred when Patriots shut down Tory sheets. Times of crisis produce increased pressures for conformity. Even before the fighting began, printers sympathetic to the British Crown faced intolerance both from Whig leaders and angry mobs. Yet, the Hartford County Committee of Observation declared:

> While contending for the liberties of British America in general, we would by no means encourage or countenance any measure that may be construed in any degree to infringe that of the press, on which the others so greatly depend: but on the contrary, conscious of the justice of our cause, and the rectitide of our views, wish to promote to the utmost, freedom of enquiry, and the fair and open discussion of every part of the present most important controversy between Great Britain and her colonies.[30]

Practice did not always follow theory. Patriot leaders thought that an inimical press could not be allowed to operate during any war. The Tory press fit into this category, constituting a threat to the American cause that had to be eradicated at any cost. Early in 1775, John Adams, writing as "Novanglus," admitted "the abuses of the press are notorious." Although he advised "that writers on all sides . . . be more careful of truth and decency," he asserted that, "upon the most impartial estimate, the tories will be found to have been the least so, of any party among us." Whig leaders agreed with Adams and urged their followers to stop supporting newspapers that did not preach the patriot cause. New England printers who received such censure were the Tory printers of Boston—Margaret Draper, John Howe, Nathaniel Mills, and John Hicks, all of whom fled from Boston with the British army in 1776. Their fates, however, proved mild compared to that of James Rivington of New York. Patriots from Maine to Georgia castigated Rivington for his support of the British cause. All this criticism reached its height in late 1775 when a group of Connecticut men rode into New York City and destroyed Rivington's press and types. Although probably not the only example of mob action against a printer during the Revolution, this incident stands as the most notorious one.[31]

If attempts to shut down newspapers favorable to the cause of the enemy might be justified during time of war, these proved to be only some of the efforts by Whig leaders to control the press, both Whig and Tory, during the Revolutionary era. Legally, newspaper printers could be charged with seditious libel anytime they criticized the government in any form. In England, use of the law of seditious libel proved useful in government attempts to control the press. In America, however, legal channels were seldom used because of the unlikelihood of finding a jury that would convict an American printer against a government accusation. Printers seldom faced court imposed jail terms, fines, or suspensions of their papers during this period. Instead, most infringements on the freedom of the press came from state assemblies that struck back at patriot printers for publishing unpopular statements. Eighteenth-century governments, including American legislatures, viewed published criticisms of their actions as threats to their ability to function because such commentaries lowered their public reputations. The possible interference with the workings of government that could result from such pieces provided the justification for legislative reprimands of printers.[32]

During the colonial era, legislatures enforced the law of seditious libel against American printers by exercising the assembly's power to punish breaches of legislative privilege. Colonial assemblies often censured printers for including accounts of their votes and proceedings. They also occasionally issued reprimands for pieces questioning or criticizing their actions. Both Thomas Fleet and Daniel Fowle spent time in jail after being arrested and imprisoned by officials of the state legislature for publishing articles that questioned government policy. Isaiah Thomas, refusing to appear before the Council when summoned in 1771, faced prosecution for libel, but the government failed to get a conviction.[33]

Throughout the Revolutionary era, New England legislatures continued to censure newspaper printers for publications they disliked. In January 1776, Daniel Fowle came under fire from the New Hampshire legislature for an essay in his *Gazette* condemning independence. The assembly, labeling the piece "ignominious, scurrilous and scandalous," ordered Fowle to appear to answer for his action. Because of this reprimand, Fowle suspended his newspaper. It resumed in May under a new name and a new editor, but Fowle did not become active again in its publication until December 1776. From time to time, the public prints of Boston came under fire from all levels of state and local government. In 1779, the Boston Selectmen censured Nathaniel Willis for publishing "a false infamous and Malicious Libel on a respectable Committee of this Town," and concluded that "this Town resents the Writing and Publishing of said Libel as affrontive to them." The Massachusetts attorney general investigated the *Independent Chronicle* in 1786 for publishing "a false and scandalous representation of certain proceedings in [the] Senate." In 1788 the convention called to consider the proposed Federal Constitution criticized the printers of the *Boston Gazette* for publishing a piece that declared that convention members were being bribed to vote for the new Constitution. In voting to prevent the sale and distribution of certain pamphlets after publication, the Connecticut legislature clearly summarized the feelings of many government leaders on the issue of what printers could and could not publish:

> Whereas it is represented to this Assembly that a certain pamphlet entitled A Discourse Upon Extortion is now in the press at Hartford, containing many insulting reflections on civil government, tending to sedition, bloodshed and domestic insurrections, and that the same is expected soon to be published and dispersed among the people, to the great danger of the public peace and the safety of the good people of these United States: It is thereupon resolved by this Assembly, that a precept be immediately issued, directed to the sheriff of the county of Hartford, requiring him to seize the said pamphlet and all the copies thereof and commit the same to the care of the Attorney for this State in the County of Hartford, who is hereby directed carefully to inspect the same and pursue such measures relative thereto as he shall judge to be reasonable and proper.[34]

Patently, New England leaders envisioned limits on what the press could do. Printers, however, strongly disagreed. They praised the benefits of a free press and supported the removal of all restrictions. In efforts to further their cause, New England newspaper proprietors often carried pieces from all over the world dealing with attacks or restrictions on printers. The *Newport Gazette* reported the threatened tar-and-feathering of William Goddard of the *Maryland Gazette* for printing pieces that apparently criticized George Washington. In its coverage of a British libel trial in 1783, the *Independent Ledger* praised the jury for its acquittal verdict: "a free and spirited people always shew . . .

their abhorrence of oppression, and of their detestation of those
tyrannic, time serving characters that invade their liberties, and in
particular that pre-eminent and inestimable privilege of every
freeman, 'The Liberty Of The Press!' "[35]

Printers also eagerly praised their fellow tradesmen wherever
and whenever they stood up to government infringements on the
press. One case that received great attention in the Boston papers
concerned Eleazer Oswald of Philadelphia. Oswald, indicted for
libeling a private individual, tried to argue that the common law of
libel violated Pennsylvania's constitution, which protected a free
press. He asserted that libel was "a doctrine incompatible with law
and liberty, and at once destructive to the privileges of a free
country." The Pennsylvania Assembly, functioning as the state's
highest court, disagreed and let Oswald's conviction stand. The
case became a cause célèbre among printers throughout the
United States. Following Oswald's imprisonment, Edward E.
Powars, printer of Boston's *American Herald*, warned that printers
had better "be extremely cautious how They think evil of Dig-
nities." Trials such as Oswald's worried newspaper proprietors in
New England, who feared that such cases could occur closer to
home.[36]

Physical attacks on printers anywhere also brought immediate
reactions in the public prints. In reporting an assault on Thomas
Greenleaf of New York, Edward E. Powars praised him as "sacri-
ficing his ease, his interest, his reputation, yea life itself, to secure
to himself, and to hand down, unsullied to posterity, a most
invaluable jewel, even 'The Liberty Of The Press!' " An attack on
the printers of the *Massachusetts Centinel* in 1785 produced a great
deal of discussion in the public prints. Benjamin Russell and
William Warden had agreed to publish a pamphlet attacking the
"Sans Souci," a gentlemen's club that recently had been formed in
Boston. Upon advertising the forthcoming production in the *Centinel*, Russell and Warden were approached by some club members wishing to stop the publication. Failing, they assaulted the
printers in their office. The printers of Massachusetts papers used
the pages of their newspapers to condemn this action. Benjamin
Edes summed up their feelings when he urged that this attack

ought to excite the serious Attention of all those who duly regard that
Bulwark of our Liberties, The Freedom of the Press. If a Printer, for
advertising that he intends to publish a certain Book for the Information or merely the Amusement or innocent Diversion of his fellow
Citizens, is to be beset and abused by a set of Club-men, because the

Title Page does not happen to hit their Taste, we may take a farewell of our Independence which we have gloriously obtained, not without great Expence of our Treasure, and the loss of some of our best Blood. A Wound in so tender a Point must surely prove fatal![37]

Printers, thus, always stood ready to fight together against a threat to their rights. Never was this trait more evident than after Massachusetts passed a stamp tax imposing a two-thirds penny duty on newspapers and a one penny duty on almanacs in March 1785. Stamp taxes had been common in Britain and her colonies since the early eighteenth century. Great Britain had had a tax on newspapers since 1712. During the French and Indian War, Massachusetts had instituted a half penny stamp tax to help pay war expenses. This provincial law remained in effect for two years and apparently aroused little opposition. Then, of course, there was the most painful precedent of all—the Parliamentary imposed Stamp Act of 1765. The 1785 legislation was designed to provide sorely needed revenue to pay the war debt and was not meant to stifle a free press. Protests, however, quickly surfaced throughout Massachusetts and other parts of the country.[38]

Many essayists who attacked the stamp act feared that the tax would reduce the spread of knowledge and information by making newspapers too expensive for most people to buy. "Lucius" declared that "ignorance will universally prevail, and slavery will advance with hasty strides, as soon as the avenues of political information are closed." Furthermore, he had difficulty believing that Massachusetts, once a great supporter of a free press, would be the first "to strike a blow at the root of this inestimable right." One reader of the *Salem Gazette,* in ending his subscription, blamed the British for the tax. He concluded that his action probably would have little impact overall, but the cancellation would keep him "from being continually haunted with an idea of supporting the wicked principle that . . . has given birth to it." One widely reprinted essay responded to the Massachusetts stamp act with surprise because of the importance of newspapers in establishing American independence. Finally, many correspondents attacked the legislation as "impolitic, as it will encourage our sister states to send their papers into this Commonwealth cheaper than can possibly be afforded here, to the ruin of a set of artisans, whose exertions in the late revolution, deserves a more liberal fate."[39]

Materials in newspapers from other states afforded ammunition in ridiculing the enactment of the Massachusetts law. Particularly

94   NEWSPAPERS AND GOVERNMENT

useful were essays and letters from Philadelphia sheets, which
were reprinted widely throughout the state. Philadelphia printers
spared no words—one writer described the Bay State stamp act as
"that paragon of ridicule, inconsistency, infamy, and tyranny."
Another, joining the act with the consecration of America's first
Anglican bishop, spoke of "Two Wonders of the World: A Stamp
Act in Boston! and A Bishop in Connecticut!" One correspondent
concluded: "it is a little extraordinary . . . that the people of
Boston, who have hitherto been accustomed to stand foremost in
the cause of justice and of liberty, should be the first to adopt the
measures of tyranny." Finally, one essayist summarized most
printers' concerns:

> May Providence avert the dire malady from sister states! May their
> crimes never entail this dreadful chastisement on them! But should
> any wretch pollute the air with such a proposal in the Pennsylvania
> senate, may the plagues of Pharoah await him! May he wander a
> vagabond about the earth like the murderous Cain! And may he be
> accurst, sitting, standing, lying, and in every action of his detested
> life.[40]

Massachusetts printers quickly added their voices to the roar of
complaints. They asserted that Massachusetts would gain little
from the tax because newspapers of neighboring states would
supplant local sheets that cost more due to the added duty.
Furthermore, printers charged that the tax clearly constituted an
attack on the freedom of the press and should be resisted as such.
John Gill sold his newspaper, the *Continental Journal,* to James D.
Griffith, declaring that he had already experienced the bad effects
of two previous stamp acts and did not care to deal with a third.
The printer of the *Essex Journal* said he would move his operation
to New Hampshire rather than "print a News-Paper burdened
with a Stamp, in a land of Liberty, and where the Press is said to
be Free!" Other editors charged that the stamp act would result in
the "suppression of public newspapers" and cut the people off
from "this only trusty channel of intelligence." They accused the
general populace of being lethargic and warned that "now, perhaps for the last time, it [the press] sounds an alarm! an alarm that
ought to arouse even those that sleep—It this day lifts up its voice,
and cries aloud, 'Your situation is perilous—Look about you—
Exert yourselves like Freemen, or your ruin is inevitable!' "[41]
The Massachusetts General Court, responding to public criticism, repealed the stamp act, replacing it with a bill placing an
advertisement tax of six pence per insertion. Although this act

received some public support, most considered the advertisement tax as bad as the previous measure. Some essayists feared a rise in newspaper prices would result, reducing the number of people who could afford to purchase one. The citizens of New Braintree considered the law an infringement of the constitutional protection afforded the press and instructed their assemblyman to work for its repeal. One essayist from Philadelphia prayed that "should the infection ever spread so far as this State, God grant that the Printers may have spirit enough to oppose such tyrannical measures in the beginning."[42]

The printers disliked the advertisement tax even more than the stamp act because it struck at their major source of newspaper income. They accurately predicted that the tax would be self-defeating by reducing the quantity of advertising inserted in the public gazettes. Publishers also fretted because they could not advertise their wares as before. Many chose the method used by the editor of the *Salem Gazette* to get around this problem. On 2 August 1785, he inserted the following paragraph in the local news column: "Were it not for the tax upon advertising good Books, the Printer hereof would inform the publick, that he has just published 'Extracts from Dr. Priestly's Catechism,' which he sells at five coppers single, and two shillings the dozen."[43]

Isaiah Thomas refused to pay the tax because he considered it an infringement on the freedom of the press. He ceased publication of the *Massachusetts Spy* because he would not be "ignominiously fettered with a SHACKLE he has been taught to abhor!" Instead, he began producing a weekly magazine, the *Worcester Magazine*, which was little more than the *Spy* under a different name. Through his public protest of the ad tax, Thomas ably summarized the feelings of the printers:

> The tax on News-paper Advertisements has a direct tendency not only to restrain, but to destroy those necessary vehicles of public information, by taking away their only support; for Advertisements are the only support of News-papers in this Country, where Newspapers are at so low a price; if therefore the Publication of Newspapers is not by Law prohibited, yet if a law is made which takes away the means of printing and circulating News-papers, it amounts to the same thing, and is of course an unconstitutional restraint on the Liberty of the Press.[44]

The ad tax had a significant impact on Massachusetts newspapers. Due to hard times and economic pressures throughout the region, all New England states experienced a drop in the

amount of overall space allotted to advertising in the years 1784–
1788. Because of the additional burden of the advertisement tax,
however, the greatest decline occurred in Massachusetts (see table
5–2). In 1784, the percentage of space devoted to advertisements
stood at the highest point in the entire Revolutionary era—34.35
percent. In 1785 it dropped to 21.23 percent, falling even further
to 12.19 percent in 1786. Many printers had to reduce the size of
their sheets or change to a magazine format, while at least six
others ceased publication altogether. At the time of Shays's Rebellion, several essayists blamed the troubles in the backcountry
on the lack of reliable information: "The cause of the . . . want of
political intelligence is manifest—their source of information has
become extinct—A large proportion of the Insurgents belong in
the vicinity of Springfield, from whence, 'till lately, they were
supplied with News-papers; but by reason of the tax . . . they,
with many others, in this State, are no more." In announcing the
end of the *Hampshire Herald,* its editor declared that "the laws of
government, under which we expected protection and support,

Table 5–2
Percentage of Available Space Allotted to Advertisements:
New England Newspapers, 1775–1789

Year	Connecticut	Maine	Massachusetts	New Hampshire	Rhode Island	Vermont
1775	19.23	——	17.48	17.19	26.31	——
1776	24.57	——	20.59	13.02	23.14	——
1777	29.34	——	24.93	17.47	24.65	——
1778	30.54	——	25.05	33.80	33.00	——
1779	26.74	——	24.88	26.04	26.39	——
1780	23.31	——	26.05	28.47	16.08	——
1781	31.55	——	26.59	27.52	28.44	——
1782	32.39	——	29.09	36.81	28.22	——
1783	30.07	——	32.66	45.49	30.30	20.42
1784	29.67	——	34.35	31.47	35.24	30.49
1785	33.09	13.37	21.23	30.84	38.19	27.47
1786	27.04	13.72	12.19	17.52	30.27	27.45
1787	26.27	17.53	11.36	20.47	29.67	31.17
1788	28.44	23.26	17.41	21.95	16.41	35.88
1789	26.76	17.88	19.99	19.14	22.25	30.52
Averages:	27.93	17.15	22.92	25.81	27.24	29.06

Note: See Appendix 1 for survey method used to acquire the data for these
averages.

have, in a great measure, driven us to this disagreeable alternative."[45]

In February 1786, the printers petitioned the General Court for repeal of the advertisement tax, asserting that the assessment greatly interfered with their businesses and gained very little for the state. A committee set up to study the issue reported that printers had lost about one half of their profits as a result of the legislation and that "the revenue arising to Government from the Duties on advertisements in newspapers is very Inconsiderable." Finally, in 1788, the General Court repealed the tax. Printers throughout Massachusetts rejoiced at the end of the act, praising the legislature for restoring "the Liberty of the Press in this Commonwealth to its original and Constitutional Freedom!" Isaiah Thomas prayed that "Heaven grant that the FREEDOM of the PRESS, on which depends the FREEDOM of the PEOPLE, may, in the United States, be ever guarded with a watchful eye, and defended from shackles, of every form and shape, until the trump of the celestial Messenger shall announce the final dissolution of all things."[46]

Throughout the Revolutionary era, the concept of freedom of the press did not mean the same thing to everyone. Sometimes it seems almost as if no one was quite sure what the concept of a free press really meant. John Adams said that "there is not in any nation of the world so unlimited a freedom of the press as is now established in every State of America, both by law and practice." Still, mobs wrecked presses and legislatures arrested printers. According to one historian, the problem lies in how eighteenth-century Americans viewed newspapers and the press. To them, the public prints were designed as a weapon to be used by the people in their constant struggle against those in power. Those in power would always become tyrannical if not closely watched by a united people. Newspapers helped to produce the necessary unity by keeping everyone informed of public happenings. However, newspapers themselves possessed power that could also be used for bad purposes, such as defaming someone's character or ruining a person's reputation. The press could, and did, abuse its special privileges. Because of this, newspapers had to be controlled by a united people. Eighteenth-century Americans felt justified in punishing printers anytime they overstepped the bounds of what the readers considered to be the public good. These ideas provided the justification for interferences in the free workings of the press throughout the Revolutionary era.[47]

Still, the printers themselves voiced a belief in a libertarian view of a free press—that one could publish without fear of censorship or reprisal. As indicated in their struggles against the Massachusetts stamp and advertisement taxes, they desired to remove all controls of any kind on what they produced. Although government officials interfered on occasion, most newspapers operated freely, and printers increasingly fought for their right to continue to do so. A statement made in the *New London Bee* in 1800, following the trials under the Alien and Sedition Acts, could easily have been applied fifteen years earlier: "Punishment only hardens printers—they come out of jail holding their heads higher than if they had never been persecuted." Leonard Levy is correct in stating that the press was not truly free during the American Revolution: both legal and extralegal press restraints existed and were invoked from time to time. Great strides, however, were made toward the establishment of a press free from official interference. Printers freely criticized their rulers, feeling confident in their right to do so without reprisals. The failure of governments to squelch such criticism—in most cases, they did not even try—set precedents for the future. The tradition of a free American press developed, becoming the expected and accepted practice even though not actually existing in law. Very few public officeholders were willing to face the possible public outcry that could result from questioning such a widely acclaimed tradition.[48]

The relationship between the newspaper press and the government during the Revolutionary era proved to be a close one, even if fraught with disagreements. A sizeable portion of a printer's income could come from government sources, such as printing contracts or appointment to a government post, often as postmaster. In return, printers provided a link of information between the people and their rulers. Relations in these areas were generally good, except when government officials pitted printers against each other in order to save money on contracts. Most of the disagreements, however, came in the area of government attempts to control or regulate the press. Official discussions concerning publications angered printers, for they considered such investigations to be infringements on the freedom of the press. They felt that the press should be free from all government regulations, including taxes. The Massachusetts stamp and advertisement taxes of 1785 created the greatest furor in this area. Although a great deal of discussion took place concerning just how free the press should be, the issue was not settled. Throughout the era, printers operated with little real government interference, but the possibility always existed. Freedom from a fear of government intervention would not be possible for many years to come.

6
The Press and Political Issues: A Time of Unity, 1775–1781

Throughout the Revolutionary era, political issues proved to be important newspaper fare. A variety of subjects came up for discussion, but not all appeared in the press. The decision concerning what topics to cover lay primarily in the hands of the printer. All subjects could not be covered, so some choices had to be made. The publisher's decision about what to include in the newspaper each week told the readership what was and was not important. In modern terminology, the newspapers helped set the public agenda by emphasizing some items and downplaying others.[1] The influence of the press is difficult to measure. However, the confluence of republican ideas expressed in the newspapers and changes brought about by the Revolution indicated agreement among the majority of Americans concerning their future.[2] How the newspapers covered political topics during the Revolutionary era provided guidance for the people as to which issues and ideas deserved attention. The press thus helped influence attitudes toward the changes occurring as the United States broke away from Great Britain to become the world's first modern republic.[3]

During the 1770s and 1780s, the coverage of political matters in the press went through a series of changes. With the disappearance of a viable Tory press in early 1775, New England's public prints presented a unified front in the face of the British foe. Although some printers questioned specific government actions or policies, they supported the war and called for a unified citizenry. This solidarity of purpose dissolved at war's end and was replaced with many-sided discussions about an assortment of issues. Each state had its own set of postwar anxieties and its own attitudes about national questions that found reflection in its weekly newspapers. These divisions continued throughout most of the 1780s, ending only with the outbreak of an armed uprising in Massachusetts in 1786. Shays's Rebellion frightened the entire country and restored the unity theme in New England's news-papers. Once more, the essays, which made up a sizeable portion of each weekly sheet, generally dealt with the same topic, an agreement on subject matter that continued through the Constitutional Convention and the ratification of the new federal charter. In many ways, the changes in political subjects covered in the press reflected American attentions as a whole: from a certain amount of oneness in facing the British enemy to the divisions of the immediate postwar years to a reunion of sorts under the Constitution.

The newspapers fulfilled a vital function during the Revolutionary War, primarily as a font of information and inspiration. The role of the press as a source of news proved so essential that Congress provided for a printer for the army so the troops could maintain access to a newspaper. George Washington also arranged to keep abreast of events throughout the colonies and Britain by exchanging, through enemy lines, local sheets for the papers of New York. By 1775, the public prints constituted the only truly national medium for news. Although pamphlets, letters, and broadsides continued to be useful methods of communication, the newspapers had become the public's major source of information.[4]

In attempting to keep their readers informed about the war, printers included accounts of battles and the actions of Congress and state legislatures in each week's production. Because many battle reports often proved unreliable, John Adams urged Nathanael Greene to arrange for publication of accurate descriptions of the actions he fought in order to prevent the spreading of false information. Along with battle tales, printers also published troop movements, a practice that concerned American leaders because they feared what the British would do if they acquired the information. George Washington once worried that "it is much to be wished, that our Printers were more discreet in many of their Publications. We see almost in every Paper, Proclamations or Accounts transmitted by the Enemy, of an injurious nature. If some hint or caution could be given them on the Subject, it might be of material service." Pleas for men and supplies became common in the newspapers. Important public documents, such as the Declaration of Independence and the Articles of Confederation, were published in full, while important essays such as "Common Sense" and "The Crisis" appeared everywhere.[5]

While not always accurate in their reports, publishers did the best with what they had. No reporters traveled with the army at this time, so much of the material printed consisted of rumor and hearsay. Delays in receiving existing information often made stories several weeks out of date. Most newspapermen, however, felt that any information was better than none at all. As one printer said, "at such a Day as this, where is the Man that is not anxious for himself, and all his Connections, and from Week to Week is uneasy till he receives his News-Paper, which these shocking Distresses has induced a much greater Number to take then [sic] was ever known before." People turned to the public prints for news of the war from other parts of the country. Inclusion of such items made readers more aware of a national war effort.[6]

More importantly, the local printers used their papers to maintain morale and public support for the war. Using both essays and regular news columns, publishers continually painted the best picture possible. They strove diligently to convince their readers that the colonies had ample justification for their revolt and that Great Britain was a "Monster of imperious domination and cruelty." Americans' rights had been violated time and again by the British Parliament, threatening the freedom so deeply cherished by the colonials. Independence was the only possible solution: "It is the opinion of many wise and sagacious men, that a connexion with Great Britain is an indissoluble bar to the prosperity of these American colonies, and that independence is the only means by which we can preserve that freedom of which we are now possessed, and which is the foundation of all national happiness." War constituted the final recourse, turned to only after all other avenues had failed.[7]

Furthermore, George III, the "whining King of Great Britain," no longer deserved American loyalty because he had failed to defend American interests against the encroachments of Parliament. In a response to a Tory defense of the British monarch, the *Boston Gazette* averred that "Tories may perhaps think the Tyrant is ill-used, but his crimes are so black and numerous, that it is perhaps impossible to represent him worse, on the whole, than he really is, or even so bad:—and the Tories may as well undertake to vindicate the conduct of the Devil, as that of the Tyrant." According to New England's public prints, Great Britain and her monarch had undermined any claims they had ever had to American support and loyalty.[8]

In addition to attempts to undermine loyalty to the British government, the newspapers tried to show that the majority of the British people did not support the war. Most of these efforts came in the form of letters from Britain that attacked the ministry and the Crown for fighting the colonies. Several pieces, including one that summarized a Parliamentary speech by General

Burgoyne, insisted that Britain could not afford to lose America's commerce. Others insisted that the government planned to enslave America first and then subdue its own people at home—"the present plan of royal despotism is a plan of general ruin." One British response to Lexington and Concord bemoaned that

> the sword of civil war is drawn, and if there is truth in Heaven, The King's Troops Unsheathed It. Will the English nation much longer suffer their fellow subjects to be slaughtered? It is a shameful fallacy to talk about the Supremacy of Parliament; it is the Despotism for the Crown and the Slavery of the people which the ministry aim at; for refusing these attempts, and for that only the Americans have been inhumanly murdered by the king's troops.[9]

As the war dragged on, some Britons expressed surprise that the island kingdom continued the effort "when all the prospects on which she so unjustly commenced it, are vanquished; and every campaign, for which she pays immense sums, only increases her humiliation, and adds to her embarrassment." In 1782, one writer summed up the feelings of many who desired an end to the long conflict: "it would ill become me to dictate to our Ministers, but humanity, love of country, and self-interest extort from me many an ardent wish for peace and an end to this diabolical unavailing war—Give the Americans their independence—give them anything—but give us peace."[10]

With the first skirmishes at Lexington and Concord, New England's Patriot printers blamed British leaders for the war. They insisted that future generations would agree with them "that Britain is guilty of waging the present war against America, not only without provocation, but in defiance of entreaties the most tender, and submission the most humiliating, faithful history will in time evince." All of them insisted that the redcoats had provoked the fighting at Lexington and Concord. The printers criticized the regulars for firing first and then trying to lay the blame on the colonials. Isaiah Thomas accused the British of plotting to fix the blame on the militiamen: "Their method of cheating the Devil, we are told, has been by some means brought out. They procured three or four traitors to their God and country, born among us, and took them with them, and they first fired upon their countrymen, which was immediately followed by the regulars." After these clashes, one printer declared

> thus, through the sanguinary measures of a wicked Ministry, and the Readiness of a standing Army to execute their Mandates, has commenced the American Civil War, which will hereafter fill an important

Page in History. That it may speedily terminate in a full Restoration of our Liberties, and the Confusion of all who have aimed at an Abridgement of them, should be the earnest desire of every real Friend to Great-Britain and America.[11]

As happens in almost any wartime situation, printers during the Revolutionary War filled their newspapers with accusations of cowardice and cruelty against the enemy. Upon the evacuation of Boston in 1776, the *Newport Mercury* declared that the redcoats left in such a panic that they were unable to carry all their military stores with them. Some believed that the British feared to fight the Americans and intended to hire others to do their fighting for them. Stories of plots to emancipate the slaves for use against the colonials became common, as well as discussions of plans to hire European mercenaries, plans that later proved to be true.[12]

Accounts of British cruelty proved even more popular than stories of their cowardice. Tales of the redcoats' plundering and pillaging the countryside appeared frequently—"One Mr. Beers, about 80 years of age, we are informed was inhumanly murdered by a British soldier, in his own house, and 'tis said, two children were burnt in the conflagration of Fairfield." One story in the *Providence Gazette* even accused the troops in Newport of grave robbing. Officers also came under attack for their supposed attempts to spread disease, particularly smallpox, among the general populace. In a reprint of a story originating in the *Maryland Gazette*, the *Salem Gazette* affirmed that "Lord Cornwallis's attempt to spread the small-pox among the inhabitants in the vicinity of York, has been reduced to a certainty, and must render him contemptible in the eyes of every civilized nation, it being a practice as inconsistent with the law of nations and, as repugnant to humanity."[13]

Perhaps the most damaging accounts, however, concerned how the British treated American prisoners. Accusations of cruelty and lack of concern for the well-being of the captives abounded. John Carter declared that many American soldiers died after their exchange "owing to the inhuman treatment they received from the enemy." At war's end, Isaiah Thomas urged all of his fellow printers to publish the following charge against the British concerning American prisoners of war:

> Tell it to the world, and let it be published in every newspaper throughout America, Europe, Asia and Africa, to the everlasting disgrace and infamy of the British King's commander at New York. That during the late war, it is said, ELEVEN THOUSAND SIX HUNDRED and FORTY-FOUR American prisoners, have suffered death by

their inhumane, cruel, savage and barbarous usage on board the filthy
and malignant "British Prison Ship" called the *Jersey*, lying at New-
York. Britons tremble lest the vengeance of heaven fall on your isle,
for the blood of these unfortunate victims![14]

More popular than castigations of the British, however, were
attacks on those Americans who remained loyal to Great Britain.[15]
Tales of Tory troubles proved very popular. One humorous piece
in the *Newport Mercury* concerned a house where a large number
of martins usually spent the spring. The house was bought by a
Tory, but the martins continued to nest there, "hoping that he
might reform; but upon their return this spring, finding that he
was incorrigible, determined no longer to build under the roof of
a Despot, and entertain him with their music, so, with one voice,
quitted his house, and flew away to the dwellings of the Sons of
Liberty." Rumors of sundry plots and conspiracies also abounded
in all the public prints. On one occasion, accusations of plans to
ruin the paper currency while spreading smallpox everywhere
resounded throughout New England.[16]

Although useful in spreading information concerning Tory activities, the newspapers proved most helpful as a means to label
publicly those who did not support the American cause. Lists of
such people appeared regularly, along with the recantations of
those who had seen the error of their ways. In 1776 the *Connecticut
Courant* declared that everyone labeled "inimical to the Country"
by the Committees of Inspection would have their names published in the paper weekly "till a deep Sense of their Guilt, and
Promise of Amendment, shall restore them to the Favour of their
insulted Country." Although desirous of aiding the cause, the
printers of the *Courant* did not forget finances. They also requested that the Committees of Inspection charge a dollar for
every confession that had to be published in order to pay the
printing costs.[17]

Public attacks against some of these people also became normal
newspaper fare. Particularly hated by New Englanders was the
former governor of Massachusetts, Thomas Hutchinson, who became a favorite target for writers in the public prints—some even
placed total blame for the war on his shoulders. Upon Hutchinson's death in 1783, John Gill insisted that he had cut his own
throat for

the probability was so great, that he could never have died a natural
death (having contracted at least as much guilt of any traitor since the

apostacy of Adam) that without any direct information, it might reasonably have been thought that this, or something equally shocking, was the manner of his exit.—May it prove to the end of time, a solemn warning to all hypocrites and traitors.[18]

Many of the accusations against the British proved groundless, but these statements still helped the war effort because colonials believed them.

While condemning the British for their plots and their inhuman treatment of the populace, the public prints had only praise for the Continentals. After the initial fighting at Lexington and Concord, one article declared that "some future historian will relate, with pleasure, and the latest posterity will read with wonder and admiration, how three hundred intrepid, rural sons of freedom drove before them more than five times their number of regular, well appointed troops, and forced them to take shelter behind their bulwarks!" Throughout the war, the newspapers expressed no doubts that the American forces would ultimately prevail. By 1779, the printer of the *American Journal* concluded that "it is allowed on all hands that the American Army is now equal at least to any in the world for discipline, activity and bravery. There are no soldiers in Europe more exemplary for subordination, regularity of conduct, patience in fatigues and hardships, perseverance in service, and intrepidity in danger."[19]

Most newspapers attributed the success of America's armed forces to the leadership of George Washington. By 1777, following the victory at Trenton, the public prints had made Washington into a national hero. He could do no wrong—"this great man was born to give a consistency and cement to the military efforts of these States, in one of the most important and honorable causes that any nation was engaged in." Praise for this almost perfect man filled the columns of the local gazettes and centinels. Numerous poems were written in his honor. In 1777 the *Independent Chronicle* printed one of the best of these efforts, an acrostic of Washington's name:

> Genuine production of the God's above,
> Emerg'd from Heav'n on Wings of sovereign love,
> Over Columbia's host to take command,
> Regain her freedom, and defend her land;
> Greatness of language can't his praise express,
> Eclipses but his fame and makes it shine the less.
> Wisdom and knowledge all his deeds inspire,
> And his vast soul warm'd with angelic fire;

Statesman accomplished, hero Brave and Bold,
His matchless virtue like the Stars untold;
In utmost perils calm and most serene,
Nor over flush'd when he's victorious been;
Godlike his mind's from common changes free,
Turns o'er the fate of nations and their end does see,
Of all the heroes, history doth record,
None ever were so great, so free from vice,
    and so well serv'd the Lord.[20]

Reports of British efforts to bribe Washington produced ridicule and laughter. So great was the aura that surrounded George Washington, his name alone was invoked as a reason for joining the army:

> Such, my countrymen, is the General who directs the military operations of America; such the glorious leaders of her armies; such the Hero whose bright example should fire every generous heart to enlist in the service of his country. Let it not be said, you are callous to the impressions of such noble considerations, but, by following his glorious example, shew yourselves worthy of possessing that inestimable jewel Liberty, and reflect that you have nothing to dread whilst you are engaged in so glorious a cause, and blessed with a Washington for a leader.[21]

If George Washington was America's national hero, then Benedict Arnold was its archfiend. Arnold's attempt to turn West Point over to the British in 1780 shocked the nation and produced a torrent of abuse in the press that has never been equalled. The newspapers made Benedict Arnold into the ultimate traitor, a reputation that still holds today. Epitaphs attached to his name included "Judas," "the meanest & basest of mankind," and "the basest villain on earth." Reproaches and recriminations flooded the public prints. The following acrostic, published in the *Boston Gazette* in 1780, was only one of many barbs that flew Arnold's way:

> BORN for a curse to virtue and mankind!
> Earth's broadest realms can't show so black a mind.
> Night's sable Veil, your crimes can never hide.
> Each is so great—they'st glut th' historic tide.
> Defunct—your memory will ever live.
> In all the glare that Infamy can give!
> Curses of ages will attend your name;
> TRAITORS alone will glory in your shame.
> Almighty Justice sternly waits to roll

> Rivers of sulphur, on your trait'rous soul—
> Nature looks back, in conscious error, sad,
> On such a tarnish'd blot, that she has made!
> Let HELL receive you rivetted in chains!
> Damn'd to the hottest focus of its FLAMES.[22]

Printers took great glee in reporting that Arnold's reception among the British army was less than cordial. They accused him of cowardice for fleeing and leaving his British contact, Major John Andre, to suffer alone. Although everyone agreed that Andre was a spy, they were full of praise for the gentlemanly manner in which he faced his execution. Many wished that the victim had been Arnold instead. Finally, many writers saw desperation in the British bribery of Arnold. One essayist concluded that

> it shows the declining power of the enemy. An attempt to bribe is a sacrifice of military fame, and a concession of inability to conquer; as a proud people they ought to be above it, and as soldiers to despise it; and however they may feel on the occasion, the world at large will despise them for it, and consider America superior to their arms.[23]

Along with accusations aimed at Benedict Arnold appeared encouragements for Americans to do their utmost for the war effort: "America has yet to learn one important lesson from the defection and treachery of General Arnold. To cultivate domestick and moral virtue as the only basis of true patriotism. Publick virtue and private vice are wholly incompatible." Such appeals had been common since the beginning of the war. In 1776 Isaiah Thomas printed the following encouragement to his readers: "Let us not busy ourselves now about our private internal affairs, but with the utmost care and caution, attend to the grand American controversy, and assist her in her earnest struggle in support of her natural rights and freedom." Benjamin Edes insisted that independence would be valued more highly if it cost dearly. Calls for increased endeavors accompanied both victory and defeat. The victory at Saratoga produced a need for more American exertions in order to encourage aid from France and Spain while the defeat at Charleston, "instead of being a Misfortune, will, it is presumed from present Appearances, turn out a real Advantage," reinstilling "the noble Spirit which invigorated these States in Seventy six."[24]

One big problem that dogged Americans throughout the war was inflation. Prices soared while the value of the paper currency plummeted. Efforts to regulate prices met with little success. The newspapers reflected public concern over this issue and tried to encourage efforts to correct the problem. In reporting a fall in produce prices west of the Connecticut River, the printer of the *Norwich Packet* hoped that "the flame" might "spread throughout the United States." One Connecticut essayist accused merchants of purchasing "necessities and luxuries of life" only to sell them "at a most exorbitant price." In reprinting this piece, Benjamin Edes commented that it was "as applicable to this State as any other, and ought to be remedied." Illicit trade with the British in New York increased, making provisions even more costly.[25]

Accompanying the rise in prices was a devaluation in the currency. Fears for the credit of the government became rampant. "The Sentinel" regretted these developments because "a depreciating paper currency is one of the greatest calamities which can happen to a state; for it not only embarrasses every public department of business, but it corrupts the morals of the people at large." Some accused the British of plotting to ruin America's finances, but insisted that, "notwithstanding all the boasts of our enemies, a little time will show that America has resources fully sufficient to retrieve her currency; and even without this, it can be demonstrated, that we are able to defend ourselves, and support our glorious cause." In an effort to encourage the people to have more faith in the government's money, several papers reported that "the Continental Currency grows every day more and more in esteem, which must consequently give great pleasure to every well-wisher to his country." Isaiah Thomas summed up the feelings of many people when he called on everyone to do all they could to maintain the government's credit rating:

> Americans! Restore the Credit of your Currency, by lowering the Prices of the Necessaries of Life, and imported Goods; placing your several Quotas in the Continental Treasury; lending Money for public Uses; and sinking the Emissions of your respective States. Fill up your Battalions. Supply well your Fleets and Armies with Provisions and Stores. Put an End to Monopolising and Oppressing. Pursue this Campaign with redoubled Vigour. Practice and encourage Virtue. And, with the Smiles of Heaven, you will secure Peace, Liberty, and Safety, with the blessings of Millions yet Unborn![26]

The public prints insisted that God had chosen America for a special mission; its effort for independence was to be a shining example for the rest of the world to follow. Many felt that another part of the British Empire, Ireland, would be the first to follow the American model. Interest in Britain's troubles in Ireland increased, because "the Independence of these States, & the Efforts of our Allies, have prepared the way for the Freedom of Ireland." In 1782, a local essayist in the *Massachusetts Spy* urged the Irish to quickly follow the American example:

> Now is the Time! Providence opened the pearly gate to America, she flew to enter, cut her way through the opposing legions of Britain, and hath taken her seat in the TEMPLE OF LIBERTY.—Shall Ireland pause, while the portals are open, and her American sister beckons her to come in and join the triumphant circle of the FREE! . . . On God and yourselves depend. Let your own counsels make your laws, and your own swords defend them; then and not until then can you be free. . . . LET IRELAND AND AMERICA TAKE CARE OF THEM-SELVES![27]

This interest in Irish efforts to gain their rights in the face of "British tyranny" continued in the years after the Revolution ended.

While encouraging everyone to continue the struggle because America was meant to be a model for all, the newspapers also reminded them not to forget their "firm reliance on the goodness of Almighty God." The Continental Congress expressed this idea best in 1778 in a call for unity and strength among the people:

> Yet do not believe that you have been or can be saved merely by your own strength. No! It is by the assistance of Heaven, and this you must assiduously cultivate, by acts which Heaven approves. Thus shall the power and the happiness of these sovereign, free and independent States, founded on the virtue of their citizens, increase, extend and endure, until the Almighty shall blot out all the empires of the earth.[28]

The end of the fighting in 1781 promised fulfillment of these dreams of future greatness expressed in New England's newspapers. The press had played an integral part in the overall war effort by making it a national concern. The widespread reprinting of essays and letters along with accounts of actions in other colonies served to create a unity of ideas and feelings about the war. This proved particularly crucial in New England because very little fighting occurred there after the British evacuated Boston in 1776. The public prints performed a crucial task in convincing their readers that the war was everyone's fight even though the center of operations had shifted southward. The over-all result was the solidarity of purpose needed for a successful revolt. This solidarity had been reflected in the press as the newspapers presented a united front in the face of the enemy. Prospects looked bright following Cornwallis's surrender in late 1781. The years immediately after the war, however, would be ones of divisiveness and indecision, a state reflected in the lack of concurrence about political issues expressed in the public prints. The unity of the war years would not be rediscovered for several years to come.

7

The Press and Political Issues: Division between the States, 1782–1786

The end of the fighting in 1781 and the official peace treaty in 1783 produced changes in the newspaper press of New England. Even though the war was followed by a predictable depression, the number of newspapers grew quickly, from nineteen in 1783 to thirty-three in 1789. Many of the new endeavors occurred in the backcountry, away from the large commercial centers. The public prints also no longer had to present a united front in the face of a common enemy; the commonality of subject matter that had held throughout the Revolutionary War dissolved. As the need for solidarity faded, the states in New England began to look inward in hopes of solving problems that had gone unsettled during the war. Many worries proved common to all of New England, but each state had its own set of issues that were of particular interest to its residents. The newspapers reflected this in their coverage of political issues, with those from each state concentrating on the questions most important to their own areas. Local printers became more vocal in this period, increasingly expressing their own opinions about issues of concern to their readers. In Maine and Vermont, the issue that came to the forefront was their desire to be separate states. In New Hampshire, public concern revolved around the nation's public credit. The people of Connecticut worried about the method proposed to pay the Continental Army, while Rhode Island reflected on the need for a national impost and a local paper currency. The weekly sheets of Massachusetts considered a variety of issues of importance to their readers, but two stood out above the rest: the state of America's foreign trade and problems in the backcountry. All of these issues provided newspapers with materials for public debate during the 1780s.

Some people in Maine had long desired to be separated from Massachusetts, but a movement to accomplish this goal did not begin until 1785. One indication of early efforts in this direction was the establishment of Maine's first newspaper, the *Falmouth Gazette*, in January 1785. The editors of the *Gazette*, Benjamin Titcomb and Thomas Wait, quickly came out in favor of separation, charging that Maine did not have fair representation in the General Court and that the Massachusetts government never considered Maine's interests. From the founding of their paper until the middle of 1786, they averaged at least one essay a week in favor of an independent Maine. One writer called on the people of Maine to united in favor of separation. Another, under the pen name of "Considerator," suggested sending a petition to Congress: "let us supplicate their interposition, and pray for their consent that we should separate ourselves from our oppressive rulers, and form a government of our own. If our cause is just, they will comply with our request; and if we act by their authority, they will support us in the important undertaking."[1]

In the face of such strong support for separation in Maine, newspapers in Massachusetts did not seem to know how to react. One stated that "an independent state seems to engross the attention of the inhabitants" of Maine while another declared that "the rage for revolution seems only confined to a few individuals." In Maine, the *Falmouth Gazette* continued to agitate, calling for a meeting to discuss the issue. In response, thirty delegates met on 5 October 1785. The result was a convention which met in January 1786, representing twenty towns. Although the conventions continued to take place periodically, very little came of them. Shays's Rebellion in the fall of 1786 scared many of Maine's leaders, and the separation movement slowly died. Even though the statehood crusade had foundered, the newspaper established to support the movement, the *Falmouth Gazette*, continued to operate for years to come.[2]

Vermont's case differed slightly from that of Maine. In 1777, Vermont declared itself to be an independent republic. Both New York and New Hampshire laid claim to the territory but proved unable to maintain control. Throughout the war, Vermont had negotiated with the British and with the Continental Congress in hopes of gaining recognition of their separation from both New York and New Hampshire. Although Vermont's leaders desired to become the fourteenth state, they would have allied themselves with the British in order to preserve their separate identity. War's end halted negotiations with the British but did not end the problem. Both New York and New Hampshire tried to govern the area, but proved incapable of doing so; their representatives found themselves fearing for their safety. The imprisonment of a

New Hampshire sheriff in his own jail resulted in a sharp response in the pages of the *New Hampshire Gazette:* "This attack upon the person of one of the Executive Officers of this State will convince the Honorable Congress of the Necessity of quelling these insurgents. . . . Nothing less than a solemn Resolve to annihilate this usurped State, can be the Consequence of an Application from this State [New Hampshire]." New York also requested that Congress settle the matter. Although Congress attempted to tell Vermont how to settle conflicting land claims in the area, Vermont's legislature insisted that to do so would abrogate Vermont law. Congress did no more to try and resolve the quandary.[3]

Even though no solution presented itself, Vermont still hoped to enter the Union. Numerous authors in the Vermont news papers expressed hopes that Vermont would become the fourteenth state. Public celebrations generally included an extra toast, in addition to the usual thirteen, which called for "the confederacy of Vermont with the United States" to "close the glorious struggle for liberty." Some editors in other parts of New England expressed a dislike for this idea because Vermont would "participate in the advantages, and have borne but a small part of the expences attending the late revolution." In response to such assertions, the printer of the *Vermont Gazette* insisted that "the British in Canada were rendered good neighbors" of America during the war because Vermont had done her share by "keeping constantly in readiness to repel attacks." Vermonters clearly desired to be in the Union, but they did not achieve their goal of becoming the fourteenth state until 1791.[4]

At the end of the Revolution, New Hampshire's economy was a shambles; the stresses of war and inflation had taken their toll. The local public prints mirrored these developments in their discussions of issues of importance to their readers. State attempts to solve the economic problems failed, so New Hampshire leaders turned to some form of interstate cooperation as a possible way to restore economic stability. Particularly important was the reestablishment of the public credit on a sound footing. As a reflection of these concerns, the newspapers of New Hampshire began to show a special interest in the efforts of the Continental Congress to shore up the national finances, particularly the plan for a federal import duty. Opinions varied from strong support to extreme dislike. Most, however, felt that something had to be done to restore the financial stature of the central government.[5]

In hopes that Congress had found another solution, many in

New Hampshire exhibited a particular regard for the efforts of Robert Morris, who had been appointed superintendent of finance in mid–1781. Numerous letters and essays appeared discussing Morris's proposals for a national bank and a federal impost. Some pieces appeared that criticized these ideas, but, overall, New Hampshire's public prints supported the superintendent, praising him for his efforts to restore the public credit. One essayist affirmed that "the bank has enabled the Financier almost to work miracles; and the public would be astonished to see, could the springs be safely disclosed, how much credit he has derived from small resources." Another author insisted that "the widow, the orphan, the aged citizen, and the half-starved soldier sing for joy at the bare mention of the name of Mr. Morris, to whose abilities and industries we are indebted for the revival of public and private credit." Daniel Fowle concluded that "to this Gentleman we are indebted in a great measure for the political salvation of this country."[6]

Robert Morris's recommendations, however, did not solve the problem of the national debt and thus did not help with New Hampshire's economic stagnation. Writers in the local press studied the problem, hoping to find an answer. "Amicus" complained "no wonder the public faith is at so low an ebb, when their public securities are despised by the lowest class of people." Several insisted that there would be no problem if all the states met their financial obligations owed to Congress. Clearly, all must do their part to pay off the national debt: "the states will forfeit their honor and plight their faith should they refuse to approve and support Congress in the public engagements; or neglect to provide resources for the payment of them." When the proposed national impost failed to pass, one author urged each state to adopt its own impost to raise money to pay the national debt. One possible solution, according to "Consideration," was the sale of public lands. All of these suggestions fell short of enactment. New Hampshire entered the last years of the 1780s with its economy still in a deplorable condition.[7]

Connecticut also faced troubles following the end of the Revolution. Early in the conflict, her people had wholeheartedly supported the war effort. All congressional requisitions prior to June 1779 had been completely met. After that time, Connecticut's ardor began to abate. Failure on the part of the national government to protect the Connecticut coast from British raids raised questions in Connecticut about whether efforts for the American cause were really worthwhile. This growing disillusionment with the war and the Continental Congress, coupled with a long-standing distrust of armies, set the stage for the bitter controversy that raged in Connecticut in the wake of the congressional commutation pay proposal.[8]

The issue of commutation pay grew out of a discussion of army pensions that had begun in 1780. Then, almost in a fit of desperation, Congress had granted half-pay pensions to all officers who remained in the service until the end of the war, hoping such a provision would encourage officers to remain in the service. As the war's end approached, however, the measure became increasingly unpopular among the people at large. The officers realized this and included in their 1782 list of grievances a request that the half-pay pensions be commuted to five years' full pay, thus the term "commutation pay." Fears aroused by the 1783 Newburgh Addresses[9] prompted Congress to grant this request on March 22.[10]

Press reaction to the congressional grant of five years' pay came quickly in Connecticut, varying widely from strong support to extreme dislike. Many supporters declared that the measure was a contract that could not be broken. Under the Articles of Confederation, Congress had the right to make contracts, commutation pay was a contract just like any other one, and the states did not have the right or power to back out of the bargain. Congress promised the officers a pension of some description, so they should get paid. They also deserved it as "a reward for their unparalleled sufferings." Many officers had ruined their fortunes by leaving their homes and jobs to join the army in America's fight for freedom. Opponents of the pension plan, however, disagreed. Many felt that the Connecticut people had already given enough to win the war and that commutation would call for more. Furthermore, the five years' pay constituted "unreasonable wages" and set a bad precedent for the future. The granting of pay to the officers was not fair to the enlisted, militia, and general citizenry who also sacrificed for the war effort, possibly resulting in the elevation of members of the army above the rest of the people, a notion unacceptable in an independent republic.[11]

The idea of freedom played an important role in several protests against the commutation pay in the Connecticut press. One essayist described the measure as "perfectly unjust and unconstitutional"—a menace to America's liberty. More importantly, commutation went against the principles upon which America was founded by threatening to establish a class of placemen, one of the issues that helped cause the American Revolution. As one historian has described the public's reaction, commutation appeared to be a device "by which a ruling few, like the ministers of the English Crown, would attach a corps of pensioners and dependents to the government and spread their influence and connections throughout the states in order 'to dissolve our present Happy and Benevolent Constitution and to erect on the Ruins, a proper Aristocracy.' "[12]

These reactions in the public prints mirrored those of the people. Responses to the Commutation Act reverberated throughout Connecticut. At town meetings convened to discuss the issue, most of those present opposed the measure and elected representatives to a convention scheduled to meet in Middletown. Over two-thirds of the towns were represented at the Middletown Convention, which took place in September 1783. The representatives discussed the best method of overruling the Commutation Act and urged the Connecticut assembly to investigate whether Congress had overstepped its powers. Several essayists decried the convention's actions because they went against the general sense of the nation, which had supported commutation. Other writers, however, supported the meeting. "A Convention Man" insisted that commutation was "without a foundation either in law or equity." Adoption of the proposal meant that the officers were being paid twice for the same services—an idea that was "abhorrent to every idea of justice."[13]

Besides essays, the Middletown Convention also inspired poetry and satire in the Connecticut press. One poet supported the convention's actions in the following satirical manner: "rejoice in this, that your children are free, / And may work all their days to support a grandee." Other efforts sarcastically attacked the convention. These included "A Political Creed by Heliogabulus Gonty, Scribe" and a poem praising the conventioneers for adjourning for the third time without accomplishing anything of substance and for spreading sedition. One man in Europe, writing to a friend in Hartford, asked, "Is it commutation that causes such a ferment? When the resolution of Congress promising halfpay to the army passed, little or no objection was made, but the service performed and the war over, now the impropriety of the measures appear very clear to the good people of Connecticut." A fake advertisement, however, contained the best satire concerning the Middletown Convention. Inserted by "Convention-Man," the piece advertised a stallion for stud: "Hobby-Horse, the famous horse, Ambition, upon the ambling Mare, Popularity, from thence in a direct line from the noted horse,

Turbulence, alias Faction. . . . He has run four heats at Middletown against the well-known Horse, Honour and Honesty."[14]

Following these strong reactions in Connecticut, a few writers expressed fears that the opposition to the Congressional measure came from those opposed to the government—"the enemies of independence." One essayist blamed the trouble on "the blustering patriots of the present times, who, being suspected of toryism and neglected in the glorious contest for freedom have made a stalking horse of commutation to ride into office, and make it their sole business to traduce Congress and the army to whom chiefly this Continent owes its independence."[15]

Most Connecticut printers expressed their opinions concerning the commutation issue, but the owners of the *Connecticut Courant*, Barzillai Hudson and George Goodwin, proved particularly vocal. They supported commutation pay as a legitimate debt of the government that had to be paid. In reporting the refusal of one town to pay the expense account of its representative to the Middletown Convention, Hudson and Goodwin said that "the churl probably did not reflect, that in teaching mankind not to pay their debts, he learnt them to cheat himself." Both printers feared that refusal to fulfill the obligation of some form of pension for the army officers would produce anarchy. They declared that the people of Connecticut had allowed "themselves to be duped out of their senses by the foes of our independence and British emissaries, who are scattering the seeds of discord in the region of tranquility." Many others probably shared these fears of possible unrest. The issue of commutation died a quiet death in the mid-1780s, but some of the discord the proposal created in Connecticut remained for years to come.[16]

The end of the fighting in 1781 found the state of Rhode Island in disorder. Having suffered greatly during the British occupation, the economy was practically at a standstill. Rhode Island had contributed a great deal to the war effort, both in money and materials, and most citizens felt that the needs of the state should come first now. Although complete unity had been necessary during the war, the approach of peace meant that Rhode Island could look after local interests for a change. As one essayist said, "nothing now remains but for every one to mind his own business." These feelings produced two major conflicts for Rhode Island during the 1780s, one external and the other internal in nature. The external question concerned the proposed congressional impost. The internal problem pertained to the desire by many for an issue of paper money to ease the debt problem in

Rhode Island. Both issues generated debates in Rhode Island's public prints that continued throughout most of the decade.[17]

On 3 February 1781, the Continental Congress requested permission to levy a continental impost, a 5 percent duty on imported goods. Proceeds from this duty would form a fund to pay the national debt. For Congress to have the proper authority, the Articles of Confederation had to be amended, which required approval by all thirteen states.[18]

Reaction to this proposal came quickly in the press. John Carter, publisher of the *Providence Gazette*, reported that the response was so heavy that he could not print everything he received. In Rhode Island, most people opposed the congressional impost because the federal tax would give the national government too much power over the state's internal affairs. One author called on the Sons of Liberty to rise and prevent the tyrannical efforts of Congress to increase its powers while "A Lover of Liberty" urged Americans not to "plunge themselves into a bondage ten thousand times worse" than that suffered under Britain. This essayist believed that adoption of the continental impost would return America to the same state that existed prior to the Revolution.[19]

Supporters of the duties dismissed these objections, declaring that the import taxes were necessary to establish a firm credit for America to pay its debts and to continue borrowing money to augment tax revenues. Adoption of the impost would complete America's financial system—"the government will be rendered firm, and the people happy" after providing for a more stable congressional revenue. More importantly, "the possession of a solid and permanent revenue in the General Congress, to be solely at their disposal, is absolutely necessary to establish and perpetuate the sovereignty of the United States."[20]

Opponents argued that rather than establishing the nation's sovereignty, the import duties would produce a tyrannical and despotic government, perhaps even resulting in a dictatorship. Impost supporters disagreed, declaring that failure to adopt the measure would be tyrannical because rejecting the proposal would "violate the spirit of the confederation." Congress formed "a supreme independent power, composed of the whole strength of all the separate states." Because Congress, as the sole representative of the United States, had contracted the obligation, only Congress could repay the debt. Failure to pay these debts would be "a breach of national faith." The impost would provide the necessary revenues; the proposal had to be adopted in order for the Confederation to function properly.[21]

Some Rhode Island newspaper correspondents foresaw bankruptcy if the impost failed to pass, but most feared the exact opposite result. "If our finances are distressed" now, declared one, the adoption of the impost would be "a ready way to distress them further." The import duties would fall heavily on all consumers, making money even more scarce. Many felt that the duty would prove particularly detrimental to Rhode Island because the economy was so dependent on commerce. "A Farmer" feared an irrevocable grant, such as the one proposed by Congress, because, "like 'Pandora's box,' once opened," it would never close. The tax could only serve to increase, rather than reduce the national debt and should be opposed for this reason. One letter in the *Providence Gazette* declared that "the only Danger on that Score is that of contracting too large a Debt." The author concluded that "instead of regretting that our credit was no better established, by an Impost, or permanent Revenue to be mortgaged for the Purpose, Posterity, when they feel the Weight of Debt thereby transmitted on them will admire at its extent, and rejoice that it went no further." "Honestus Politicus" declared that, in honor of those "patriots of great zeal and abilities" who opposed the impost, "future generations may rise up and call their names blessed."[22]

Because of the strong anti-impost sentiment, the Rhode Island government declared the measure to be a violation of the Confederation and refused to ratify the proposal. Without the approval of all thirteen states, the amendment could not take effect, so Rhode Island's refusal killed the measure. Congressional supporters failed to understand Rhode Island's reasoning and severely castigated the state legislature for not bending to the rule of the majority. Some felt that the real reason for the refusal lay in the fact that since Rhode Island raised a good deal of money through its own impost, state leaders did not want to lose any of the revenue to Congress. A resident of Rhode Island lamented his state's action: "The voice of our legislature has reprobated the measure; as a citizen therefore of the state, I acquiesce in their determination; but as a citizen of the United States, I deeply regret the consequences."[23]

In an effort to understand Rhode Island's reasoning and also to get its citizens to change their minds, Thomas Paine wrote a series of essays in December 1782–February 1783 under the pseudonym of "A Friend to Rhode Island and the Union." He supported the impost, declaring that the tax would lie equally on all the states and all classes of people. The wealthy would pay more because they used more imported goods. The necessity of paying the

public debt made the adoption of the duties essential. Paine
accused the merchants of Rhode Island of opposing the measure
in order to protect their commerce from all taxation. If twelve
states had approved the proposal, how could Rhode Island dare
to reject it? Paine concluded that "more injury has arisen to the
United States, by the conduct of Rhode Island in this instance;
than lies in her power to repair."[24]

While Paine condemned Rhode Island for hurting the Confederation, a number of New Englanders praised its stand as
noble and justified. Congressman David Howell of Rhode Island
praised his home state for the action: "Your early, decided and
persevering opposition to British claims, will not rank you higher
in the annals of America, than the temper, firmness and unanimity, with which you rejected the recommendation for a Continental impost of five per cent. on the memorable first of November, 1782." "A Bayman" thanked the people of the state to the
south for having taken a stand that "hath gone far towards saving
the liberties of America, without which the name of independence would have been nugatory." Perhaps "Cato" summed up
best the feelings of those who supported Rhode Island's rejection
of the impost: "I look upon Rhode Island as the poor wise man
that saved the city. Her name will go down to posterity with the
highest renown and honor—she hath saved America."[25]

The conflict did not end with Rhode Island's rejection of the
impost. Castigations and defenses of the action filled the press for
months to come. New impost proposals, introduced by Congress
in 1783, reheated the debate, which continued through 1784 and
1785. Rhode Island's citizens, however, had turned most of their
attention to solving state problems, and the national issue of the
impost was slowly displaced by one of a more local nature dealing
with paper money.[26]

By the mid–1780s, many people in Rhode Island had decided
that the way to ease economic troubles was to issue paper currency and make the money a legal tender for the payment of all
debts. The years 1785–1786 saw a great deal of discussion of this
idea in all the Rhode Island newspapers. Although many supported this idea, the merchants came out strongly against the
proposal. In a memorial to the state assembly, the town of Providence assured the legislature that its citizens were "sincerely disposed to contribute their best endeavours to give effect to all
measures calculated to promote and perpetuate the prosperity of
this State, and of the United States; But That They Do Not Con-

sider An Emission Of Paper Money As Coming Within That Description."[27]

Although the merchants clearly opposed paper money, a majority in Rhode Island endorsed the proposal and the legislature responded to this support by providing for an emission in May 1786. This currency constituted a legal tender and had to be accepted in payment of any legal debt. Criticism of this plan came quickly in the Rhode Island press. One writer feared that "the whole scheme is pregnant with Mischief, and inadequate to the Purpose it is proposed to answer." An essayist in the *Providence Gazette* insisted that paper money could not pay a nation's debts, while another asserted that "paper money, in any light it can be viewed, . . . is at best a bubble." No one benefited except "the horse jockey, the mushroom merchant, the running and dishonest speculator, who after they have run a debt must continue to pay without money, or be obliged to run their country." Peter Edes, editor of the *Newport Mercury*, railed against paper money for months, describing the Rhode Island system as a "deviation . . . from justice and honor." Creditors would be cheated out of the money rightfully owed to them because the paper money system was an "uncheery labyrinth" producing "injuries arising from sporting with public faith and infringing upon the sacred rights of private contracts."[28]

Supporters of the paper money system scoffed at these objections, believing that most creditors were really speculators who had acquired their securities at below-par rates and that paying them in paper money seemed only just. Many of these securities had originally belonged to Revolutionary soldiers, men who deserved better treatment than they had received from the speculators. A poem published in the *United States Chronicle* of Providence ably summarized the moral convictions of many concerning the issue: "In times of war, we fought and bled, / For fine times which they promised; / And since the jewel we did gain, / We'll bleed again, or it sustain. / Stock-jobbers did not fight at all, / Hawkers and sharpers got our all; / And now we'd rather die like men, / Than be slaves to such as them."[29]

Rhode Island's leaders continued to back their paper money system as the only means to pay off the state debt in any reasonable length of time. By late 1788 and early 1789, interest in the new federal government replaced much of the discussion of paper money in the Rhode Island public prints. Some historians have speculated that a desire to finish paying the state debt delayed

Rhode Island's approval of the Constitution until 1791. Whether this is true or not, the entire state debt was paid off by 1790.[30]

Massachusetts faced many problems following the end of the Revolution, but most questions concerned economic matters in one form or another. In the early 1780s, people worried about the state of America's foreign commerce, in which Massachusetts had a great personal interest, and what should be done to restore the trade to a stable and profitable level. An excess of imports threatened to drain the state of specie, leading to requests for paper money in order to have some form of circulating currency. Money became tight, particularly in the backcountry, leading to liens for back taxes and mortgage foreclosures. These occurrences, accompanied by growing discontent over an apparent lack of concern by the Massachusetts government for the backcountry's problems, helped spark Shays's Rebellion in the fall of 1786. This revolt alarmed the entire country and sparked a great deal of discussion in the public prints, restoring a preoccupation with a single subject—a phenomenon that had been absent since the end of the fighting in 1781. The first economic problem that Massachusetts faced, however, was the stagnation of trade following the end of the war.[31]

With the approach of peace in 1783, Massachusetts's citizens had believed they faced a bright future because America's merchants would now be able to trade all over the world. In reporting the sailing of a ship from Boston to China, the printer of the *Salem Gazette* exclaimed: "We have, at an earlier period than the most sanguine Whig could have expected, or even hoped, or the most inveterate Tory feared, very pleasing prospects of a very extensive commerce with the most distant parts of the globe." This optimism soon faded, as imports began to greatly outnumber exports. Trade stagnated and many began to fear that, "should this continue to be the case, cold Poverty and meagre Want will soon stare us in the face."[32]

Some people blamed all this trouble on the British, insisting that continued British restrictions on American trade, particularly in the West Indies, stifled any chance of a recovery. Clearly the British intended to abide by their navigation system, a form of oppression that Americans could not tolerate. Benjamin Russell felt that the British consciously intended to ruin America and called on the Continental Congress to do something:

> It evidently appears to be the policy of Great Britain to do every thing to injure these States. She is determined that British vessels only

shall be carriers of all exports and imports, both to and from Great-Britain, the West-Indies and these States. All American vessels being obliged to pay heavy duties on their bottoms and cargoes in all British ports where they are allowed to enter. Surely the great Council of our Nation will not fail to do all in their power, and the several States individually to take effectual measures to frustrate such a ruinous plan to our country.[33]

Even more troublesome than the overall state of foreign trade was the fact that a great deal of America's commerce was being taken over by British representatives in the United States, to the detriment of American merchants. Writers in the Massachusetts newspapers, particularly in Boston, decried this development as "glaringly repugnant to the welfare of the community" and called for action of some kind to forestall the ruin of American merchants. Benjamin Russell complained that British traders unfairly monopolized trade in America while American ships could not even enter parts of the British empire. According to Russell,

> while those infamous paricides, the Refugees and English Factors, are permitted quietly to contaminate the air of a land of Freedom—to impede the wheels of government with their gold—and to ruin our Merchants and Tradesmen by their importations, our Trade is suffering every restriction, and as a nation we are treated with every indignity and insult that ignorance, ingratitude or verociousness can invest.[34]

A letter to the editor of the *Exchange Advertiser* of Boston urged that a town meeting be held and that "these BRITISH Factors, those Miscreants, those infernal Bloodsuckers, be commanded forthwith to depart; and if they accept not of this friendly advice, then let the DIRE VENGEANCE OF AN INCENSED, DETERMINED PEOPLE, fall on their guilty heads."[35]

Some writers in the public prints worried about the large number of foreign imports, declaring that America was trading the political oppression of the British for commercial tyranny through dependence on foreign manufactured goods. Several people called for a national agreement against using imported items in order to escape the problem. Through "a Union in such measures, on which the safety and welfare of our country so much depend, our enemies may be convinced, that we have wisdom to develop, and firmness to counteract, their deep laid designs against the happiness, and indeed against the existence of the Commonwealth." The printer of the *Independent Chronicle* felt that such an association was the only hope, for "if we should unhappily continue in the present prevailing taste for foreign tinsel, and for extravagant dress and equipage, which are a dishonor to Republicans, and inconsistent with every idea of republicanism, it must prove the ruin of the Commonwealth."[36]

Apprehensive that the strong desire for British goods indicated a decline in public virtue, many of Boston's intellectual leaders overreacted in 1785 to the formation of a club by some of the young men of the town. Named the "Sans Souci Club" or "Tea Assembly," the organization proposed to offer refreshments, dancing, and card-playing for its members and their guests. Horrified by this supposed attempt to copy "the vices of degraded Britain," several writers attacked the club as being "pregnant with fatal consequences . . . leading the way to vice." The first essayist to enter the fray, "Observer," charged that Americans were "exchanging prudence, virtue and economy, for those glaring spectres luxury, prodigality and profligacy" and were "prostituting" their "glory as a people, for new modes of pleasure, ruinous in their expences, injurious to virtue, and totally detrimental to the well being of society." "Nestor Ironside," summing up the fears of many, charged that "empires have been sunk by the sons of pleasure and dissipation. This will finally be our history."[37]

Members of the Sans Souci did not allow these accusations to go unanswered. They defended their organization, describing it as a "laudable institution," "a very harmless meeting, decent even to dullness." Furthermore, the group was "a company whose whole deportment bespeaks purity of mind and manners in the highest degree—evinces such a portion of republican virtue as places the inhabitants of this town (here beheld) on a par with the most celebrated either of Sparta or Lacedaemon."[38]

These arguments continued in the Boston press for two months, growing ever more abusive. Becoming bored with the fight, one reader of the *Exchange Advertiser* wrote "I am tired and disgusted with 'Sans Souci' bubbles, noise and nonsense; and heartily wish our folks would employ their time, and pen, and paper, and tongues, to better purpose." Such petty disagreements were a waste of time when more pressing issues needed resolution. Rather than railing at each other, "let every head and pen by employed to promote frugality, industry, national union, the love of our country, and the other virtues which are necessary for public happiness—to suggest the best way and means to pay our state and national debt, to promote learning and all useful arts, etc. is the work of patriots."[39]

Concern over public debts abounded in Massachusetts in the mid–1780s. Money was scarce, according to many, "on account of our numerous imports, and internal extravagance." Most of the state's specie was going overseas, leaving Massachusetts with very little money in circulation. Many people feared the results of this lack of funds, but one writer in the *Massachusetts Centinel* felt that the scarcity of money might be a good thing, forcing "all ranks of people, to resign their respective luxuries, one by one; to discharge the lazy vermin of the hall; to retrench all superfluous expences; to become economical and temperate; to devote themselves to industry; and, in fine to free themselves from the slavery of habits which accord but indifferently with an infant country, like America."[40]

Some people, however, declared that "a circulating medium is much wanted" and insisted that something had to be done. Several essayists called for an emission of paper money to ease the tight money situation. Many of the newspaper printers opposed this idea, insisting that a paper currency would "entirely put a stop to all Credit" because those with money would be scared to lend it for fear of losing it. The result would only be "pernicious effects, and public distresses." Isaiah Thomas maintained that, if the state turned to paper money, "an immediate and general stagnation of business, and suspension of justice, would follow, and anarchy and confusion, with all their horrid train of attendants, reign triumphant!" According to Thomas, "Industry, Economy and honest principles, with the aid of a little patience and perseverance will only, and will assuredly, bring the relief we seek for."[41]

Scarcity of money, intensified by a severe taxation and debt retirement program instituted by the state, created severe hardships for rural debtors in Massachusetts. Trouble had been brewing throughout rural New England ever since the end of the war. Attempts to force favorable legislation out of state governments occurred in Connecticut and Vermont; in New Hampshire, the general assembly was held prisoner for several hours by a mob of disgruntled farmers. The greatest unrest, however, occurred in the frontier counties of western Massachusetts. Trying to stave off losing their property for failure to pay their taxes, residents met in several county conventions in the summer and fall of 1786 to petition the General Court for help. Failing to get a sympathetic hearing in Boston, these men rebelled. Led by Daniel Shays, an ex-Continental Army captain, close to two thousand of them joined together in a makeshift army that closed the courts and prevented government officials from foreclosing on anyone's property. Finally, in February 1787, the militia under General Benjamin Lincoln clashed with Shays's men near Petersham, bringing an end to the rebellion.[42]

The newspaper printers of New England recoiled in horror at the lawlessness of these events because they considered such actions to be adding to, rather than solving, America's postwar problems. Blame for the insurrection was attributed to a variety of causes. After the disturbance was put down, one Boston printer asserted that the "late irregularities have proceeded from want of true information respecting the doings of the General Court." A piece reprinted from a Philadelphia paper declared that Massachusetts's troubles were punishment for her continued participation in the slave trade. Many, however, placed blame for the insurrection on the shoulders of a group of essayists who had spoken out against the legal system. "Honestus," an essayist in the *Independent Chronicle*, received particular criticism. During March and April of 1786, he had written a series of pieces condemning lawyers and the legal system as too expensive and time-consuming: "Are the 'PEOPLE' of this Commonwealth reduced to so dreadful a state as to give one quarter part of their property to secure the remainder when they appeal to the laws of their country?" He called for reform of the entire system. Many in the backcountry agreed with Honestus and the Shaysites called for similar changes in their demands. The similarity in proposals between Honestus and the insurrectionists resulted in the accusations against the essayist. Honestus defended himself in print, insisting that the grievances he wrote of had existed for a long time and that the failure to solve the problems, rather than his writing about them, produced the insurrection.[43]

Newspaper pieces attacked the rebellion participants for taking the law into their own hands. Essayists denounced the county conventions as "unconstitutional from the very nature of such assemblies, because they weaken the government, which is feeble at best." Furthermore, "these conventions are void of all authority, and when they assume to give law or direction to the people, or to any branch of government, they usurp the lawful powers of the legislature and are guilty of injuring the majesty of the people." "A Yeoman" asserted that he hated "tyranny, and will ever oppose it, be it in the government, or the people." He felt that the legislature should listen to the people's complaints and do what it could to help solve their problems; however, he did not want a government that anyone could "insult with impunity." He called on everyone "to rouse, the safety of the Commonwealth demands our help." Isaiah Thomas strongly urged that "all orders of people in this Commonwealth would use their utmost endeavours to restore the publick tranquility, that peace and harmony may again prevail, and our numerous inhabitants be united and happy. It cannot be doubted but our legislature will immediately attend to all just complaints of the people, and exert themselves for the general good."[44]

One direct result of Shays's Rebellion in the backcountry of Massachusetts was the establishment of a newspaper in Northampton in September 1786, the *Hampshire Gazette*. William Butler, editor of the new venture, filled the pages of his sheet with pieces against the actions of Shays and his followers. At least one essay on the subject appeared every week from September 1786 to the end of March 1787. Writers in Butler's paper called on the insurrectionists to desist, insisting they had no real reasons for complaint. One essayist, concluding that rebellion was more costly than the taxes complained about, insisted that "industry, frugality and economy, and not mobbing or breaking up courts, is the way to pay debts and taxes." When some compared the rebellion to the revolt against Great Britain, "Grapteer" cried that this was "highly injurious" to the glory of the Revolution: "the conduct of the insurgents must be represented in the opposite view, as succeeding to the place of British usurpation, and not as supporting liberty, which is inseparably connected with government."[45]

Finally, some feared that the revolt in Massachusetts would create trouble for the entire United States, possibly even resulting in European intervention: "They will say our division is our weakness; our aversion to taxation is our determination to cheat them; the instability of the confederation, and our diversity of sentiment is our greatest curse; the whole renders them without a friend to assist in case of attack, let us therefore but step forth and that very moment they are conquered." Fearing the worst and urging that something be done to solve the grievances that produced the rebellion, one writer concluded that "our country has stood upon the edge of ruin." "Camillus" cried that "this is a crisis in our affairs, which requires all the wisdom and energy of government: For every man of sense must be convinced that our disturbances have arisen, more from the want of power, than the abuse of it; from the relaxation, and almost annihilation of our federal government; from the feeble, unsystematic, temporising, inconsistent character of our own State." The editor of the *Norwich Packet* voiced the hopes of many when he prayed that "proper measures may speedily be adopted (for under God they may) to strengthen the declining, jarring, convulsive empire, as well the whole confederate body as the constituent parts."[46]

Shays's Rebellion restored the unity of subject matter to the newspapers that had existed during the Revolutionary War. The years after 1781 had witnessed a splintering of interests among the states, a development reflected in the division of political issues covered in the public prints of the various states. Shays's Rebellion changed all this. The rebellion sent shock waves throughout the country, producing anxiety over the nation's future. One result of this concern was an intensification of the movement for an alteration in the national government, which led to the Constitutional Convention in 1787. Another result was that all the newspapers were once more talking about the same thing. This oneness—a concern for national issues as opposed to local and regional themes—would continue throughout the remainder of the decade.

8

The Press and Political Issues: Return to Common National Concerns, 1787–1789

Shays's Rebellion restored the unity of subject matter in the newspapers that had existed during the Revolutionary War. This commonality in political topics in the newspapers continued to be the norm until after the inauguration of George Washington as president in 1789. The widespread circulation of information about the happenings in Massachusetts also aided the move for a stronger national government. For some time, many of America's leaders had wished that something could be done to strengthen the Confederation. Following Shays's Rebellion, this group succeeded in getting a convention called to meet in Philadelphia in May 1787 to discuss ways to improve the government.

The Constitutional Convention met in secret session in an attempt to invoke an air of openness and honesty in its deliberations. Surprisingly, the nation's newspaper printers complained little, even though reports of state legislative debates had appeared throughout the 1780s. Peter Edes, publisher of the *Newport Herald*, had begun to print a detailed record of the actions of the Rhode Island assembly in the spring of 1787. Concerning the Convention debates, however, printers published whatever rumors they received and apparently let matters go at that. They did not even speculate very much about the outcome; most just stated that the results would be beneficial for the nation. Some, in fact, insisted that "the profound secrecy . . . observed" by the Convention was a good sign, showing "that the spirit of party, on any great and essential point, cannot have arisen to any height."[1]

Hopes were high in the press concerning the outcome of the Philadelphia meeting. A writer in the *Providence Gazette* observed "that on the Proceedings of the Federal Convention . . . must these United States depend for political Happiness, and national

Honour." The editors of the *Connecticut Courant* insisted that one result of the Convention must be a strong executive power in the national government: "How widely different would have been the character of the union, if in Congress had resided a power to control the selfish interests of a single state, and to compel the sacrifice of partial views, in order to promote the common weal." They reported that "the greatest unanimity subsists in the councils of the Federal Convention" and prayed that "the United States will discover as much wisdom in receiving from them a suitable form of government to preserve the liberties of the people, as they did fortitude in defending them against the arbitrary and wicked attempts of Great Britain" because "nothing but union and a vigorous continental government, can save us from destruction." Upon reporting the adjournment of the Convention to allow a committee to write up the results, the *Independent Chronicle* declared that "the public curiosity will soon be gratified; and it is hoped, from the universal confidence reposed in this delegation, that the minds of the people throughout the United States are prepared to receive with respect, and to try with a fortitude and perseverance, the plan which will be offered to them by men distinguished for their wisdom and patriotism." Clearly,

> whatever measure may be recommended by the federal convention, whether an addition to the old constitution, or the adoption of a new one, it will, in effect, if agreed to, of which there can be no reasonable doubt, be a Revolution in Government, Accomplished by Reasoning and Deliberation; an event that has never occurred since the formation of society, and which will be strongly characteristic of the philosophic and tolerant spirit of the age.[2]

The Constitutional Convention adjourned on September 17th, its work done. The result of its deliberations was a brief document, which began appearing in the public prints on September 19th. Following the four-month news drought, the printers snapped up this document quickly. Every newspaper of the period published the complete Constitution. The newspapers soon inundated their readers with discussions of the proposed new government. Whereas pamphlets had functioned along with the weekly sheets as sources of political information in earlier years, the debates over the Constitution witnessed the establishment of the supremacy of the newspaper as a public forum, a domination that would last into the twentieth century. *The Federalist Papers*, so famous to modern readers, constituted only the best-known of hundreds of essays that appeared in the public prints during the ratification struggle.[3]

Even before the Convention completed its task, some newspapers heaped praise on its members. Referring to the delegates as "sages and patriots," the *New Hampshire Gazette* asserted that "an union of the abilities of so distinguished a body of men, among whom will be a Franklin and a Washington, cannot but produce the most salutary measures. These names affixed to their recommendations . . . will stamp a confidence in them" that the opposition "will not dare to attack, or endeavour to nullify." The invocation of George Washington's name in support of the Convention and its recommendations occurred from the time of the first session in Philadelphia until the Constitution was ratified: "Who can read or hear, that the immortal Washington has again quitted his beloved retirement, and obeyed the voice of God and his country, by accepting the chair of this illustrious body of patriots and heroes, and doubt of the safety and blessings of the government we are to receive from their hands?" Other members of the Convention also received commendations from the press. In general, the public prints applauded them because "they have shown themselves no less wise in council than brave in the field; they have calmly and deliberately formed and adopted a plan of government, which (when we consider the heterogeneous materials afforded for its construction by thirteen distinct states, almost all of them different in their interests, manners and customs) may justly be called a master-piece of human wisdom." Furthermore, "while the revolutions of government in other countries, have given rise to the most horrid scenes of carnage and bloodshed," only the United States could "boast of a Constitution formed by her chosen sages."[4]

Many writers at the time realized the uniqueness of the situation. In urging adoption of the Constitution, "Publius" insisted that "America can scarcely hope ever to see so respectable a body of her citizens convened on a similar occasion—so great an unanimity we cannot expect again." "A Landholder" warned that this might be America's last opportunity "to adopt a government which gives all protection to personal liberty and, at the same time, promises fair to afford you all the advantages of a sovereign empire." Such a meeting as the Convention was "quite novel in the history of government" while "the establishment of a Free and Efficient Government by the unbiased suffrages of an extended and numerous people, is without precedent in the old world, and will be an immortal honor to the new." According to one New England correspondent,

> the United States of America . . . now exhibits to the world a most unusual spectacle—that of a great and numerous people, calmly and deliberately, in time of peace, unawed by arms, and uninfluenced by party faction, appointing their wisest and best men to form a constitution of government, adequate to the great purposes of the general confederacy, and most productive of the prosperity, felicity, safety and welfare of the whole.[5]

The newspapers of New England were overwhelmingly in favor of the Constitution. In fact, many of them had long been urging a more consolidated national government. At the time of the final approval of the Articles of Confederation in 1781, printers praised the establishment of a government for the United States. Soon, however, some complained that the system was inadequate and that some changes needed to be made. These comments increased during the mid–1780s until, by the time the Constitutional Convention met, most of the printers had concluded that any change at all from the weak Articles of Confederation would be beneficial.[6]

Fears concerning the effectiveness of the Articles had appeared as early as 1782 and slowly increased in number and intensity throughout the decade. In April 1782, one essayist declared that "the political machine has been improved of late; but it is not yet perfected. It does not answer fully the cogs of national government. The defects are felt in many pernicious consequences." A correspondent in the *Independent Chronicle* expressed surprise that such great care would be taken in forming state governments while so little time was spent in formulating the national system. He concluded that a flawed government had been the result, indicated by the fact that "our national honour, character, and abilities have declined, and are declining under it." He urged a change because "there is a defect somewhere" and "it is our duty, interest and happiness to remove it."[7]

The weakness of Congress and the need to enlarge its powers produced most of the worries about the national government expressed in the newspapers. An essay in the *Freeman's Oracle* concluded that "they may DECLARE every thing but can DO nothing." Benjamin Russell, while lamenting the state of the nation, declared that "the Confederated States in Congress assembled have not the power to apply to effect any remedy, however salutary, to cure our national disorders." The editor of the *Hampshire Herald* averred "how absurd, to endow them with power to levy war, to contract loans, and then deprive them of their resources necessary for the discharge of such debts, which the faith of the nation is pledged for." One editor feared that the United States, "by neglecting to vest Congress with necessary powers, are precipitating themselves into an imperial government." "A.B." concluded that "every one must be convinced of the utility, nay absolute necessity of the powers of Congress being either enlarged, or entirely annihilated—either to support our national dignity, or confess we have none."[8]

Some writers urged changes in the Articles because of concerns over the country's international reputation. Lack of a recognizable and functional central government would produce European laughter and ridicule: "The Confederal Constitution, while it presents a Comedy to the rest of the world, will prove in the end a Tragedy to ourselves—and our distress will be attended with so much ridicule, that we shall lose the consolation of pity." Several writers concluded that only a strong national government could defend America's interests abroad and "protect the United-States from the insults and abuses of barbarians, whether civilized or uncivilized."[9]

Whatever the reason for their anxiety, most newspaper writers who urged changes in the Confederation clearly felt that all the country's problems were the result of a weak government. The Articles of Confederation had failed. The individual states had acted in their own selfish interests, threatening to ruin everything that had been gained during the war with Britain. The editor of the *New Hampshire Recorder* compared the states to the Prodigal Son: "They have taken of the portion of their Independence, that should have been lodged forever in Congress, and spent it in riotous living in a far country." The establishment of a stable national government was essential for America's survival. In fact, this action would constitute the final chapter of the American Revolution. "Nestor" insisted that

> there is nothing more common than to confound the term of the American revolution with that of the late American war.—The American war is over, but this is far from being the case with the American revolution; On the contrary, nothing but the first act of the great drama is closed. It remains yet to establish and perfect our new forms of government, and to prepare the principles, morals and manners, of our citizens.[10]

Many printers saw the proposed Constitution as the means for carrying out this final chapter of the Revolution. Because of this, they almost assumed that all good patriots would support the measure. They endeavored to convince their readers to approve the proposal because a large majority of the American people supported the recommended new government. The *New Hampshire Gazette* reported that

> the public prints from every quarter of the United States are filled with accounts of the unanimity with which the new federal constitution has been received, and the great happiness the people feel in the glorious prospect of being speedily relieved from their present feeble and declining state, and being put on a respectable footing among the nations, by the adoption of a united government, founded on so much wisdom, and so well calculated to preserve the rights of mankind, and raise to opulence and power the vast extended empire of America.[11]

Constitution supporters urged support for the proposal in order to end the suspense over America's future. "A Freeman" affirmed that "our country now seems to hang in anxious suspense, not knowing whether she is to have a good and efficient government or none at all, or a despotic one imposed upon her by some daring adventurer." Describing the Constitution as "the best plan of government that ever graced the ancient or modern world," the *Massachusetts Centinel* warned that "the consequence of the people's rejecting the federal Constitution, will be Anarchy in the extreme." Furthermore, it affirmed that, "in anticipating the acceptance of the American Constitution every countenance brightens with the full glow of hope and animating expectation of publick honour, peace and lasting prosperity to our 'Dear Country.'" Several other Boston papers reported that "many people look upon the adoption of the new constitution, as the millennium of virtue and wealth." An anonymous essayist in the *Independent Chronicle* summed up the feelings presented by the New England printers in their papers:

> Let us then be of one heart, and of one mind. Let us seize the golden opportunity to secure a stable government, and to become a respectable nation. Let us be open, decided and resolute in a good cause. Let us render our situation worthy the ashes of our slaughtered brethren, and our own sufferings. Let us remember our emblem, the twisted serpent, and its emphatical motto, unite or die! This was once written in blood; but it is as emphatical now as then. A house divided

against itself, cannot stand. Our national existence depends as much as ever upon our union; and its consolidation most assuredly involves our posterity, felicity and safety.[12]

Many writers praised the Constitution because it offered the "prospect of our national reputation being rescued from approbrium and disgrace" by preventing breaches of public contracts. According to "Common Sense," one of the best parts of the proposal was "power, adequate power, to manage the great affairs of the nation, conferred upon the Congress." An author in the *Boston Gazette* insisted that the economic evils that had plagued America since the end of the Revolution would disappear once the Constitution was adopted. "Connecticutensis" insisted that taxes under the new system would be fairer because they would be raised in an indirect manner. Praising the proposed government for its "wisdom and sound judgment," the editor of a Connecticut paper rejoiced over America's possibilities if the Constitution were adopted:

> It will set all the springs of action in motion. The government will be able to counteract the oppressive acts of other nations respecting our trade, our own ships and seamen will be employed in exporting our own produce. This will revive ship-building; and we may soon expect to see our rivers lined, as heretofore, with new ships; this gives employment to carpenters, joiners, blacksmiths, and even to every species of tradesmen; . . . to which I may add this happy and agreeable circumstance, that we shall be one people, and governed by the same general laws from New Hampshire to Georgia.[13]

Some Constitution supporters commended the document, declaring its adoption would "raise us from the lowest degree of contempt, into which we are now plunged, to an honorable, and consequently equal station among the nations." In fact, institution of a new government would produce surprise in Europe and bring praise to America: "The philosophers will no longer consider a republic as an impracticable form of government; and pious men of all denominations will thank God for having provided, in our federal Constitution an Ark, for the preservation of the remains of the justice and liberties of the world." A correspondent in the *Boston Gazette* declared that

> it was reserved for us, in the annals of fate, to open an ASYLUM for the oppressed in every quarter of the Globe; but it remains to complete the noble work, by establishing a government which shall secure

the blessings of liberty to ourselves, our posterity, and the emigrant, from tyranny who may fly to these hospitable shores. Heaven, to all its other favours, now presents the golden opportunity.[14]

Everyone, however, did not wholeheartedly support the proposed new plan of government. Some pieces raising serious objections against the Constitution appeared in all the New England newspapers. One author charged that the Constitution removed the seat of power too far from the people. Others insisted that it would take away the right to trial by jury, that it did not provide enough protection for a free press, and that it abolished free elections. A writer in the *Freeman's Journal* insisted that "the great names of Washington and Franklin have been taken in vain, and shockingly prostituted to effect the most infamous principles"— just because they both signed the Constitution did not mean that they both gave the document their complete support. Finally, "Algernon Sidney" worried that, "if we suffer it to be established, the world will, on account of the gross tyranny which it holds forth, be inclined to suspect, rather than our understandings, our integrity and courage."[15]

In overall numbers, however, very few essays against the Constitution appeared in the New England press. The Anti-Federalists expressed great concern over their inability to get their ideas included in the public prints, revealing their belief in the definite impact of newspapers on the general public. Constitution supporters clearly agreed because they used economic pressure against Anti-Federal printers. Only about a dozen opposition sheets existed in the entire country, with only one of any importance in New England—Boston's *American Herald*. Edward E. Powars, editor of the *Herald*, attempted to keep up the fight, but canceled subscriptions and declining advertising forced him to cease his efforts against the Constitution and move his operation to Worcester in June 1788. At approximately the same time, Massachusetts ratified the Constitution.[16]

Because of the lack of Anti-Federalist essays in the newspapers, opponents of the Constitution accused printers of being partial in the way they conducted their businesses. All hotly denied the charge, insisting that they published everything they were given and that their papers were "open to all parties." John Carter of Providence asserted that "whatever may have been my private sentiments respecting public measures, I have never suffered them to interfere with what I conceive to be the indispensible duty of an impartial Printer; nor have I at any time suffered myself to become the 'dupe' or 'tool' of a party." Furthermore, he concluded that

> on the Subject of Paper Money—on the Subject of the proposed new Constitution, and other interesting political questions, he has faithfully and impartially handed to the Public every Performance, pro and con, that has been committed to him; and persevering in this Line of Rectitude, and discharging what he conceives to be the indispensible Duty of an impartial Printer, he shall ever with great Cheerfulness submit his conduct to the Judgement of the Public, and by the Decision of that respectable and revered Tribunal stand acquitted or condemned.[17]

Whatever the accuracy of Carter's defense, few pieces appeared in opposition to the Constitution. In many cases, ardent Federalist printers probably found reasons for not publishing Anti-Federalist pieces. In Connecticut, for example, there really was no public debate because so few opposition essays appeared. Between the publication of the Constitution in September 1787 and its ratification by Connecticut fifteen weeks later, only six articles criticizing the proposed new government appeared in Connecticut newspapers. A historian of the Anti-Federalists found only twenty-eight original pieces against the Constitution from New England. Some essays from other parts of the country also appeared, but these were also few in number. "Candidus," an essayist in the *Independent Chronicle*, decried this situation:

> the adoption of the proposed Constitution, being a concern of such magnitude, we are in duty bound to hear with patience, the observations of our fellow citizens, provided their remarks are delivered with calmness and propriety; this candid disposition towards each other, cannot at this time injure us, but would be the means to unite every man, in embracing a system of Government, which might forever secure the liberties of this Country.[18]

The Anti-Federalists also had to face the problems of delays in the circulation of newspapers. Postmaster General Ebenezer Hazard, in an effort to save money, had restricted the free carriage of newspapers by postal riders. He could not have chosen a worse time for such changes. Printers depended almost completely on mail exchanges for their news. Anti-Federal writers suspected a conspiracy and castigated Hazard and his employees for attempting to muzzle them. Complaints from opposition printers alone would lend support to the conspiracy theme, but Federalist publishers also complained of delays in the mails. In February 1788, the *Independent Chronicle* of Boston stated that "Printers in the northern States have received scarce a single paper, printed beyond the Hudson" since the beginning of the year. A bottleneck had developed somewhere, but its source was never clearly ascertained. Because of his inability to solve this problem, Hazard lost his job after George Washington became president.[19]

Although they accorded precious little space to Anti-Federal pieces, New England's printers did not seem to mind using part of their papers to castigate those who opposed the new government. The newspapers freely attacked those who criticized the Constitution, even impugning the characters of such Revolutionary heroes as Richard Henry Lee and Patrick Henry. Equating Anti-Federalists with Tories and insurgents—"enemies of good government" and "Shaysites"—the newspapers pictured these people as dishonest and ignorant men who desired to squelch on their legal obligations. One correspondent in the *Massachusetts Gazette* assured everyone that the supporters of the Constitution had nothing to worry about: "if the anti-federal cause . . . is as base and contemptible as the scribblers who advocate it, the federalists have very little to fear, for certainly a more despicable junto than the herd of anti-federal writers, were never leagued together." Following approval of the Constitution by the necessary nine states, the *Connecticut Courant* used a fake advertisement to poke fun at the losing Anti-Federalists:

> On the 4th of July next, will be sold, for the benefit of the Anti-federalists, the old Articles of Confederation. That no one may have cause to plead ignorance of their condition, to have an excuse for returning them, the intended purchasers are informed, that they have been found much the worse for wear, and that having been patched up in a hurry, to answer a purpose during the war, they are defective in every part. However, sold they must be—and as a little encouragement to buyers, the purchaser will have the State of Rhode Island thrown into the bargain.[20]

Throughout the ratification struggle, the public prints of New England took a keen interest in the state conventions called to consider the Constitution. They wished for wisdom and understanding to be showered on the delegates:

> May the Great Idea fill the mind of every member of this honourable body, that Heaven on this auspicious occasion favours America, with an opportunity never before enjoyed by the sons of men, of establish-

ing a form of government peaceably and deliberately, which will secure to these states all those blessings which give worth to existence, or dignity to man, Peace, Liberty, and Safety![21]

The *Newport Herald* warned that "should any state reject this salutary system, unbiased posterity will consign their names to an infamous immortality." Joyfully, printers reported the ratification of the Constitution by each state. Benjamin Russell, editor of Boston's *Massachusetts Centinel*, introduced an illustration of ratification's progress that became popular throughout the United States. Following Connecticut's approval in early January 1788, Russell printed a cartoon of five pillars, one for each state that had ratified. He added another pillar each time a new state voted in favor of the Constitution. Newspapers all over the country reprinted this journalistic innovation—illustrations were rare in the public prints and a continuing one such as this was unheard of. A particularly happy day came when news of New Hampshire's approval, the ninth state to do so, arrived, for "by this fortunate Event we expect an efficient just and lasting Government will very soon take Place upon such a Foundation as no other Nation can boast of." Many prayed "may every other State erect a pillar to strengthen this noble building; and may it secure the freeborn sons of Columbia from every attempt to interrupt their peace— and last as long as the sun and moon endure." Isaiah Thomas insisted that "this great event will stand unrivalled in history—a revolution of the kind we have no record of. The present era is one of the most important of our country, and bids fair greatly to promote our political happiness."[22]

In covering the ratification conventions in each state, the New England public prints ridiculed those states that refused to approve the Constitution, namely North Carolina and Rhode Island. The printer of the *New Hampshire Spy* reported that "the rejection of the new government by the state of North Carolina is not considered as an affair of the first magnitude. Few tears have been shed in consequence of it, and but few people have troubled themselves much about it." Rhode Island, as a New England state, received more barbs for throwing "the shadow of a schism on the Bond that unites the great Federal Republic." Rhode Island's reputation had suffered during the 1780s because of its paper money laws and the state legislature's refusal to ratify the continental impost. Some felt that Rhode Island's opposition was an "infallible sign of the justice and utility" of the Constitution. Many felt no great loss that Rhode Island was not a part of the new union. The problem was a big one, because Rhode Island could not really chart an independent course of its own; the possibility of invasion and dismemberment by neighbors was a very real threat. Even prior to the Convention, an out-of-state correspondent in the *Newport Herald* warned that "matters have come to such an alarming crisis, that the confederation must take notice of you, and it seems the opinion of many here, that when the convention meets in Philadelphia, that measures will be taken to reduce you to order and good government, or strike your State out of the union, and annex you to others." Rhode Island eventually bowed to the inevitable, ratifying the Constitution in 1790.[23]

All through the debates over the Constitution, New England's newspaper printers joined together in praising the document and the possibilities it promised for the future. Benjamin Russell referred to the situation as "one of those few opportunities which occur in the revolution of human affairs, for the unfolding and displaying the amazing powers of the human mind." Following ratification and the institution of the new form of government, several editors considered the events of the last several years. The pages of the *Salem Mercury* summed up the reflections of countless persons on the dangers avoided and their prayers for the future:

> On contemplating our country, just arrived upon the solid and uniform tract of regular, equitable and effectual government, after having so narrowly escaped the dreadful calamity of anarchy and disunion; while, on one hand, civil disunion yawned for our peace and safety, and on the other, foreign subjugation watched, to devour all that was valuable in life, the present pleasing reverse of affairs must yield delight to every beholder. . . . May the national blessings resulting from this political revolution, continue, and continually expand, from generation to generation, till the last shock of Time buries the Empires of the world in one undistinguished ruin.[24]

With the inauguration of the new government in 1789, the *Herald of Freedom* painted a glorious picture of what the future held for America:

> Trade and commerce now raise their drooping heads, the Mechanick brandishes the tool of industry in triumph, and the husbandman repairs to the field with vigour; justice, from her sacred seat, views with pleasure the once benighted prospect, now dawning into brightness resplendent as nature's purest light; while publick faith and

honour gladden at the thought of our reviving credit. May America never cease to pay the tribute of gratitude she owes to the bountiful Parent of the Universe; may her citizens prove themselves worthy to enjoy the blessings heaped upon them: and may our country increase in splendour and glory 'till the "course of nature changes, and the sun shall have finished its last diurnal rotation round the skies."[25]

Most of New England's newspaper printers would have agreed. With the new form of government, America was now ready to take its rightful place in the world.

The newspaper discussions of the Constitution were the last of many political debates that had filled the pages of New England's public prints during the Revolutionary era. Throughout the entire period, New England's printers paid attention to political matters and included materials on them in their newspapers. The issues changed as the years passed, producing variations in coverage in the press. During the war itself, newspapers presented a united front, preaching solidarity in the face of the British enemy. Following the end of the war, this oneness in subject matter fractured, reflecting strains on the union itself, as the states looked inward to issues of concern within their own boundaries. Each New England state addressed certain issues on both the national and local levels, but concerns of each state differed. The newspapers reflected this, with those of each state concentrating on the issues of interest in their state. The last few years of the 1780s saw an end to this variety and a return to a unity of subject matter in the public prints. Shays's Rebellion in Massachusetts in late 1786, riveting the attention of the entire nation and becoming a subject of interest to everyone, restored concurrence to the New England press. From this point to George Washington's inauguration as president in 1789, all the newspapers discussed the same political issues: Shays's Rebellion and the fear of anarchy, the Philadelphia Convention, and the Constitutional ratification struggle. This topical solidarity continued into the 1790s as everyone took a keen interest in the new government established under the Constitution.

9

The Role of the Newspaper during the Revolutionary Era

New England's newspapers played a variety of roles from 1775 to 1789. Obviously they provided news and entertainment to their readers, and their readership increased as the number of newspapers grew. The public prints spread into the countryside, offering more people an outlet to the world at large. Accompanying newspaper growth were changes in the printing fraternity. The number of people involved increased, but more importantly, they began to exhibit a sense of professionalism, indicated by the slow development of ethical standards for printers. The public prints had a hand in the leveling influences that grew out of the Revolution. Furthermore, the newspapers set the public agenda by telling their readers what was significant and what was not. They preached the importance of a free and open press and urged their readers to take advantage of it to keep informed. Finally, the newspaper fulfilled a role in American society that was new and unprecedented by extending a public forum to the general populace for debate on issues of interest and concern. By emphasizing the importance of an informed citizenry under a republican government, the newspapers furthered the idea that public opinion reigned supreme in a free society.

The public prints of New England experienced growth during the Revolutionary years, although the total number actually decreased by one between Lexington and Yorktown. After the return of peace, however, newspapers mushroomed. By 1789, thirty-two different newspapers were published in New England. Most of this growth occurred outside of the large port cities. Many smaller ports and inland towns gained their first weekly sheets during the 1780s.

Other roles that the newspapers played were those of educator and entertainer. Printers consciously used the pages of their weekly productions to publish useful materials for their readers, besides the latest news. They contributed essays about issues pertinent to their communities. They reprinted literary works in serial form, many taking weeks to complete. Humorous stories appeared to cheer and amuse readers. Eighteenth-century publishers, realizing that most of their subscribers had access to few printed materials except the newspaper, strived to make their sheets more than just sources of news. They hoped to brighten and enrich their readers' lives as well. In doing so, they filled a need that would later be undertaken by magazines and still later by radio and television—relieving the dreariness of hard work and long days. By printing such a variety of materials, the eighteenth-century newspaper provided the means for many to discover the parts of the world that they would never see.

The newspapers also encouraged the development of local industries. The cessation of trade with Britain forced printers to turn to local sources to supply their needs. They promoted all types of local manufactures, but they placed greatest emphasis on the infant paper industry, the mainstay of their own business. Printers continually urged their readers to save rags for making paper, often paying cash or trading stationery supplies for rags brought to their offices. Saving such materials became a patriotic duty that no one could fail to do. These efforts gave paper mills the needed assistance for survival during the war. Although printers clearly pushed the development of the industry for selfish motives, their support still constituted a valuable boost for the paper industry and American manufacturing in general.

Ninety-three people printed seventy-one different New England newspapers between 1775 and 1789 (see Appendix 2 for a list of the newspapers and their printers). In 1775, twenty-four printers produced fifteen sheets. By 1789, these numbers had risen to forty-five printers and thirty-two newspapers. All of them experienced different degrees of success. Printing generally constituted a stable profession, but nothing was guaranteed. Roger Storrs died broke in 1820 with assets of only $175.90, while Barzillai Hudson left an estate worth $115,029.18 in 1823. Most newspaper printers, however, managed to provide a moderately comfortable living for themselves and their families.[1]

Although New England's Revolutionary printers constituted a basically homogeneous group in terms of their origins and the conduct of their businesses, several individuals are uniquely interesting. The most out-of-the-ordinary Revolutionary printer in New England was Isaiah Thomas, successful publisher of Worcester's *Massachusetts Spy*. Thomas was one of the most important

American printers of the eighteenth century because of his efforts to preserve historical artifacts of his time. With a keen sense for the future, he urged the saving of newspapers because of the record of events they contained. To that end, in 1812 he founded the American Antiquarian Society. Daniel Fowle, publisher of the *New Hampshire Gazette*, trained at least nine apprentices who went on to print their own newspapers. Fowle represented the mainstream of Patriot printers, concentrating his efforts on his business, particularly the publication of his newspaper. One of the Boston printers, Benjamin Edes, typified the arch-Whig publisher. Edes, a member of the Sons of Liberty, used the pages of his *Boston Gazette* to push the American cause. Following the war, a new generation of printers appeared on the scene. Benjamin Russell, publisher of Boston's *Massachusetts Centinel*, was the most successful among this group. Russell, strongly in favor of the Constitution of 1787, published a staunchly Federalist sheet after the inauguration of the new government in 1789.

The Revolutionary era witnessed the slow development of professionalism within New England's printing fraternity. Business networks, usually based on family relationships or apprenticeship ties, became common and widespread. These provided useful support for the printers during the trials and tribulations of the war and the depression that followed it. Other signs that printing was becoming more than a trade appeared: concerns over the use of unknown sources, plagiarism, and copyright. Increasingly, printers refused to publish pieces without knowing who wrote them, and they began to credit the original sources for materials clipped from other journals. Printers expressed the belief that copyright laws were needed in order to clear up confusion by clarifying the legal rights of authors and printers. New England's printers, in short, were beginning to see themselves as professionals with similar interests and goals best met through a common set of ethics and standards for their work.

Because of the possible influence of the press upon the public at large, political leaders tried not to antagonize the printers. The fact that the printer was listened to by local leaders made him a respected person in the community. Printers still worked with their hands, however, and this created confusion concerning their rightful place in society. The uncertainty over whether or not a newspaper publisher was truly a mechanic underlined the breakdown of social barriers in Revolutionary America. Furthermore, many printers aspired to a better station in life and used their newspapers to improve their overall position in their community.

Such efforts aided in the growth of a more egalitarian society throughout America.

Printers used the pages of their weekly productions to keep their customers abreast of events occurring in America and the rest of the world, although choices had to be made about what went into the paper each week. Just by what he chose to include, the printer made a statement on what issues were important. By emphasizing some topics and downplaying or ignoring others, a printer instructed his readers what they should be thinking about, a concept known to modern-day journalists as agenda-setting. Theorists of agenda-setting have disagreed concerning whether newspapers originate the public agenda, but they have agreed that the press affects what people talk about through the attention given certain events and topics. The Revolutionary press fits this model. Through the emphasis placed on various issues, the New England press played an important role in shaping the agenda of public discussion. As a result, newspaper publishers impacted the people's view of the conflict with Great Britain and the development of the United States following the acquisition of independence.

After 1776, the New England states—except for Rhode Island—suffered little directly from the actions of the British army and navy. Throughout the conflict, however, New England's public prints gave ample coverage to military events, and more importantly, to reasons why Americans would ultimately prevail in such a just war.

The early years of peace produced a plethora of issues in the press, many local in nature. At the same time, there was always an undercurrent of concern over the viability of the Articles of Confederation as a national government. These apprehensions reached a crescendo in 1787 and 1788 when the movement for a new national instrument reached fruition. In retrospect, it seems surprising that Americans would accept another charter so quietly after only seven years under the old system. The newspapers, however, had been discussing such a possibility for most of that time so many people had grown somewhat accustomed to the idea. Although some disagreed with the results of the Constitutional Convention, few denied that the meeting was necessary. The public agenda concerning a need to alter the American political union had been set by the press during the mid–1780s.

Newspapers of the Revolutionary era also contributed to the development of a theory of a free press. A dynamic tension existed between the press and government during the eighteenth century—they needed each other. Printers published records, documents, and announcements for state and national officials. But if government provided employment for printers, government also sometimes tried to control the presses. In response, printers declared that their sheets should be free from all outside interference, particularly from the civil authority. They insisted that a truly free press was "essential to the support of a republican government," and without it, any government would eventually become a tyranny. The Massachusetts stamp act of 1785 was cited as proof that "Power may rise into Tyranny, whether it be intrusted in the hands of Republican or Monarchical governments." According to the printers, the tax was clearly meant "to shackle the means of political knowledge and necessary learning." The only solution to such threats was to protect the liberty of the press, which was "so necessary to prevent or remove public evils, that no people can long continue free or happy without it." Furthermore, "the liberty of the Press has ever been held as one of the most sacred rights of a free people, and when we are abridged of that invaluable privilege, farewell to Peace, Liberty, and Safety, farewell to Learning, Knowledge, and Truth, farewell to all that is dear to us; we must ever after grope in darkness, thick darkness, that may even be felt: may Heaven forbid such a deprivation." Statements such as these provided the basis for the fight against later government encroachments, especially the Alien and Sedition Acts of 1798. If a libertarian theory of a free press would not become commonplace until the nineteenth century, the groundwork was assuredly laid by Revolutionary era printers.[2]

By eighteenth-century standards, the Revolutionary press was free. Privately owned and operated, New England's weekly sheets were clearly not controlled by a political party. During the 1790s, all this changed. With the rise of a national debate between Federalists and Republicans, newspaper printers took sides and no longer pretended to be nonpartisan. Some papers even came into existence for the sole purpose of representing a political party's interests. Although the public prints of the Revolutionary era did take stands on various issues, none undertook efforts comparable to that of the partisan sheets of the 1790s. In fact, printers declared that their papers were "open to all parties, and influenced by none" and that the press was open to anyone who wished to submit a piece for publication, regardless of political persuasion. John Carter insisted that "whatever may have been my private sentiments respecting public measures, I have never suffered them to interfere with what I conceive to be the indispensible duty of an impartial Printer"—to publish submitted essays dealing with all aspects of an issue. Although not always followed in practice, these statements helped develop the idea that newspapers were for everyone and not just those who supported a certain viewpoint.[3]

The public view of newspapers changed during the Revolutionary era. No longer were they just purveyors of news and information to the "better sort"; now they belonged to everyone. Much of this change resulted from the part played by the press in bringing about a successful separation from Great Britain. Many people, both contemporaries and historians, have praised the public prints for their efforts on behalf of American independence. One essayist exclaimed, "what inflamed with a holy enthusiasm of liberty such numbers of intrepid patriots as dared death in defence of America, during the late sanguinary contest? In a word, to what does this country owe the establishment of her independence? Surely to the illumination of the understanding" that comes from reading newspapers. Truly, the papers were considered to be influential.

Suggestions and accusations abounded on both sides concerning the possible propaganda uses of the press during the war. Anti-Federalist concerns over their inability to get their views into the public prints during the late 1780s underscore the value of the press in the eyes of Revolutionary leaders. The Anti-Federalists clearly felt they could not win if they could not get their ideas published in the weekly sheets. The newspapers were the key to success because they provided the best way to inform and influence the general populace.[4]

Increasingly, however, newspapers came to be seen as a means for the people to keep tabs on their government and its officials. The 1780s witnessed the occasional publication of legislative debates in the newspapers. Peter Edes, editor of the *Newport Herald*, published a series of reports on the actions of the Rhode Island General Assembly from the spring of 1787 to January 1790. This type of detailed coverage, however, was unusual. Most newspaper coverage of state legislatures consisted of the publication of speeches from time to time. Detailed reports of state and federal legislative debates and actions became common after the adoption of the Constitution. Following the inauguration of the new federal legislature in March 1789, the majority of New England's public prints carried Congressional debates regularly.[5]

The debate over the Constitution in 1787–1788 transformed the public prints into the dominant public forum, outdistancing pamphlets and broadsides. From this point until at least the early twentieth century, newspapers constituted the major means of disseminating information to the people. Thomas Jefferson said that, given the choice between a government or newspapers, he would choose the latter because they provided the only means for the public to keep truly informed. In urging printers to rouse the people to solve the country's problems, "Acirema" asserted that "without political knowledge the people cannot secure their liberties, and this necessary information they receive by the medium of News-Papers."[6]

America had always been a more egalitarian society than Europe. In reality, there was only one class, what contemporary political thinkers called the democratical element. No royalty or nobility existed. The press has been referred to as the "fourth estate," but in eighteenth-century America, it actually constituted a "second estate." The press complimented democracy by providing the major source of political information. American newspapers therefore constituted a unique institution, unlike any other in the Western world. More and more, newspapers reached out to inform an ever-growing readership about its country and the world it lived in.[7]

The widening of the gazettes, chronicles, and journals enabled the press to perform its vital role. The press became increasingly democratized during the Revolutionary era; it reflected developments in the political arena as more and more people not only voted, but also became more directly involved in government, instructing their representatives and seeking offices previously held by their social betters. The public prints likewise contributed to political change. By proclaiming that newspapers were essential for people to keep informed about the doings of their rulers, they inferred that all had a right to participate in government to protect their liberties. Historian Gordon Wood has asserted that the Revolutionary era produced "a democratization of the mind" whereby public opinion replaced the social and intellectual elite as the guiding force in political circles.[8] No institution compared to the American newspaper in the Europe of the *ancien régime*. Even in Britain, hailed by continental thinkers such as Montesquieu as the most enlightened of nations, the press amounted to little more than scandal sheets or government organs. As both reflectors and formers of public opinion, American newspapers— "this popular engine"[9]—played an essential role in the democratic evolution of the United States.

Appendix 1: Content Survey

The following survey was used to acquire the data for the figures in tables 4–1 and 5–2. It was developed with the aid of Dr. John Adams and Dr. Donald Shaw, professors in the University of North Carolina School of Journalism. The survey was designed to provide some indication as to the amount of space allotted to various types of items published in the newspapers of the period under consideration. The sample consisted of the issues of the first week of every month, whether weekly, biweekly, or tri-weekly. This produced a yearly sample of twelve issues for week-lies, twenty-four for biweeklies, and thirty-six for triweeklies. The survey measured the percentage amount of column space allotted to various types of items. The results combined findings from weekly and nonweekly publications, but this is not a problem for two reasons. First, although this was the era when nonweekly sheets began to emerge, they remained highly similar in content to the weeklies. Several studies have shown that the content differences in dailies and nondailies, which are so striking to us today, did not begin to appear until the Civil War era.[1] Second, the results emphasize the percentages of overall available space used for a particular type of item rather than the actual amount of space used. Although a rough measure in some respects, it provides some indication as to what types of items were most important, or, perhaps a better way to put it might be what types of items were more frequently published in the newspapers of the period.

Survey Problem:

What types of materials did the American newspapers provide to their readers between the beginning of the American Revolution in 1775 and the inauguration of the Constitutional government in 1789? Specifically, at any one particular time, what percentage amount of space was allotted in newspapers to the various types of items that were carried between the Battle of Lexington and George Washington's inauguration? Also, what changes, if any, occurred in the average percentage amount of space allotted to each type of item included?

Appendix 2: New England Newspapers, 1775–1789

Connecticut

Fairfield
  Fairfield Gazette, 1786–1789
    Printers: Stephen Miller, 7/1786–8/1787
    Francis Forque, 7/1786–9/1789
    Peter Bulkeley, 2/1787–9/1789

Hartford
  American Mercury, 1784–1789 +
    Printers: Joel Barlow, 7/1784–11/1785
    Elisha Babcock, 7/1784–1789 +
  Connecticut Courant, 1764–1789 +
    Printers: Ebenezer Watson, 4/1768–9/1777
    George Goodwin, 1/1778–1789 +
    Hannah Watson, 1/1778–2/1779
    Barzillai Hudson, 3/1779–1789 +
  Freeman's Chronicle, 1783–1784
    Printers: Bavil Webster, 9/1783–6/1784
    Zephaniah Webster, 6/1784–7/1784

Litchfield
  Litchfield Monitor, 1784–1789 +
    Printers: Thomas Collier, 12/1784–1789 +
    William Copp, 12/1784–12/1785
    Robert Adam, 9/1788–6/1789

Middletown
  Middlesex Gazette, 1785–1789 +
    Printers: Moses H. Woodward, 11/1785–1789 +
    Thomas Green, 11/1785–6/1789

New Haven
    Connecticut Journal, 1767–1789 +
        Printers: Thomas Green, 10/1767–1789 +
                Samuel Green, 10/1767–1789 +
    New Haven Chronicle, 1786–1787
        Printer: Daniel Bowen, 4/1786–4/1787
    New Haven Gazette, 1784–1786
        Printers: Josiah Meigs, 5/1784–2/1786
                Daniel Bowen, 5/1784–2/1786
                Eleutheros Dana, 5/1784–2/1786
    New Haven Gazette, and Connecticut Magazine, 1786–1789
        Printers: Josiah Meigs, 2/1786–1789
                Eleutheros Dana, 2/1786–8/1787

New London
    Connecticut Gazette, 1763–1789 +
        Printers: Timothy Green, 11/1763–1789 +
                Samuel Green, 3/1789–1789 +

Norwich
    Norwich Packet, 1773–1789 +
        Printers: Alexander Robertson, 10/1773–5/1776
                James Robertson, 10/1773–5/1776
                John Trumbull, 10/1773–1789 +

Maine

Falmouth (renamed Portland in 1786)
    Falmouth Gazette (later *Cumberland Gazette*), 1785–1789 +
        Printers: Benjamin Titcomb, 1/1785–2/1786
                Thomas B. Wait, 1/1785–1789 +

Massachusetts

Boston
    American Journal, 1785
        Printer: William Barrett, 2/1785–7/1785
    Boston Gazette, 1719–1789 +
        Printers: John Gill, 4/1755–4/1776
                Benjamin Edes, Sr., 4/1755–1789 +

Peter Edes, 4/1779–11/1784
Benjamin Edes, Jr., 4/1779–1789+
Boston News-Letter, 1704–1776
Printers: Margaret Draper, 6/1774–2/1776
John Howe, 9/1775–2/1776
Boston Post Boy, 1734–1775
Printers: Nathaniel Mills, 4/1773–4/1775
John Hicks, 4/1773–4/1775
Boston Evening Post, 1735–1775
Printers: Thomas Fleet, Jr., 7/1758–4/1775
John Fleet, 7/1758–4/1775
Boston Evening Post (later *American Herald*), 1781–1788
Printers: Edward E. Powars, 10/1781–6/1788
Nathaniel Willis, 4/1784–7/1786
Continental Journal, 1776–1787
Printers: John Gill, 5/1776–4/1785
James D. Griffith, 4/1785–6/1787
Courier de Boston, 1789 (published for Joseph Nancrede)
Printer: Samuel Hall, 4/1789–10/1789
Evening Post (later *Morning Chronicle*), 1778–1780
Printers: James White, 10/1778–5/1780
Thomas Adams, 10/1778–5/1780
Exchange Advertiser, 1784–1787
Printer: Peter Edes, 12/1784–4/1787
Herald of Freedom, 1788–1789+
Printers: Edmund Freeman, 9/1788–1789+
Loring Andrews, 9/1788–9/1789
Independent Chronicle (originally *New England Chronicle*), 1776–1789+
Printers: Samuel Hall, 4/1776–6/1776
Edward E. Powars, 6/1776–2/1779
Nathaniel Willis, 6/1776–12/1783
Thomas Adams, 1/1784–1789+
John Nourse, 1/1784–1789+
Independent Ledger, 1778–1786
Printers: Edward Draper, 6/1778–11/1783
John W. Folsom, 6/1778–10/1786
Massachusetts Centinel, 1784–1789+
Printers: William Warden, 3/1784–3/1786
Benjamin Russell, 3/1784–1789+
Massachusetts Gazette, 1785–1788
Printers: Samuel Hall, 11/1785–9/1787
John W. Allen, 6/1787–11/1788

Massachusetts Spy, 1770–1775
    Printer: Isaiah Thomas, 7/1770–4/1775

Cambridge
  New England Chronicle, 1775–1776
    Printers: Samuel Hall, 5/1775–4/1776
                    Ebenezer Hall, 5/1775–2/1776

Charlestown
  American Recorder, 1785–1787
    Printers: John W. Allen, 12/1785–5/1787
                    Thomas C. Cushing, 12/1785–9/1786

Newburyport
  Essex Journal, 1773–1777
    Printers: Henry-Walter Tinges, 12/1773–1/1776
                    Ezra Lunt, 8/1774–7/1775
                    John Mycall, 7/1775–2/1777
  Essex Journal, 1784–1789 +
    Printers: John Mycall, 9/1784–7/1787, 7/1789–1789 +
                    William Hoyt, 7/1787–7/1789

Northampton
  Hampshire Gazette, 1786–1789 +
    Printer: William Butler, 9/1786–1789 +

Pittsfield
  American Centinel, 1787–?
    Printers: Elijah Russell, 9/1787–?
                    Roger Storrs, 9/1787–?
  Berkshire Chronicle, 1788–1789 +
    Printer: Roger Storrs, 5/1788–1789 +

Plymouth
  Plymouth Journal, 1785–1786
    Printer: Nathaniel Coverly, 3/1785–6/1786

Salem
  American Gazette, 1776
    Printers: John Rogers, 6/1776–7/1776
                    Ezekiel Russell, 6/1776–7/1776
  Essex Gazette, 1768–1775
    Printers: Samuel Hall, 8/1768–5/1775

154 APPENDIX 2

Ebenezer Hall, 1/1772–5/1775
Salem Chronicle, 1786
  Printer: George Roulstone, 3/1786–8/1786
Salem Gazette, 1774–1775
  Printer: Ezekiel Russell, 7/1774–4/1775
Salem Gazette, 1781
  Printer: Mary Crouch, 1/1781–9/1781
Salem Gazette, 1781–1785
  Printer: Samuel Hall, 10/1781–11/1785
Salem Mercury, 1786–1789+
  Printers: John Dabney, 10/1786–11/1789
       Thomas C. Cushing, 10/1786–1789+

Springfield
  Hampshire Chronicle, 1787–1789+
    Printers: John Russell, 3/1787–10/1787
         Zephaniah Webster, 5/1787–12/1787
         Isaiah Thomas, 1/1788–9/1788
         Ezra W. Weld, 1/1788–1789+
  Massachusetts Gazette (later *Hampshire Herald*), 1782–1786
    Printers: Elisha Babcock, 5/1782–5/1784
         Anthony Haswell, 5/1782–5/1783
         ? Brooks, 5/1784–6/1785
         John Russell, 5/1784–9/1786
         Gad Stebbins, 9/1785–9/1786

Stockbridge
  Western Star, 1789–1789+
    Printer: Loring Andrews, 12/1789–1789+

Worcester
  American Herald, 1788–1789
    Printer: Edward E. Powars, 8/1788–10/1789
  Massachusetts Herald, 1783
    Printer: Isaiah Thomas, 9/1783
  Massachusetts Spy, 1775–1789+
    Printers: Isaiah Thomas, 5/1775–5/1776, 6/1778–1789+
         William Stearns, 5/1776–8/1777
         Daniel Bigelow, 5/1776–8/1777
         Anthony Haswell, 8/1777–6/1778

New Hampshire

Hanover (formerly Dresden, Vermont)
  Dresden Mercury, 1779
    Printers: Judah P. Spooner, 5/1779–9/1779
              Alden Spooner, 5/1779–9/1779

Exeter
  Exeter Chronicle, 1784
    Printers: John Melcher, 6/1784–12/1784
              George J. Osborne, Jr., 6/1784–12/1784
  Exeter Journal, 1778–1779
    Printer: Zechariah Fowle, 2/1778–2/1779
  Freeman's Oracle, 1786–1789
    Printers: John Lamson, 7/1786–12/1789
              Henry Ranlet, 7/1786–8/1789
  New Hampshire Gazette, 1776–1777
    Printer: Robert Luist Fowle, 5/1776–7/1777
  New Hampshire Gazetteer, 1789–1789+
    Printer: Henry Ranlet, 8/1789–1789+

Keene
  New Hampshire Recorder, 1787–1789+
    Printer: James D. Griffith, 8/1787–1789+

Portsmouth
  Freeman's Journal, 1776–1778
    Printers: Benjamin Dearborn, 5/1776–12/1776
              Daniel Fowle, 12/1776–6/1778
  New Hampshire Gazette, 1756–1776, 1779–1789+
    Printers: Daniel Fowle, 10/1756–1/1776, 2/1779–6/1787
              Robert Gerrish, 1/1781–12/1784
              John Melcher, 12/1784–1789+
              George J. Osborne, Jr., 12/1784–1/1786
  New Hampshire Mercury, 1784–1788
    Printer: Robert Gerrish, 12/1784–3/1788
  New Hampshire Spy, 1786–1789+
    Printer: George J. Osborne, Jr., 10/1786–1789+

Rhode Island

Newport
  Gazette Française, 1780–1781
    Printer: John Jastram, 11/1780–1/1781
  Newport Gazette, 1777–1779
    Printer: John Howe, 1/1777–10/1779
  Newport Herald, 1787–1789 +
    Printer: Peter Edes, 1/1787–1789 +
  Newport Mercury, 1758–1789 +
    Printers: Solomon Southwick, 3/1768–12/1776, 5/1785–
              12/1788
              Henry Barber, 1/1780–12/1786, 1/1788–1789 +

Providence
  American Journal, 1779–1781
    Printers: Solomon Southwick, 3/1779–11/1779
              Bennett Wheeler, 3/1779–8/1781
  Providence Gazette, 1762–1789 +
    Printer: John Carter, 11/1768–1789 +
  United States Chronicle, 1784–1789 +
    Printer: Bennett Wheeler, 1/1784–1789 +

Vermont

Bennington
  Vermont Gazette, 1783–1789 +
    Printers: Anthony Haswell, 6/1783–1789 +
              David Russell, 6/1783–1789 +

Westminster
  Vermont Gazette, 1780–1781
    Printers: Judah P. Spooner, 12/1780–7/1781
              Timothy Green IV, 12/1780–7/1781

Windsor
  Vermont Journal, 1783–1789 +
    Printers: George Hough, 8/1783–12/1788
              Alden Spooner, 8/1783–1789 +

Notes

Chapter 1. Growth and Development of New England Newspapers prior to 1775

1. Connecticut's first printer, Thomas Short, established his business in 1709. James Franklin moved to Rhode Island in 1727, and Daniel Fowle became New Hampshire's first printer in 1756. Vermont acquired printers Judah Paddock Spooner and Alden Spooner in 1778. Maine got its first printing office under Thomas Baker Wait and Benjamin Titcomb in 1785. Lawrence C. Wroth, *The Colonial Printer* (Portland, Me.: The Southworth-Anthoensen Press, 1938), 16–29; Isaiah Thomas, *The History of Printing in America* (Worcester, Mass.: Isaiah Thomas, Jr., 1810; reprint ed. edited by Marcus A. McCorison, Barre, Mass.: Imprint Society, 1970), 13–14, 234–42, 326–27.

2. James Parker published the *Connecticut Gazette* in New Haven beginning in 1755. The *Rhode Island Gazette*, published by James Franklin, first appeared in Newport in 1732. Daniel Fowle began publication of the *New Hampshire Gazette* in Portsmouth in 1756. The *Vermont Gazette*, published by Timothy Green IV and Judah Paddock Spooner, first appeared in Westminster in 1780. Wait and Titcomb began the *Falmouth Gazette* in 1785. Douglas C. McMurtrie, *The Beginnings of the American Newspaper* (Chicago: The Black Cat Press, 1935), 8–12; Wroth, *Colonial Printer*, 18–19; Jarvis Means Morse, *Connecticut Newspapers in the Eighteenth Century* (New Haven, Conn.: Published for the Tercentenary Commission of the State of Connecticut by the Yale University Press, 1935), 1–12; Frank W. Miller, "The *New Hampshire Gazette*," *New England Historical and Genealogical Register* 26 (1872): 132–33; J. Kevin Graffagnino, " 'We Have Long Been Wishing for a Good Printer in This Vicinity': The State of Vermont, the First East Union, and the Dresden Press, 1778–1779." *Vermont History* 47 (1979): 21–36; John Spargo, "Early Vermont Printers and Printing," *Proceedings of the Vermont Historical Society* 10 (1942): 214–21; Frederick G. Fassett, Jr., "Maine's First Newspaper," in *A History of Maine: A Collection of Readings on the History of Maine, 1600–1976,* ed. by Ronald F. Banks, 4th ed. (Dubuque, Ia.: Kendall/Hunt Publishing Company, 1976 [1969]), 154–55; Philip M. Marsh, "Maine's First Newspaper Editor: Thomas Wait," *New England Quarterly* 28 (1955): 519–21.

3. Wroth, *Colonial Printer*, 233–34; Kenneth A. Lockridge, *Literacy in Colonial New England: An Enquiry into the Social Context of Literacy in the Early Modern West* (New York: W. W. Norton & Company, Inc., 1974), 13–43.

4. Charles Wheeler Wetherell, "Brokers of the Word: An Essay in the Social History of the Early American Press, 1639–1783" (Ph.D. dissertation, University of New Hampshire, 1980), 33, 48; U.S. Bureau of the Census, *Historical Statistics of the United States, Colonial Times to 1970,* 2 vol. (Washington, D.C.: United States Department of Commerce, Bureau of the Census, 1975), 2:1168; Evarts B. Greene and Virginia D. Harrington, *American Population Before the Federal Census of 1790*

158 NOTES

(New York: Columbia University Press, 1932), 19, 57; Jere Daniell, *Colonial New Hampshire: A History* (Millwood, N.Y.: KTO Press, 1981), 184.

5. The growth of newspapers followed this trend throughout the mainland colonies. Outside of New England, the number of papers published grew from sixteen in 1765 to twenty at the end of 1774. The growth spurt came at the end of the Revolution. (See chapter 2 for a discussion of postrevolutionary growth.)

Chapter 2. Printing as a Business: One Problem after Another

1. Lawrence C. Wroth, *The Colonial Printer* (Portland, Me.: The Southworth-Anthoensen Press, 1938), 79–80; Sidney Kobre, *Development of American Journalism* (Dubuque, Ia.: William C. Brown Company, Publishers, 1969), 49–50; Charles L. Cutler, *Connecticut's Revolutionary Press* (Chester, Conn.: Pequot Press, 1975), 13.

2. Wroth, *Colonial Printer*, 61–62, 65–67; Kobre, *American Journalism*, 50, 61; Alan Kulikoff, "The Progress of Inequality in Revolutionary Boston," *William and Mary Quarterly* 28 (1971): 385–87.

3. Rollo G. Silver, "Aprons Instead of Uniforms: The Practice of Printing, 1776–1787," *Proceedings of the American Antiquarian Society* 87 (1977): 172–73; Wroth, *Colonial Printer*, 41; Rollo G. Silver, *The American Printer, 1787–1825* (Charlottesville: University Press of Virginia, 1967), 38–40; Kobre, *American Journalism*, 50–51; Isaiah Thomas, *The History of Printing in America* (Worcester, Mass.: Isaiah Thomas, Jr., 1810; reprint ed. edited by Marcus A. McCorison, Barre, Mass.: Imprint Society, 1970), 35–36, 40–41n.

4. Silver, "Aprons Instead of Uniforms," 173; *New Hampshire Gazette*, 13 April 1786; Silver, *American Printer*, 40–41; Thomas, *History of Printing*, 35–36, 40–41n; Kobre, *American Journalism*, 61; Wroth, *Colonial Printer*, 84; Thompson R. Harlow, "Connecticut's Contribution to Printing," An Article Prepared for the 500th Anniversary of Printing, November 1940, ms., Connecticut Historical Society, Hartford, Conn., 1.

5. Rollo G. Silver, *Typefounding in America, 1787–1825* (Charlottesville: University Press of Virginia, 1965), 54, 91–92, 109–11; Wroth, *Colonial Printer*, 90–93, 171–72; Bill to Isaiah Thomas from Joseph Fry & Sons, 16 August 1786, Isaiah Thomas Papers, American Antiquarian Society, Worcester, Mass.

6. Silver, *Typefounding*, 54, 91–92, 109–11; Wroth, *Colonial Printer*, 90–93, 171–72; Isaiah Thomas and Zechariah Fowle, 23 October 1770, Isaiah Thomas Papers, American Antiquarian Society, Worcester, Mass.; Isaiah Thomas to George Goodwin, 19 October 1780, Isaiah Thomas to Hudson & Goodwin, 8 December 1785, copies in Isaiah Thomas Papers, American Antiquarian Society, Worcester, Mass., originals at the New York Historical Society, New York, N.Y.; *Massachusetts Spy*, 12 February 1778; *United States Chronicle*, 26 November 1783; *American Herald*, 13 November 1786.

7. Several type foundries began operation in other parts of the country between Buell's two attempts—(1) 1772—Christopher Sower, Jr. established a foundry in Germantown, Pennsylvania, for manufacturing German types; (2) 1775—Jacob Bay opened a second foundry in Germantown, but never developed a large clientele; (3) 1775—with the help of his famous grandfather, Benjamin Franklin Bache opened a typemaking business, but soon turned to printing as the preferable career.

8. Silver, *Typefounding*, 3–8, 18–20; Wroth, *Colonial Printer*, 40–56; Thomas, *History of Printing*, 28–33; Harlow, "Connecticut's Contributions," 3–4; *Newport Mercury*, 6 August 1787.

9. Silver, "Aprons Instead of Uniforms," 174; Wroth, *Colonial Printer*, 115, 120–21; Kobre, *American Journalism*, 51.

10. Silver, "Aprons Instead of Uniforms," 174; Wroth, *Colonial Printer*, 122–24, 152–53, 169–71; Lyman Horace Weeks, *A History of Paper-Manufacturing in the United States, 1690–1916* (New York: The Lockwood Trade Journal Company, 1916), 9, 15.

11. The first paper mills in America were built in Germantown, Pennsylvania in 1690 and 1710.

12. Wroth, *Colonial Printer*, 151; Thomas, *History of Printing*, 21–28, 38–39n; Weeks, *Paper-Manufacturing*, 3–4, 6–13; Frank Luther Mott, *American Journalism: A History of Newspapers in the United States Through 250 Years, 1690 to 1940* (New York: The Macmillan Company, 1962 [1941]), 97–98; William Whiting, "Paper Making in New England," in William T. Davis, ed., *The New England States*, 3 vols. (Boston: D. H. Hurd, & Company, 1897), 1:307–8.

13. Wroth, *Colonial Printer*, 140; Arthur M. Schlesinger, *Prelude to Independence: The Newspaper War on Britain, 1764–1776* (New York: Alfred A. Knopf, 1958), 305–8; John Bard McNulty, *Older than the Nation: The Story of the Hartford Courant* (Stonington, Conn.: The Pequot Press, Inc., 1964), 10; Marcus A. McCorison, "Vermont Papermaking, 1784–1820," *Vermont History* 31 (1963): 209–45; *Connecticut Courant*, 14 November 1776; *Connecticut Journal*, 30 January 1777; *Massachusetts Spy*, 9 May 1777, 21 May 1778; *Independent Ledger*, 2 October 1780; *American Journal*, 30 December 1780.

14. Weeks, *Paper-Manufacturing*, 18–21, 35–37; Silver, "Aprons Instead of Uniforms," 174–75; Kobre, *American Journalism*, 60; Mott, *American Journalism*, 98; Don Higginbotham, *The War of American Independence: Military Attitudes, Policies, and Practice, 1763–1789* (New York: Macmillan Publishing Company, Inc., 1971), 259; Philip Gardiner Nordell, "Vermont's Early Lotteries," *Vermont History* 35 (1967): 46; No Author Given, "Early Paper Mills in Massachusetts and New England," *Massachusetts Magazine* 10 (1917): 180–81; Charles J. Hoadley and Leonard W. Labaree, eds., *The Public Records of the State of Connecticut*, 6 vols. (Hartford: State Printer, 1894–1945), 1:503; Isaac Hammond, ed., *Documents Relating to Towns in New Hampshire*, vol. 11 of Nathaniel Bouton *et al.*, eds., *State Papers of New Hampshire*, 40 vols. (Nashua and elsewhere: State Printer, 1870–1895), 11:658; *Essex Journal*, 1 March 1776; *Connecticut Courant*, 10 February 1778; *Vermont Gazette*, 30 October 1783, 11 October 1784; Josiah Meigs to Jeremiah Wadsworth, 7 August 1787, Jeremiah Wadsworth Papers, Connecticut Historical Society, Hartford, Conn.

15. Wroth, *Colonial Printer*, 143–44; Weeks, *Paper-Manufacturing*, 72; J. Eugene Smith, *One Hundred Years of Hartford's Courant: From Colonial Times Through the Civil War* (New Haven, Conn.: Yale University Press, 1949), 11; *Connecticut Courant*, 30 October 1781; *Vermont Gazette*, 10 July and 9 October 1783, 23 May 1785, 26 February 1787; *Newport Mercury*, 12 June 1775, 5 January and 5 May 1780, 27 January, 18 August, and 4 November 1781, 5 January, 14 and 21 June, and 17 August 1782, 9 October 1784, 9 April 1785; *Boston Gazette*, 19 February and 30 September 1776, 24 December 1781, 18 February, 15 April, 22 July, and 12 August 1782; *New Hampshire Gazette*, 22 June 1776; *Connecticut Journal*, 12 June 1776, 12 January 1780; *Norwich Packet*, 26 May 1777; *Massachusetts Spy*, 30 October 1777; *Independent Chronicle*, 14 August and 25 December 1777, 20 August 1778, 12

August 1779, 11 May 1780; *Providence Gazette*, 2 May 1778; *Independent Ledger*, 15 June 1778, 5 June 1780, 1 January 1781; *Connecticut Gazette*, 22 September 1780; *American Journal*, 30 March 1780; *Boston Evening Post*, 15 June 1782, 18 September 1788; *Falmouth Gazette*, 22 January 1785; *New Haven Gazette*, 10 March 1785; *American Mercury*, 18 September 1786; *New Haven Chronicle*, 23 May 1786; *Hampshire Gazette*, 30 September 1786, 25 July 1787, 25 February 1789; *New Hampshire Spy*, 10 November 1786; *Salem Mercury*, 4 November 1787; Diaries of Isaiah Thomas, 1781–1789, Isaiah Thomas Papers, American Antiquarian Society, Worcester, Mass.

16. *Boston Evening Post*, 6 March 1775; *Connecticut Courant*, 16 June 1778; *Connecticut Journal*, 30 January 1777; *New Hampshire Gazette*, 21 January 1777, 25 March 1780; *Vermont Gazette*, 29 November 1784; *Salem Mercury*, 20 May 1788; *Newport Herald*, 29 May 1788.

17. Mary Beth Norton, *Liberty's Daughters: The Revolutionary Experience of American Women, 1750–1800* (Boston: Little, Brown and Company, 1980), 163–70; Linda K. Kerber, *Women of the Republic: Intellect and Ideology in Revolutionary America* (Chapel Hill: Published for the Institute of Early American History and Culture, Williamsburg, Virginia, by the University of North Carolina Press, 1980), 41–45; *Essex Journal*, 22 July 1775; *Connecticut Courant*, 22 September 1777; *Norwich Packet*, 30 March 1778.

18. *Massachusetts Spy*, 26 November 1778.

19. *Vermont Gazette*, 30 October 1783, 13 September 1784; *Massachusetts Gazette*, 21 October 1788; *American Mercury*, 10 November 1788; *Newport Herald*, 11 December 1788; *Connecticut Courant*, 27 April 1789.

20. For examples, see *Connecticut Courant*, 21 August 1775; *Connecticut Gazette*, 12 January 1776; *Norwich Packet*, 10 November to 22 December 1777; *Providence Gazette*, 15 August 1778; *New Hampshire Gazette*, 19 February to 15 April 1780; *Connecticut Journal*, 31 October to 5 December 1782; *Vermont Gazette*, 6 November 1783; *Vermont Journal*, 21 December 1784; *New Haven Gazette*, 31 March 1785; *New Hampshire Mercury*, 18 October 1786; *New Hampshire Spy*, 28 December 1787; *Middlesex Gazette*, 28 January 1788; *American Herald*, 26 February 1789.

21. Smith, *Hartford's Courant*, 14; McNulty, *The Hartford Courant*, 14; *Connecticut Courant*, 21 August and 11 September 1775, 3 February 1778; *New Hampshire Gazette*, 3 October 1775; *Middlesex Gazette*, 27 December 1788.

22. Mott, *American Journalism*, 50–51, 99, 155; Wroth, *Colonial Printer*, 172–73; John Bixler Hench, "The Newspaper in a Republic: Boston's *Centinel* and *Chronicle*, 1784–1801" (Ph.D. dissertation, Clark University, 1979), 125–26; *Newport Mercury*, 11 November 1776, 2 February 1782, 21 November 1785; *New Hampshire Mercury*, 24 February 1785, 14 December 1786; *Continental Journal*, 6 January 1780, 16 January 1783; *Independent Ledger*, 22 February 1779, 17 January, 20 March, and 2 October 1780; *Connecticut Gazette*, 19 January 1780; *Boston Gazette*, 10, 17, and 24 January and 14 February 1780; *Independent Chronicle*, 13 January 1780; *Salem Gazette*, 1 January 1784; *Vermont Gazette*, 23 October 1783, February 1784, and 19 and 26 March 1787; *Falmouth Gazette*, 2 and 23 April 1785; *Essex Journal*, February to April 1785, December 1786.

23. *Boston News-Letter*, 19 May and 26 October 1775; *Independent Ledger*, 27 July 1778; *Newport Herald*, 1 March 1787; John Carter to Joseph Trumbull, 6 March 1776, Joseph Trumbull Papers, Connecticut Historical Society, Hartford, Conn.; Thomas B. Wait to George Thacher, 15 April 1789, Thomas B. Wait Letters, Massachusetts Historical Society, Boston, Mass.

24. *Independent Ledger*, 4 July 1785; *Falmouth Gazette*, 21 January 1786.

25. *Falmouth Gazette*, 23 February 1786; *United States Chronicle*, 29 May 1788.

26. Thomas, *History of Printing*, 319; Clarence S. Brigham, ed., *History and Bibliography of American Newspapers, 1690–1820*, 2 vols. (Worcester, Mass.: American Antiquarian Society, 1947), 2:998; *Boston Evening Post*, 24 April 1775; *New Hampshire Gazette*, 2 November 1775; *Newport Mercury*, 6 November 1775; *Connecticut Gazette*, 6 December 1776, 11 September 1778; *Connecticut Journal*, 7 July 1779; William Cheever, "A Journal—Commencing May 19, 1775," 4 August and 2 October 1775 entries, Massachusetts Historical Society, Boston, Mass.; Peter Edes, "Diary, June 19 to October 3, 1775," Massachusetts Historical Society, Boston, Mass.

27. Albert C. Bates, "Thomas Green," *Papers of the New Haven Colony Historical Society* 8 (1914): 306–7; Gilbert L. Streeter, *An Account of the Newspapers and Other Periodicals Published in Salem, from 1768 to 1856* (Salem, Mass.: William Ives and George W. Pease, Printers, 1856), 9–10.

28. Charles L. Nichols, "Fowle, Daniel," *Dictionary of American Biography*, 10 vols. (New York: Charles Scribner's Sons, 1927–1936), 3 (pt. 2):560–61; Benjamin Franklin, V, ed., *Boston Printers, Publishers, and Booksellers: 1640–1800* (Boston: G. K. Hall & Company, 1980), 181–86; Robert Wilson Kidder, "The Contribution of Daniel Fowle to New Hampshire Printing, 1756–1787" (Ph.D. dissertation, University of Illinois, 1960), 132–34; Frank W. Miller, "The *New Hampshire Gazette*," *New England Historical and Genealogical Register* 26 (1872): 135.

29. Edward France Edgett, "Edes, Benjamin," *Dictionary of American Biography*, 10 vols. (New York: Charles Scribner's Sons, 1927–1936), 3(pt. 2):17–18; Franklin, *Boston Printers*, 117–35; Rollo G. Silver, "Benjamin Edes, Trumpeter of Sedition," *Papers of the Bibliographical Society of America* 47 (1953): 248–68; Thomas, *History of Printing*, 134–38; Joseph T. Buckingham, *Specimens of Newspaper Literature*, 2 vols. (Boston: Charles C. Little and James Brown, 1850), 1:197.

30. Wroth, *Colonial Printer*, 158–61; Silver, *American Printer*, 111; Harlow, "Connecticut's Contribution," 4; *Connecticut Journal*, 1 January 1776, 23 December 1778; *New England Chronicle*, 22 February 1776; *Independent Chronicle*, 20 June 1776; *Connecticut Gazette*, 12 July 1776; *Boston Evening Post*, 3 November 1781, 7 March 1785, 24 September 1787; *Boston Gazette*, 27 December 1782; *Vermont Gazette*, 7 and 14 August 1783, 4 July 1785, 11 September 1786, 14 May and 8 October 1787; *New Haven Gazette*, 26 August and 21 October 1784; *United States Chronicle*, 6 January 1785; *Newport Mercury*, 15 October 1785, 15 October and 22 December 1787; Poem, n.d., Isaiah Thomas Papers, American Antiquarian Society, Worcester, Mass.

31. Revolutionary printers' copyright troubles and concerns will be discussed further in chapter 3.

32. Joel Barlow to Elias Boudinot, 10 January 1783, National Archives, *Papers of the Continental Congress, 1774–1789*, Microfilm—204 rolls (Washington, D.C.: National Archives, National Archives and Records Service, General Services Administration, 1958–1959), #4, Item 78; *Daily Hampshire Gazette*, 5 September 1936 (anniversary issue); *Essex Journal*, 12 September 1787.

33. For examples of complaints about overdue payments, see Isaiah Thomas to Samuel Avery, 12 November 1783, MS 73425, Connecticut Historical Society, Hartford, Conn.; Jonathan W. Jackson to Isaiah Thomas, 13 September 1789, Isaiah Thomas Papers, American Antiquarian Society, Worcester, Mass.; *Boston News-Letter*, 26 October 1775; *Boston Gazette*, 30 September 1776; *Norwich Packet*, 22 September 1777; *Independent Chronicle*, 12 March 1778; *New Hampshire Gazette*, 18 May 1779; *Massachusetts Spy*, 4 May 1780; *Providence Gazette*, 3 November 1781;

Newport Mercury, 28 September 1782; *Connecticut Courant,* 30 December 1783; *Vermont Gazette,* 24 January 1784; *Independent Ledger,* 10 January 1785; *United States Chronicle,* 30 November 1786; *Essex Journal,* 27 June 1787; *Newport Herald,* 28 August 1788; *Cumberland Gazette,* 5 June 1789.

34. *Norwich Packet,* 5 October 1787.

35. Silver, "Aprons Instead of Uniforms," 169; *Massachusetts Spy,* 31 May 1776, 18 March 1779, 2 November 1780, 19 April 1781; *Boston Gazette,* 3 June 1776, 3 November 1777, 4 and 25 January 1779, 31 December 1787; *Norwich Packet,* 4 October and 20 December 1781; *Massachusetts Gazette,* 22 August 1786; *Cumberland Gazette,* 24 November 1786, 22 November 1787, 19 June and 3 July 1788, 28 August 1789.

36. Silver, "Aprons Instead of Uniforms," 164–72; Petition of the Tradesmen to the Merchants of Boston, 8 November 1779, Smith-Carter Papers, Massachusetts Historical Society, Boston, Mass.; *Connecticut Journal,* 18 February 1778; *Continental Journal,* 18 February, 14 May, and 25 November 1779; *Boston Gazette,* 22 February and 15 May 1779, 21 May 1781, 8 August 1785; *Providence Gazette,* 27 April 1776, 27 June 1778, 12 February 1780; *Independent Chronicle,* 2 May and 22 August 1777; *Connecticut Courant,* 28 April 1777, 30 December 1783; *Independent Ledger,* 18 February, 22 March, 17 May, and 29 November 1779, 29 March 1784, 7 August 1786; *Norwich Packet,* 26 May 1777, 21 September 1778; *Massachusetts Spy,* 26 June and 23 October 1777, 25 June 1778; *Newport Mercury,* 19 February 1787.

37. Isaiah Thomas to George Goodwin, 19 October 1780, copy in Isaiah Thomas Papers, American Antiquarian Society, Worcester, Mass., original at the New York Historical Society, New York, N.Y.; Noah Webster to Isaiah Thomas, 23 February 1784, Benjamin West to Isaiah Thomas, 13 August 1784, Diaries of Isaiah Thomas, 1781–1789, Attachment of the property of Isaiah Thomas, 9 June 1791, Isaiah Thomas Papers, American Antiquarian Society, Worcester, Mass.; Accounts of Isaiah Thomas, 1778–1783, Account Book, Salisbury Family Papers, American Antiquarian Society, Worcester, Mass.

38. Silver, "Aprons Instead of Uniforms," 169–70; Milton W. Hamilton, *The Country Printer: New York State, 1785–1830* (Port Washington, Long Island, N.Y.: Ira J. Friedman, Inc., 1964 [1936]), 59–64; Wroth, *Colonial Printer,* 224–50; Mott, *American Journalism,* 47; Robert A. Rutland, *Newsmongers: Journalism in the Life of the Nation, 1690–1972* (New York: The Dial Press, 1973), 31–32; Hench, "The Newspaper in a Republic," 108–9.

39. For examples of other printing ventures undertaken by newspaper printers, see Thomas B. Wait to George Thacher, 25 March 1789, Thomas B. Wait Letters, Massachusetts Historical Society, Boston, Mass.; *Essex Gazette,* 24 November 1775; *Boston Gazette,* 18 March 1776, 17 November 1777, 23 December 1782; *New England Chronicle,* 22 August 1776; *Continental Journal,* 28 May 1778; *Providence Gazette,* 7 November 1778; *Newport Gazette,* 25 March 1779; *Newport Mercury,* 5 January 1780, 5 July 1783; *Connecticut Courant,* 30 October 1781; *Salem Gazette,* 25 October 1781; *Norwich Packet,* 1 November 1781; *Boston Evening Post,* 22 June 1782; *Vermont Gazette,* 4 December 1783; *United States Chronicle,* 8 April 1784; *Massachusetts Spy,* 28 October 1784; *New Haven Gazette,* 3 November 1785; *American Mercury,* 25 December 1786; *Hampshire Gazette,* 5 December 1787; *American Herald,* 7 January 1788; *Herald of Freedom,* 28 April 1789.

40. For examples of the variety of materials sold in a printing shop, see *Providence Gazette,* 7 January 1775; *New England Chronicle,* 25 April 1776; *Newport Gazette,* 16 January, 6 March, 7 and 28 August, 11 September, and 26 December 1777, 8 January, 5 and 12 February, 12 and 19 March, 28 May, 25 June, and 22

NOTES   **163**

October 1778, 25 March, 29 July, and 16 September 1779; *Connecticut Gazette,* 7 August 1778; *Newport Mercury,* 15 July 1780; *American Journal,* 18 August 1781; *Independent Ledger,* 23 December 1782; *Vermont Gazette,* 12 June 1783; *Boston Gazette,* 1784; *Continental Journal,* 9 September 1784; *Middlesex Gazette,* 15 November 1785; *Hampshire Gazette,* 20 September 1786; *Salem Mercury,* 27 November 1787; *Newport Herald,* 22 May 1788; *Independent Chronicle,* 5 February 1789.

41. *Massachusetts Spy,* 1 March and 12 April 1776; Isaiah Thomas to Hudson & Goodwin, 8 December 1785, copy in Isaiah Thomas Papers, American Antiquarian Society, Worcester, Mass., original at the New York Historical Society, New York, N.Y. For a good discussion of the economics of being a printer in Boston just prior to the Revolutionary War, see Mary Ann Yodelis, "Who Paid the Piper? Publishing Economics in Boston, 1763–1775," *Journalism Monographs* 38 (1975).

42. Benjamin Edes quoted in Silver, *American Printer,* 63–64.

Chapter 3. Producers of the "Popular Engine": New England's Revolutionary Newspaper Printers

1. Carl Bridenbaugh, *The Colonial Craftsmen* (Chicago: University of Chicago Press, 1950), 66, 123, 126–27, 129, 134–35, 156–57, 162–63; Ian M. G. Quimby, "Introduction: Some Observations on the Craftsmen in Early America," in *The Craftsman in Early America,* edited by Ian M. G. Quimby (New York: W. W. Norton and Company for the Henry Francis du Pont Winterthur Museum, 1984), 5–6; Thomas J. Schlereth, "Artisans and Craftsmen: A Historical Perspective," in *The Craftsman in Early America,* edited by Ian M. G. Quimby (New York: W. W. Norton and Company for the Henry Francis du Pont Winterthur Museum, 1984), 38–39; Jackson Turner Main, *The Social Structure of Revolutionary America* (Princeton, N.J.: Princeton University Press, 1965), 274–75.

2. Bridenbaugh, *The Colonial Craftsman,* 148–49, 169, 176.

3. Rollo G. Silver, *The American Printer, 1787–1825* (Charlottesville: University Press of Virginia, 1967), 3; Milton W. Hamilton, *The Country Printer: New York State, 1785–1830* (Port Washington, Long Island, N.Y.: Ira J. Friedman, Inc., 1964 [1936]), 25–27.

4. Benjamin Titcomb to Andrew Titcomb, September 1776, Andrew Hawes Collection: Titcomb Family Papers, Maine Historical Society, Portland, Me.

5. Silver, *American Printer,* 3; Hamilton, *Country Printer,* 25–27.

6. Indenture of Isaiah Thomas, 4 June 1756, Isaiah Thomas Papers, American Antiquarian Society, Worcester, Mass. The punctuation has been modernized to make the indenture easier to read and understand.

7. Silver, *American Printer,* 1–2, 5–6; Hamilton, *Country Printer,* 29–30, 39.

8. Indenture of Isaiah Thomas, 4 June 1756.

9. Silver, *American Printer,* 1–2, 5–6; Hamilton, *Country Printer,* 29–30, 39.

10. Silver, *American Printer,* 4–8; Hamilton, Country Printer, 31–34, 39–40.

11. Silver, *American Printer,* 7, 26; Hamilton, *Country Printer,* 39–40, 45–46.

12. Summary of material gleaned from the Printers' File, American Antiquarian Society, Worcester, Mass., and Isaiah Thomas, *The History of Printing in America* (Worcester, Mass.: Isaiah Thomas, Jr., 1810; reprint ed. edited by Marcus A. McCorison, Barre, Mass.: Imprint Society, 1970), 42–339.

13. Printers' File, American Antiquarian Society; Thomas, *History of Printing*, 42–339.

14. James Rivington to Isaiah Thomas, 11 August 1783, Hugh Gaine to Isaiah Thomas, 10 November 1788, John Carter to Isaiah Thomas, 6 February 1789, John Mycall to Isaiah Thomas, 22 February 1789, Isaiah Thomas Papers, American Antiquarian Society, Worcester, Mass.; Isaiah Thomas to George Goodwin, 19 October 1780, Isaiah Thomas to Hudson & Goodwin, 13 and 14 April and 8 May 1786, 9 June, 27 July, and 28 December 1789, 27 January and 8 and 22 March 1790, 3 February and 19 July 1791, 20 July and 3 November 1795, 1 and 8 February, 29 August, 26 and 31 September, and 22 November 1796, 1 February 1797, 24 and 28 January, 2, 8, 17, and 26 February, 1 and 20 November, and 17 and 31 December 1798, 7 January, 30 June, 5 August, and 12 December 1799, copies in Isaiah Thomas Papers, American Antiquarian Society, Worcester, Mass., originals at New York Historical Society, New York, N.Y.

15. Stephen Botein, " 'Meer Mechanicks' and an Open Press: The Business and Political Strategies of Colonial Printers," *Perspectives in American History* 9 (1975): 152–60; Thomas, *History of Printing*, 179, 182, 277; Joseph T. Buckingham, *Specimens of Newspaper Literature*, 2 vols. (Boston: Charles C. Little and James Brown, 1850), 2:5–9.

16. Charles L. Nichols, "Fowle, Daniel," *Dictionary of American Biography*, 10 vols. (New York: Charles Scribner's Sons, 1927–1936), 3(pt. 2):560–61.

17. Thomas B. Wyman, *The Genealogies and Estates of Charlestown, Massachusetts*, 2 vols. (Boston: D. Clapp and Son, 1879), 1:368, 371; William C. Kiessel, "The Green Family: A Dynasty of Printers," *New England Historical and Genealogical Register* 104 (1950): 81–93; Thomas Spooner, ed., *Records of William Spooner of Plymouth, Massachusetts* (Cincinnati: Press of F. W. Freeman, 1883), 73, 99, 150–54, 157–58.

18. For example, see John M. Murrin, "The Legal Transformation: The Bench and Bar of Eighteenth-Century Massachusetts," in *Colonial America: Essays in Politics and Social Development*, edited by Stanley N. Katz and John M. Murrin, 3rd ed. (New York: Alfred A. Knopf, 1983), 540–71; and Donald M. Scott, *From Office to Profession: The New England Ministry* (Philadelphia: University of Pennsylvania Press, 1978). My phrase "from trade to profession" is a reworking of Scott's title to fit my subject.

19. *Boston Gazette*, 18 May 1778, 28 May 1781, 23 June 1782, 3 October 1785; *Independent Ledger*, 3 December 1781; *Essex Journal*, 27 August 1784, 3 December 1788; *Cumberland Gazette*, 30 March and 13 April 1786; *Vermont Gazette*, 29 May 1786; *New Hampshire Mercury*, 30 August 1786; *Independent Chronicle*, 22 May and 11 and 18 December 1788; *Herald of Freedom*, 8, 11, and 15 December 1788, 17 March 1789.

20. *Continental Journal*, 14 November 1782.

21. Frank Luther Mott, *American Journalism: A History of Newspapers in the United States Through 250 Years, 1690 to 1940* (New York: The MacMillan Company, 1962 [1941]), 132–33.

22. For examples of increased crediting of sources, see *Newport Mercury*, 1775; *Vermont Journal*, 1784; *Continental Journal*, 1784-1785; *Herald of Freedom*, 1789.

23. *Herald of Freedom*, 6 March 1789.

24. Silver, *American Printer*, 111; *Boston Gazette*, 18 October 1784; Isaiah Thomas to Hudson & Goodwin, 8 May 1786, 8 March 1790, copies in Isaiah Thomas Papers, American Antiquarian Society, Worcester, Mass., originals at New York Historical Society, New York, N.Y.; John Carter to Isaiah Thomas, 15 November

1792, Isaiah Thomas Papers, American Antiquarian Society, Worcester, Mass.; Joel Barlow to Elias Boudinot, 10 January 1783, National Archives, *Papers of the Continental Congress, 1774–1789*, Microfilm—204 rolls (Washington, D.C.: National Archives, National Archives and Records Service, General Services Administration, 1958–1959), #4, item 78.

25. On 2 July 1785, the Massachusetts General Court instituted a duty on all nonofficial newspaper advertisements. The act was designed to raise money to pay off the state war debt. It operated until 26 March 1788. This will be discussed further in chapter 5.

26. John B. Hench, "Massachusetts Printers and the Commonwealth's Newspaper Advertisement Tax of 1785," *Proceedings of the American Antiquarian Society* 87 (1977): 199–211; Rollo G. Silver, "Aprons Instead of Uniforms: The Practice of Printing, 1776–1787," *Proceedings of the American Antiquarian Society* 87 (1977): 177–79; John Clyde Oswald, *Printing in the Americas* (New York: The Gregg Publishing Company, 1937), 501–2; *New Hampshire Gazette*, 20 May 1785.

27. Summary of material gleaned from Clarence S. Brigham, ed., *History and Bibliography of American Newspapers, 1690–1820*, 2 vols. (Worcester, Mass.: American Antiquarian Society, 1947).

28. Printers' File, American Antiquarian Society.

29. *Ibid.*; Susan Henry, "Work, Widowhood and War: Hannah Bunce Watson, Connecticut Printer," *The Connecticut Historical Society Bulletin* 48 (1983): 25–39.

30. In his study of American journalism, Robert Rutland noted that Isaiah Thomas made numerous references to the funerals of fellow printers in his *The History of Printing in America*. He also cites Clarence Brigham's reference to thirty-six widows who became printers as evidence of the early deaths of many colonial printers. Robert A. Rutland, *Newsmongers: Journalism in the Life of the Nation, 1690–1972* (New York: The Dial Press, 1973), 13–14.

31. Average age at death figures reached by computing the average age of all who died prior to 1800 (20) and all who died after 1800 (63). Figures not available for ten out of the ninety-three printers studied.

32. Rutland, *Newsmongers*, 13–14. One example indicates that life could still be rough in frontier areas. George Roulstone, originally a printer in Salem, Massachusetts, pioneered printing in the state of Tennessee, arriving in 1791. He died in 1804 at the age of thirty-seven. Samuel C. Williams, "George Roulstone, Father of the Tennessee Press," *The East Tennessee Historical Society's Publications* 17 (1945): 51–60; Printers' File, American Antiquarian Society.

33. Kiessel, "The Green Family," 85; Robert Earle Moody and Charles Christopher Crittenden, "The Letter-Book of Mills & Hicks," *North Carolina Historical Review* 14 (1937): 39–83; J. J. Stewart, "Early Journalism in Nova Scotia," *Nova Scotia Historical Society Collections* 6 (1888): 118–20; Marion Robertson, "The Loyalist Printers: James and Alexander Robertson," *Nova Scotia Historical Review* 3 (1983): 83–93.

34. Thomas, *History of Printing*, 333–34; Ralph Adams Brown, "New Hampshire Editors Win the War: A Study in Revolutionary Press Propaganda," *New England Quarterly* 12 (1939): 36; *Providence Gazette*, 10 May 1777.

35. Summary of material gleaned from Brigham, *American Newspapers*.

36. Frank W. Scott, "Russell, Benjamin," *Dictionary of American Biography*, 10 vols. (New York: Charles Scribner's Sons, 1927–1936), 8(pt. 2):238–40; Benjamin Franklin, V, ed., *Boston Printers, Publishers, and Booksellers: 1640–1800* (Boston: G. K. Hall & Company, 1980), 433–37; Buckingham, *Specimens of Newspaper Literature*, 2:9.

37. John Spargo, *Anthony Haswell: Printer—Patriot—Ballader* (Rutland, Vt.: The Tuttle Company, 1925); Poem by Anthony Haswell, Haswell Family Papers, American Antiquarian Society, Worcester, Mass.

38. *New Hampshire Gazette*, 20 May 1785.

39. Clifford K. Shipton, *Isaiah Thomas: Printer, Patriot, and Philanthropist, 1749–1831* (Rochester, N.Y.: The Printing House of Leo Hart, 1948).

40. Thomas S. Lunt, *A History of the Lunt Family in America* (Salem, Mass.: The Salem Press Company, 1914), 27, 48–50.

41. Joseph Griffin, *History of the Press in Maine* (Brunswick, Me.: The Press, 1872), 34; Henry S. Burrage, *History of the Baptists in Maine* (Portland, Me.: Marks Printing House, Printers, 1904), 139.

42. Emma Forbes Waite, "Benjamin Dearborn: Teacher, Inventor, Philanthropist," *Old Time New England* 42 (1951): 44–47; *New Hampshire Gazette*, 31 December 1776, 20 April 1779, 29 September 1781, 28 October 1785, 13 April 1786; *New Hampshire Mercury*, 26 April 1785; *New Hampshire Spy*, 30 January and 24 April 1787, 28 June and 21 November 1788, 3 April 1789; Albert Stillman Batchelor, ed., *Early State Papers of New Hampshire, 1784–1790*, vols. 20–21 of Nathaniel Bouton et al., eds., *State Papers of New Hampshire*, 40 vols. (Nashua and elsewhere: State Printer, 1870–1895), 20:457, 478, 489, 542, 586, 629, 727, 731, 736, 738, 770, 775, 781.

43. Gilman Bigelow Howe, *Genealogy of the Bigelow Family in America* (Worcester, Mass.: C. Hamilton, 1890), 74, 143–44; Clifford K. Shipton, ed., *Sibley's Harvard Graduates: Biographical Sketches of Those Who Attended Harvard College*, 17 vols. (Cambridge, Mass.: Harvard University Press, 1933–1975), 17:436–38.

44. Franklin B. Dexter, *Biographical Sketches of the Graduates of Yale College with Annals of the College History*, 6 vols. (New York: H. Holt and Company, 1885–1912), 4:43–47.

45. Dexter, *Graduates of Yale*, 4:3–16; Elias Boudinot to Governor William Livingston, 25 November 1782, Joel Barlow to William Livingston, 21 July 1785, William Livingston Papers, Massachusetts Historical Society, Boston, Mass.

46. Shipton, *Isaiah Thomas*, 36; *American Journal*, 1 April 1779.

47. Joel Barlow's Appointment as Chaplain for the 3rd Massachusetts Brigade, 25 November 1782, Joel Barlow Papers, American Antiquarian Society, Worcester, Mass.; Scott, "Russell, Benjamin," 238–240; Isaac Hammond, ed., *Rolls of the Soldiers in the Revolutionary War*, vols. 14–17 of Nathaniel Bouton et al., eds. *State Papers of New Hampshire*, 40 vols. (Nashua and elsewhere: State Printer, 1870–1895) 14:239, 255–56, 17:23, 31, 38.

48. Marylouise Dunham Meder, "Timothy Green III, Connecticut Printer, 1737–1796: His Life and Times" (Ph.D. dissertation, University of Michigan, 1964), 97.

49. Record Commissioners of Boston, *Reports of the Record Commissioners of Boston—Town Records*, 39 vols. (Boston: City Printer, 1876–1909), 25:20–23.

50. John Russell Bartlett, ed., *Records of the Colony of Rhode Island and Providence Plantations, 1636–1792*, 10 vols. (Providence: State Printer, 1856–1865), 8:356, 9:81, 162, 254; Solomon Southwick to Jeremiah Wadsworth, 23 and 26 May, 17 July, and 27 November 1778, 22, 26, and 31 March and 7 April 1779, Solomon Southwick to Peter Colt, 19 and 26 September, 7, 26, and 31 October, 5, 10, 21, and 25 November, and 2, 4, 13, 18, and 25 December 1778, 27 January and 31 October 1779, Solomon Southwick to Andrew Huntington, 25 July 1778, Solomon Southwick to John Sullivan, 29 November 1778, Jeremiah Wadsworth Papers, Connecticut Historical Society, Hartford, Conn.; *American Journal*, 23 September 1779.

51. Edna L. Jacobsen, "Southwick, Solomon," *Dictionary of American Biography*, 10 vols. (New York: Charles Scribner's Sons, 1927–1936), 9(pt. 1):413–14.

52. Alan Kulikoff, "The Progress of Inequality in Revolutionary Boston," *William and Mary Quarterly* 28 (1971): 376, 384–85, 389–90, 409–10.

53. Sidney I. Pomerantz, "The Patriot Newspaper and the American Revolution," in *The Era of the American Revolution*, edited by Richard B. Morris, 2nd ed. (New York: Harper & Row, Publishers, 1965 [1939]), 330–31; Robert Wilson Kidder, "The Contribution of Daniel Fowle to New Hampshire Printing, 1756–1787" (Ph.D. dissertation, University of Illinois, 1960), 102; Meder, "Timothy Green III," 115–16, 125; *Boston Town Records*, 14:293–94, 16:34–35, 49, 69, 82, 107, 130, 150, 158, 167, 289, 18:9, 243, 275, 277, 296, 25:6, 36, 49, 26:7, 36–37, 46, 47, 88, 89, 90, 99-100, 118, 123, 184, 185, 228, 262, 31:15, 210, 247, 305, 35:117, 119–20, 139–40, 167, 197, 211–14, 232, 251–52, 265–66, 285, 311, 326, 332, 334, 339, 37:7, 24, 30, 55, 66, 70, 74, 86, 93, 98, 110–11, 113–14, 115, 117, 127, 128, 135, 144, 160–61, 167, 172, 174, 176, 199, 223, 254, 275; *New Hampshire Gazette*, 4 May 1779, 17 April 1784, 2 April 1788; Receipts for Services as Coronor, October 1795, April 1796, John Mycall Letters, Essex Institute, Salem, Mass.

54. Meder, "Timothy Green III," 115–16, 125; *American Mercury*, 4 April 1785.

55. Meder, "Timothy Green III," 115–16, 125.

56. *Connecticut Journal*, 18 February 1784; *Connecticut Gazette*, 19 March 1784; *New Haven Gazette*, 3 June 1784, 9 June 1785, 8 June 1786, 7 June 1787, 5 June 1788.

57. John Hancock to Isaiah Thomas, 14 December 1788, Isaiah Thomas Papers, American Antiquarian Society, Worcester, Mass.

58. Rutland, *Newsmongers*, 10, 11; Bernard A. Weisberger, *The American Newspaperman* (Chicago: The University of Chicago Press, 1961), 9–10; John Bixler Hench, "The Newspaper in a Republic: Boston's *Centinel* and *Chronicle*, 1784–1801" (Ph.D. dissertation, Clark University, 1979), 30.

59. George Hough to Simeon Baldwin, 8 April 1781, Baldwin Family Papers, Manuscripts and Archives, Yale University, New Haven, Conn.

60. *Boston Gazette*, 29 August 1785; *Independent Chronicle*, 1 September 1785.

61. *New Hampshire Gazette*, 16 June 1787; *Newport Mercury*, 25 June 1787; *Vermont Gazette*, 23 July 1787.

62. Hamilton, *Country Printer*, 211; Lawrence C. Wroth, *The Colonial Printer* (Portland, Me.: The Southworth-Anthoensen Press, 1938), 177; Stephen Botein, "Printers and the American Revolution," in *The Press and the American Revolution*, edited by Bernard Bailyn and John B. Hench (Worcester, Mass.: American Antiquarian Society, 1980), 19, 45; Main, *Social Structure in America*, 215–19; Pomerantz, "The Patriot Newspaper," 330–31; Kidder, "Daniel Fowle," 165. Norman H. Dawes, in studying the use of honorary titles in colonial New England, concluded that the title of Esquire had lost all the specific political significance it once held by the late seventeenth century, but that it continued to indicate a certain amount of social standing in the community, Norman H. Dawes, "Titles as Symbols of Prestige in Seventeenth-Century New England," *William and Mary Quarterly* 6 (1949): 92.

63. Rollo G. Silver, "Abstracts from the Wills and Estates of Boston Printers, 1800–1825," *Studies in Bibliography* 7 (1955): 212–18.

64. Estate Inventories of John Gill, William Warden, John Nourse, Ezekiel Russell, Thomas Adams, John Fleet, John W. Folsom, Thomas B. Wait, Benjamin Russell, Files # 18510, 18652, 19431, 20613, 21043, 22599, 27497, 29214, 34226, copies in Book Trades Collection, American Antiquarian Society, Worcester, Mass., originals at Suffolk County Probate Court, Boston, Mass.; Estate Invento-

ries of Thomas Green, Samuel Green, New Haven Probate Records, Timothy Green, New London Probate Records, John Trumbull, Norwich Probate Records, Barzillai Hudson, Roger Storrs, Ebenezer Watson, Hartford Probate Records, Connecticut State Library, Hartford, Conn.; Estate Inventory of Benjamin Edes, Jr., copy in the Boston Printers Collection, Massachusetts Historical Society, Boston, Mass., original at the Suffolk County Probate Court, Boston, Mass.; Estate Inventory of Isaiah Thomas, copy in the Isaiah Thomas Papers, American Antiquarian Society, Worcester, Mass., original at the Worcester County Probate Court, Worcester, Mass.

65. Taxes of Timothy Green, 1787–1790, New London, Connecticut, Tax Lists, 1787–1790, American Antiquarian Society, Worcester, Mass.

66. Valuation Lists for 1778 and 1783, Worcester, Massachusetts Collection, 1686–1801, American Antiquarian Society, Worcester, Mass.

67. Federal Taxes of Isaiah Thomas for 1815, Worcester County, Massachusetts Collection, Isaiah Thomas Letterbook Entry for 1 February 1822, Isaiah Thomas Papers, List of Societies of which Thomas was a member, 10 April 1822, Isaiah Thomas Papers, American Antiquarian Society, Worcester, Mass.

68. Kulikoff, "Progress of Inequality in Boston," 385–87.

Chapter 4. The Printer and His Public

1. G. A. Cranfield, *The Development of the Provincial Newspaper, 1700–1760* (Oxford: Clarendon Press, 1962), 93–116.

2. Isaiah Thomas, *The History of Printing in America* (Worcester, Mass.: Isaiah Thomas, Jr., 1810; reprint ed. edited by Marcus A. McCorison, Barre, Mass.: Imprint Society, 1970), 3; *Worcester Magazine*, August 1787; *Newport Herald*, 16 April 1789.

3. *Independent Chronicle*, 8 July 1779; *Independent Ledger*, 26 January 1784; *New Hampshire Gazette*, 14 February 1784; *Essex Journal*, 29 June 1785; *Boston Gazette*, 3 September 1787; *Vermont Gazette*, 7 July 1788; *Herald of Freedom*, 15 December 1788.

4. *New Hampshire Gazette*, 6 July 1782; *Boston Gazette*, 15 July 1782; *Massachusetts Spy*, 12 September 1782; *Cumberland Gazette*, 1 November 1787; *Salem Mercury*, 20 November 1787; *Norwich Packet*, 10 January 1788.

5. *Independent Ledger*, 1 September 1783; *American Herald*, 14 November 1785; *Continental Journal*, 18 May 1786; *Boston Gazette*, 2 March 1789.

6. *Continental Journal*, 30 March 1786; *Norwich Packet*, 30 March 1786; *Massachusetts Gazette*, 15 May 1786; *Independent Chronicle*, 25 May 1786.

7. *American Gazette*, 18 June 1776; *Essex Journal*, 8 June 1785; *New Hampshire Mercury*, 14 June 1785; *Falmouth Gazette*, 25 June 1785; *Vermont Journal*, 5 July 1785; *Vermont Gazette*, 11 July 1785; *Independent Ledger*, 5 and 28 September 1785; *New Hampshire Gazette*, 11 September 1785; *Norwich Packet*, 22 September 1785; *American Herald*, 19 December 1785, 6 November 1788; *Cumberland Gazette*, 17 November 1786.

8. *Continental Journal*, 3 July 1783; *Vermont Gazette*, 2 October 1783; *Norwich Packet*, 25 December 1783; *Falmouth Gazette*, 15 January 1785; *Independent Ledger*, 6 June 1785; *Salem Mercury*, 17 June 1788; *New Hampshire Spy*, 17 June 1788; *American Mercury*, 23 June 1788; *Norwich Packet*, 26 June 1788; *Herald of Freedom*, 11 December 1788; *United States Chronicle*, 6 August 1789.

9. *New England Chronicle,* 13 June 1776; *Massachusetts Spy,* 21 June 1776; *Independent Chronicle,* 12 March 1778.

10. *Newport Mercury,* 6 March 1775; *Massachusetts Spy,* 11 December 1776.

11. Newspaper coverage of Shays's Rebellion will be treated more fully in chapter 7.

12. *Independent Ledger,* 25 February 1782; *Massachusetts Spy,* 7 March 1782; *American Mercury,* 6 September 1784; *Hampshire Gazette,* 13 September 1786; *Salem Mercury,* 14 October 1786; *New Hampshire Spy,* 16 February 1787; *Boston Gazette,* 26 February 1787; *New Hampshire Recorder,* 8 April 1788; *Western Star,* 1 December 1789.

13. *Massachusetts Spy,* 14 August 1783; *Freeman's Chronicle,* 10 November 1783; *Connecticut Courant,* 27 July 1784; *Exchange Advertiser,* 30 December 1784; *Plymouth Journal,* 19 March 1785; *Middlesex Gazette,* 8 November 1785; *Freeman's Oracle,* 1 July 1786; *Newport Herald,* 1 March 1787; *Massachusetts Centinel,* 17 March 1787.

14. *Independent Ledger,* 15 June and 16 February 1784; *Independent Chronicle,* 17 September 1778; *Massachusetts Gazette,* 14 May 1782; *Freeman's Chronicle,* 10 November 1783; *United States Chronicle,* 19 February 1784; *Connecticut Courant,* 2 March and 27 July 1784, 17 July 1786; *Exchange Advertiser,* 30 December 1784; *Plymouth Journal,* 19 March 1785; *Salem Chronicle,* 30 March 1786; *Freeman's Oracle,* 1 July 1786.

15. For examples, see *Connecticut Journal* and *New Hampshire Gazette,* January to July 1777 ("The Crisis"); *Independent Chronicle,* January to June 1786 (Lawyers and the Judicial System); *Boston Gazette,* 29 May 1780, 22 April 1782, 10 January, 28 March, and 28 November 1785, 17 July 1786, 24 March 1788; *New Hampshire Gazette,* 10 May 1783; *Essex Journal,* 22 February 1786; *Freeman's Oracle,* 8 July 1786.

16. Mary Beth Norton, *Liberty's Daughters: The Revolutionary Experience of American Women, 1750–1800* (Boston: Little, Brown and Company, 1980), 256–94; Linda K. Kerber, *Women of the Republic: Intellect and Ideology in Revolutionary America* (Chapel Hill: Published for the Institute of Early American History and Culture, Williamsburg, Virginia, by the University of North Carolina Press, 1980), 185–232.

17. *Continental Journal,* 26 April 1781, 8 August 1782, 11 August 1785, 1 June 1786; *Independent Ledger,* 17 July 1786; *Independent Chronicle,* 13 July 1786.

18. *New Haven Gazette, and Connecticut Magazine,* 31 August 1786, 7 August 1788; *Middlesex Gazette,* 17 March 1788.

19. *Newport Mercury,* 7 July 1782; *Boston Gazette,* 20 June 1785; *Freeman's Oracle,* 3 February 1787.

20. *Continental Journal,* 10 May 1781, 25 December 1783; *Exeter Chronicle,* 1 July 1784; *American Herald,* March to July 1786; *Cumberland Gazette,* 21 June 1787.

21. Beginning in mid–1787, an increasing number of essays dealing with slavery and the slave trade began to appear in the Rhode Island papers, the *Providence Gazette* and the *Newport Mercury. Independent Chronicle,* 28 November 1776, 20 March 1788; *Independent Ledger,* 16 and 23 February 1784, 19 December 1785; *American Herald,* 27 February 1786; *New Hampshire Spy,* 26 December 1786; *Massachusetts Centinel,* 9 May 1787; *Providence Gazette,* 6 October 1787, 14 June 1788; *Newport Mercury,* 28 April 1788; *New Haven Gazette, and Connecticut Magazine,* 30 October 1788.

22. *Boston Gazette,* 9 October 1775; *Herald of Freedom,* 30 October 1788.

23. Frank Luther Mott, *American Journalism: A History of Newspapers in the*

United States Through 250 Years, 1690 to 1940 (New York: The MacMillan Company, 1962 [1941]), 101; *Connecticut Gazette*, 23 February 1776; *Massachusetts Spy*, 14 October 1779.

24. Milton W. Hamilton, *The Country Printer: New York State, 1785–1830* (Port Washington, Long Island, N.Y.: Ira J. Friedman, Inc., 1964 [1936]), 139–55.

25. David J. Russo, "The Origins of Local News in the United States Country Press, 1840s–1870s," *Journalism Monographs* 65 (1980): 2–4; John Bard McNulty, *Older than the Nation: The Story of the Hartford Courant* (Stonington, Conn.: The Pequot Press, Inc., 1964), 6; *Massachusetts Centinel*, 8 October 1788.

26. In an attempt to raise money to pay off the war debt, Massachusetts passed a stamp tax in 1785. Because of great public protest, the stamp tax was replaced by an advertisement tax in 1786. Printers in Massachusetts complained loudly that both of these actions were detrimental to their business.

27. Mott, *American Journalism*, 104–5, 159; Sidney Kobre, *Development of American Journalism* (Dubuque, Ia.: William C. Brown Company, Publishers, 1969), 75, 78–79; Susan Henry, "Work, Widowhood and War: Hannah Bunce Watson, Connecticut Printer," *The Connecticut Historical Society Bulletin* 48 (1983): 30; *Massachusetts Spy*, 21 December 1780; *New Haven Gazette, and Connecticut Magazine*, 18 January and 14 May 1787.

28. Clarence S. Brigham, *Journals and Journeymen: A Contribution to the History of Early American Newspapers* (Philadelphia: University of Pennsylvania Press, 1950), 19–20; Mary Ann Yodelis, "Who Paid the Piper? Publishing Economics in Boston, 1763–1775," *Journalism Monographs* 38 (1975): 36–37; John Bixler Hench, "The Newspaper in a Republic: Boston's *Centinel* and *Chronicle*, 1784–1801" (Ph.D. dissertation, Clark University, 1979), 105; Ralph A. Brown, "The New Hampshire Press, 1775 to 1789," chapter 7, 1, Typed Ms., Connecticut Historical Society, Hartford, Conn.; E. Wilder Spaulding, "The *Connecticut Courant*, a Representative Newspaper in the Eighteenth Century," in *Selected Readings in the History of American Journalism*, edited by Edwin H. Ford (Minneapolis: University of Minnesota, 1939), 83.

29. Charles L. Cutler, *Connecticut's Revolutionary Press* (Chester, Conn.: Pequot Press, 1975), 8; Hamilton, *The Country Printer*, 216; No Author Given, *History of the Connecticut Valley in Massachusetts*, 2 vols. (Philadelphia: L. H. Everts, 1879), 1:214–15.

30. Timothy M. Barnes, "The Loyalist Press in the American Revolution, 1765–1781" (Ph.D. dissertation, The University of New Mexico, 1970), 3–4.

31. Mott, *American Journalism*, 108; Richard D. Brown, "From Cohesion to Competition," in *Printing and Society in Early America*, edited by William L. Joyce, David D. Hall, Richard D. Brown, and John B. Hench (Worcester, Mass.: American Antiquarian Society, 1983), 303; Stephen Botein, " 'Meer Mechanicks' and an Open Press: The Business and Political Strategies of Colonial American Printers," *Perspectives in American History* 9 (1975): 216; Carl Bridenbaugh, *Cities in Revolt: Urban Life in America, 1743–1776* (New York: Alfred A. Knopf, 1955), 388–89; *Freeman's Chronicle*, 10 November 1783; *Independent Ledger*, 16 February 1784; *United States Chronicle*, 19 February 1784; *Connecticut Courant*, 2 March 1784; *Exchange Advertiser*, 30 December 1784; *Plymouth Journal*, 19 March 1785; *Newport Herald*, 1 March 1787.

32. Cranfield, *Provincial Newspaper*, 93; *Continental Journal*, 30 March 1786; *Norwich Packet*, 30 March 1786; *Massachusetts Gazette*, 15 May 1786; *Independent Chronicle*, 25 May 1786.

Chapter 5. Newspapers and Government: A Tension-Filled Relationship

1. *Newport Mercury,* 4 December 1775; *Independent Ledger,* 26 April 1779, 2 and 30 December 1782, 10 May 1784; *New Hampshire Gazette,* 23 April 1781; *Continental Journal,* 18 December 1783, 8 April 1784, 10 February 1785; *Massachusetts Centinel,* 28 April 1784, 3 March 1787; *American Herald,* 10 May 1784; *Boston Gazette,* 25 July 1785; *Independent Chronicle,* 18 January 1786, 23 April 1789; *Salem Mercury,* 25 December 1787; James Phinney Baxter *et al.,* eds., *Documentary History of the State of Maine,* 24 vols. (Portland: State Printer, 1869–1916), 21:127, 173, 228, 316, 22:201, 348; E. P. Walton, ed., *Records of the Governor and Council of the State of Vermont,* 8 vols. (Montpelier, Vt.: J. and J. M. Poland, 1873–1880), 3:22, 85, 108, 110–11; David Syrett, "Town-Meeting Politics in Massachusetts, 1776–1786," *William and Mary Quarterly* 21 (1964): 356.

2. *Boston Gazette,* 22 January 1776; *Independent Chronicle,* January–April 1778; *Independent Ledger,* 31 July 1780, 18 August 1783; *Continental Journal,* 15 November 1781, 22 April 1784, 9 July 1788; *Newport Mercury,* 17 November 1781, 23 February and 2 November 1782, 17 April 1784, 25 June 1785; *New Hampshire Gazette,* 8 February 1783; *New Haven Gazette,* 22 July 1784; *Herald of Freedom,* November 1788, February–April 1789.

3. Rollo G. Silver, "Government Printing in Massachusetts: 1751–1801," *Studies in Bibliography* 16 (1963): 166, 176; William Lincoln, ed., *The Journals of Each Provincial Congress of Massachusetts in 1774 and 1775* (Boston: Dutton and Wentworth, State Printers, 1838), 527, 542; Charles J. Hoadley and Leonard W. Labaree, eds., *The Public Records of the State of Connecticut,* 6 vols. (Hartford: State Printer, 1894–1945), 1:377; Edmund C. Burnett, ed., *Letters of Members of the Continental Congress, 1774–1789,* 8 vols. (Washington, D.C.: Carnegie Institution of Washington, 1921–1936), 8:52, 832; Worthington C. Ford *et al.,* eds., *Journals of the Continental Congress, 1774–1789,* 34 vols. (Washington, D.C.: United States Government Printing Office, 1904–1937), 33:465.

4. Albert Carlos Bates, "Fighting the Revolution with Printer's Ink in Connecticut: The Official Printing of the Colony from Lexington to the Declaration," *Papers of the New Haven Colony Historical Society* 9 (1918): 129–60; Albert Carlos Bates, "Some Notes on Early Connecticut Printing," *Papers of the Bibliographical Society of America* 27 (1933): 5; Silver, "Government Printing in Massachusetts: 1751–1801," 161–200.

5. In his study of Revolutionary Philadelphia, Dwight L. Teeter concluded that printers exercised freedom in their dealings with government because the government needed them more than they needed the government. Since both the Continental Congress and the Pennsylvania state assembly met in Philadelphia, official printing contracts were plentiful. If one lost a job because of unfavorable reactions to newspaper essays, other contracts were readily available. Dwight L. Teeter, "Press Freedom and the Public Printing: Pennsylvania, 1775–1783," *Journalism Quarterly* 45 (1968): 445–51.

This state of affairs did not exist in New England. With only one government to deal with, printers could not always afford to speak or print their mind. Still, many took the risk.

6. Rollo G. Silver, "Aprons Instead of Uniforms: The Practice of Printing, 1776–1787," *Proceedings of the American Antiquarian Society* 87 (1977): 136–41; Marylouise Dunham Meder, "Timothy Green III, Connecticut Printer, 1737–

1796: His Life and Times" (Ph.D. dissertation, University of Michigan, 1964), 123; Ted N. Weissbuch, "A Chapter in Vermont's Revolutionary War Finance," *Vermont History* 29 (1961): 9; Silver, "Government Printing in Massachusetts: 1751–1801," 169; Walton, *Records of Vermont*, 3:27, 151; Nathaniel Bouton et al., eds., *State Papers of New Hampshire*, 40 vols. (Nashua and elsewhere: State Printer, 1870–1895), 7:313; Baxter, *Documentary History of Maine*, 22:188–89; *Boston Gazette*, 1 July 1776; *New Hampshire Gazette*, 11 and 25 February 1777; *Independent Chronicle*, 26 November 1784; Benjamin Franklin, V, ed., *Boston Printers, Publishers, and Booksellers: 1640–1800* (Boston: G. K. Hall & Company, 1980), 493; John Bixler Hench, "The Newspaper in a Republic: Boston's *Centinel* and *Chronicle*, 1784–1801" (Ph.D. dissertation, Clark University, 1979), 84. The published records of the New England states contain numerous references to printing contracts. See the indexes of the following: Record Commissioners of Boston, *Reports of the Record Commissioners of Boston—Town Records*, 39 vols. (Boston: City Printer, 1876–1909); Charles J. Hoadley and James H. Trumbull, eds., *The Public Records of the Colony of Connecticut*, 15 vols. (Hartford: State Printer, 1850–1890); Hoadley and Labaree, *State Records of Connecticut*; Walton, *Records of Vermont*; Bouton, *State Papers of New Hampshire*; John Russell Bartlett, ed., *Records of the Colony of Rhode Island and Providence Plantations, 1636–1792*, 10 vols. (Providence: State Printer, 1856–1865).

7. Lawrence C. Wroth, *The Colonial Printer* (Portland, Me.: The Southworth-Anthoensen Press, 1938), 13; Meder, "Timothy Green III," 81, 83–84, 86, 88–89, 93–95, 111, 122; Mary Ann Yodelis, "Who Paid the Piper? Publishing Economics in Boston, 1763–1775," *Journalism Monographs* 38 (1975): 23–30, 42–43; Silver, "Government Printing in Massachusetts: 1751–1801," 175, 180; G. Thomas Tanselle, "Some Statistics on American Printing, 1764–1783," in *The Press and the American Revolution*, edited by Bernard Bailyn and John B. Hench (Worcester, Mass.: American Antiquarian Society, 1980), 340–44; *Continental Journal*, 31 July 1777; Hoadley and Labaree, *State Records of Connecticut*, 1:457, 462, 467, 577, 4:333; Record Commissioners of Boston, *Town Records*, 19:85, 20:144, 25:246, 290; Bouton, *State Papers of New Hampshire*, 9:837, 18:546, 676–77, 20:542, 590, 636; Bartlett, *Records of Rhode Island*, 7:327, 338–39, 420, 495; John Avery to Isaiah Thomas, 30 April 1788, Isaiah Thomas Papers, American Antiquarian Society, Worcester, Mass.

8. Daniel J. Boorstin, *The Americans: The Colonial Experience* (New York: Random House, Inc., 1958), 337–40; Willard Grosvenor Bleyer, *Main Currents in the History of American Journalism* (Boston: Houghton Mifflin Company, 1927), 47–52; Sidney Kobre, *Development of American Journalism* (Dubuque, Ia.: William C. Brown Company, Publishers, 1969), 16; Wroth, *Colonial Printer*, 187–88; Jim Allee Hart, *The Developing Views on the News: Editorial Syndrome, 1500–1800* (Carbondale: Southern Illinois University Press, 1970), 95–96; Robert A. Rutland, *Newsmongers: Journalism in the Life of the Nation, 1690–1972* (New York: The Dial Press, 1973), 8–9; Arthur M. Schlesinger, *Prelude to Independence: The Newspaper War on Britain, 1764–1776* (New York: Alfred A. Knopf, 1958), 53; Frank Luther Mott, *American Journalism: A History of Newspapers in the United States Through 250 Years, 1690 to 1940* (New York: The MacMillan Company, 1962 [1941]), 60–63; Edwin Emery, *The Press and America: An Interpretative History of the Mass Media* (Englewood Cliffs, N.J.: Prentice-Hall, Inc., 1972 [1954]), 29, 37, 54; S. N. D. North, "The Newspaper and Periodical Press," *Tenth Census of the United States, 1880*, vol. 8 (Washington, D.C.: United States Government Printing Office, 1884), 12; Wallace Eberhard, "Press and Post Office in Eighteenth-Century America: Origins of a Public Policy," in *Newsletters to Newspapers: Eighteenth-Century Journalism*,

edited by Donovan H. Bond and W. Reynolds McLeod (Morgantown: School of Journalism, West Virginia University, 1977), 145–46, 151; Sidney Kobre, "The Revolutionary Colonial Press—A Social Interpretation," *Journalism Quarterly* 20 (1943): 199; Robert Wilson Kidder, "The Contribution of Daniel Fowle to New Hampshire Printing, 1756–1787" (Ph.D. dissertation, University of Illinois, 1960), 165–66; Lawrence C. Wroth, "The First Press in Providence," *Proceedings of the American Antiquarian Society* 51 (1941): 379.

9. *Massachusetts Spy*, 13 March 1777; *Newport Mercury*, 7 August 1784, 19 January 1786; *Providence Gazette*, 1779; Lincoln, *Provincial Congresses of Massachusetts*, 223; Bartlett, *Records of Rhode Island*, 7:352; Ebenezer Hazard to Isaiah Thomas, 4 March 1786, Certificate from United States Postmaster General to Isaiah Thomas, 2 December 1789, Isaiah Thomas Papers, American Antiquarian Society, Worcester, Mass.; Hugh Finlay, *Journal Kept by Hugh Finlay, Surveyor of the Post Roads on the Continent of North America, during His Survey of the Post Offices between Falmouth and Casco Bay in the Province of Massachusetts and Savannah in Georgia; begun the 13th September 1773 and ended 26th June 1774* (Brooklyn, N.Y.: Frank H. Norton, 1867), 16–17, 22–25, 30–33, 37, 40, 43, 46, 49, 54, 63, 67, 72, 74–75, 80, 85–86, 89, 91, 93–94; John C. Fitzpatrick, *The Spirit of the Revolution* (Boston: Houghton Mifflin Company, 1924), 244–46; "List of Postmasters, 1788," National Archives, *Papers of the Continental Congress, 1774–1789*, Microfilm—204 rolls (Washington, D.C.: National Archives, National Archives and Records Service, General Services Administration, 1958–1959), #61, items 587–588.

10. Eberhard, "Press and Post Office," 147–50; Oliver W. Holmes, "Shall Stagecoaches Carry the Mail?—A Debate of the Confederation Period," *William and Mary Quarterly* 20 (1963): 570–71; Ford, *Journals of Congress*, 34:144; *New Hampshire Spy*, 28 March and 11 April 1788; *Newport Mercury*, 19 May 1788; Walton, *Records of Vermont*, 3:45.

11. Clyde Augustus Duniway, *The Development of Freedom of the Press in Massachusetts* (Cambridge, Mass.: Harvard University Press, 1906), 104–30; Livingston R. Schuyler, *The Liberty of the Press in the American Colonies Before the Revolutionary War* (New York: Thomas Whittaker, 1905), 7–10, 72–76; Isaiah Thomas, *The History of Printing in America* (Worcester, Mass.: Isaiah Thomas, Jr., 1810; reprint ed. edited by Marcus A. McCorison, Barre, Mass.: Imprint Society, 1970), 5–6.

12. Zechariah Chafee, Jr., *Free Speech in the United States* (Cambridge, Mass.: Harvard University Press, 1941), 16–17; Leonard W. Levy, *Emergence of a Free Press* (New York: Oxford University Press, 1985), 173–74; Duniway, *Freedom of the Press in Massachusetts*, 132–36; Schuyler, *Liberty of the Press*, 76–78; Bernard A. Weisberger, *The American Newspaperman* (Chicago: University of Chicago Press, 1961), 55; Francis Newton Thorpe, ed. *The Federal and State Constitutions*, 7 vols. (Washington, D.C.: United States Government Printing Office, 1909), 1:537, 3:1647, 1892, 4:2456, 6:3244, 3741; General Court of Massachusetts, *The Perpetual Laws of the Commonwealth of Massachusetts, 1780–1788* (Worcester: Isaiah Thomas, 1788), 7; General Assembly of New Hampshire, *The Laws of the State of New-Hampshire* (Portsmouth: John Melcher, 1792), 26; Allen Soule, ed., *State Papers of Vermont*, 16 vols. (Montpelier: Secretary of State, 1964–1968), 12:10, 18.

13. *Independent Ledger*, 7 August 1780; *Norwich Packet*, 8 March 1781; *American Herald*, 3 April 1786; *American Mercury*, 8 May 1786; *Connecticut Journal*, 12 July 1786; *Continental Journal*, 3 August 1786; *New Hampshire Mercury*, 23 August 1786; *Newport Mercury*, 28 August 1786; *Vermont Journal*, 26 February 1787; *Massachusetts Spy*, 4 December 1788; *Cumberland Gazette*, 15 January 1789.

14. *Providence Gazette*, 2 February 1782; *Massachusetts Centinel*, 19 January 1785; *Continental Journal*, 20 January 1785; *American Herald*, 22 August 1785; *Salem*

Gazette, 23 August 1785; *American Mercury*, 29 August 1785; *Falmouth Gazette*, 3 September 1785; *Massachusetts Gazette*, 1 January 1788; *Herald of Freedom*, 15 September 1788.

15. Clifton O. Lawhorne, *Defamation and Public Officials: The Evolving Law of Libel* (Carbondale: Southern Illinois University Press, 1971), 1–37; Levy, *Emergence of a Free Press*, 7–9.

16. *Boston Gazette*, 4 February 1782; *Vermont Gazette*, 18 September 1783; *Independent Ledger*, 4 April 1785; *Massachusetts Gazette*, 7 October 1788; *Newport Mercury*, 17 November 1788.

17. *Boston Gazette*, 25 August 1777.

18. *Providence Gazette*, 15 February 1783; *Hampshire Herald*, 28 June 1785; *Continental Journal*, 14 July 1785; *New Hampshire Mercury*, 2 August 1785; *United States Chronicle*, 2 July 1789.

19. *New Hampshire Gazette*, 25 May 1776; *Massachusetts Spy*, 16 October 1783; *Independent Chronicle*, 1 January 1784; *Massachusetts Centinel*, 11 March 1784; *Exeter Chronicle*, 10 June 1784; *Boston Gazette*, 3 January 1785.

20. *New Hampshire Gazette*, 1 June 1776; *Salem Chronicle*, 30 March 1786; *New Hampshire Recorder*, 9 September 1788; *Herald of Freedom*, 11 December 1788.

21. "Massachusettensis" and "Novanglus" were the pen names of Daniel Leonard and John Adams, respectively. In 1774–1775, these two essayists engaged in a newspaper debate in the *Massachusetts Gazette* over the origins of the conflict with Great Britain. Leonard upheld the policies of the Crown, while Adams supported the actions of the colonies.

22. *New Hampshire Gazette*, 10 March 1775; *Boston Gazette*, 7 February 1780; *Providence Gazette*, 30 March 1782; *Vermont Gazette*, 13 March 1786; *Exchange Advertiser*, 6 July 1786; *American Herald*, 15 October and 17 December 1787, 21 August 1788; *Newport Herald*, 2 October 1788.

23. *Boston Gazette*, 25 September 1780, 7 January 1782; *New Haven Gazette*, 19 and 26 August 1784; *Cumberland Gazette*, 20 April 1786.

24. Clifford K. Shipton, *Isaiah Thomas: Printer, Patriot, and Philanthropist, 1749–1831* (Rochester, N.Y.: The Printing House of Leo Hart, 1948), 36; *Massachusetts Spy*, 3 November 1775; *New Haven Gazette*, 7 July 1785; *Connecticut Courant*, 12 December 1785; *Herald of Freedom*, 16 January 1789; *Boston Gazette*, 30 March 1789.

25. *Massachusetts Centinel*, 22 August 1787; *Herald of Freedom*, 27 February, 31 March, and 14 April 1789.

26. *New Hampshire Gazette*, 10 August 1776; *New Hampshire Gazette* (Exeter), 3 December 1776; *Massachusetts Spy*, 11 September 1777; *Boston Evening Post*, 9 February 1782; *Falmouth Gazette*, 5 February 1785; *New Haven Gazette*, 23 June 1785; *Cumberland Gazette*, 30 March 1786; *Vermont Gazette*, 4 February 1788.

27. Hench, "Newspaper in a Republic," 155–58; J. Eugene Smith, *One Hundred Years of Hartford's Courant: From Colonial Times Through the Civil War* (New Haven, Conn.: Yale University Press, 1949), 10; *Boston Gazette*, 18 May 1778, 28 May 1781, 23 June 1782, 3 October 1785; *Continental Journal*, 14 November 1782; *Independent Ledger*, 17 April 1786; *New Hampshire Mercury*, 30 August 1786; *Independent Chronicle*, 4 and 18 October 1787, 22 May and 11 and 18 December 1788; *Massachusetts Centinel*, 10 and 17 October 1787; *Essex Journal*, 3 December 1788; *Herald of Freedom*, 8, 11, and 15 December 1788, 17 March 1789.

28. *Independent Chronicle*, 29 August 1777, 14 August 1788; *Independent Ledger*, 3 December 1781; *Cumberland Gazette*, 13 April 1786; *Boston Gazette*, 28 January 1788.

29. Duniway, *Freedom of the Press in Massachusetts*, 131–32; Schuyler, *Liberty of the Press*, 21; Thomas, *History of Printing*, 319; *Newport Mercury*, 5 January 1780.

30. Levy, *Emergence of a Free Press*, 174–75, 177; Duniway, *Freedom of the Press in Massachusetts*, 131–32; John Tebbel, *The Compact History of the American Newspaper* (New York: Hawthorn Books, Inc., Publishers, 1963), 37–38, 51; Rutland, *Newsmongers*, 46–47; Charles L. Cutler, *Connecticut's Revolutionary Press* (Chester, Conn.: Pequot Press, 1975), 22–25.

31. Duniway, *Freedom of the Press in Massachusetts*, 131–32; Tebbel, *Compact History of the American Newspaper*, 37–38, 51; Rutland, *Newsmongers*, 46–47; Richard Buel, Jr., *Dear Liberty: Connecticut's Mobilization for the Revolutionary War* (Middletown, Conn.: Wesleyan University Press, 1980), 60; John Adams, *Papers of John Adams*, edited by Robert J. Taylor, Gregg L. Lunt, and Celeste Walker, 8 vols. to date (Cambridge, Mass.: Belknap Press of Harvard University Press, 1977–), 2:245; *Boston News-Letter*, 2 March 1775; *Independent Ledger*, 23 October 1780.

32. Levy, *Emergence of a Free Press*, 8, 14.

33. Duniway, *Freedom of the Press in Massachusetts*, 114–19, 130–32; Schuyler, *Liberty of the Press*, 14–21; Levy, *Emergence of a Free Press*, 16–18; Leonard W. Levy, "Did the Zenger Case Really Matter? Freedom of the Press in Colonial New York," *William and Mary Quarterly* 17 (1960): 38–43; Rutland, *Newsmongers*, 34–37; Thomas, *History of Printing*, 164–69, 251–53, 266–69; Donald L. Shaw and Stephen W. Brauer, "Press Freedom and War Constraints: Case Testing Siebert's Proposition II," *Journalism Quarterly* 46 (1969): 243–54.

34. Levy, *Emergence of a Free Press*, 174–75; Jere Daniell, *Experiment in Republicanism: New Hampshire Politics and the American Revolution, 1741–1794* (Cambridge, Mass.: Harvard University Press, 1970), 112; Hoadley and Labaree, *State Records of Connecticut*, 1:377; Record Commissioners of Boston, *Town Records*, 26:85; Bouton, *State Records of New Hampshire*, 8:24–27; *American Herald*, 30 October 1786; *Independent Chronicle*, 24 January 1788.

35. *Boston Gazette*, 5 August 1779; *Independent Ledger*, 15 December 1783; *American Herald*, 10 March 1788.

36. *Independent Chronicle*, 14 August 1788; *American Herald*, 4 September 1788.

37. Schuyler, *Liberty of the Press*, 21–22; *Boston Gazette*, 17 January 1785; *Massachusetts Centinel*, 19 January 1785; *Falmouth Gazette*, 22 January 1785; *Salem Gazette*, 25 January 1785; *American Herald*, 21 August 1788.

38. Duniway, *Freedom of the Press in Massachusetts*, 119–22, 136; Thomas, *History of Printing*, 259; Bleyer, *Main Currents in American Journalism*, 77; James Melvin Lee, *History of American Journalism* (Garden City, N.Y.: The Garden City Publishing Company, Inc., 1923 [1917]), 109–10; Emery, *The Press and America*, 15; Van Beck Hall, *Politics Without Parties: Massachusetts, 1780–1791* (Pittsburgh: University of Pittsburgh Press, 1972), 117.

Only Massachusetts passed a stamp act that affected newspapers. Virginia passed a stamp tax in 1784, but it dealt only with legal documents.

39. Joseph T. Buckingham, *Specimens of Newspaper Literature*, 2 vols. (Boston: Charles C. Little and James Brown, 1850), 1:33; *Essex Journal*, 6 April 1785; *Salem Gazette*, 19 April and 23 August 1785; *Exchange Advertiser*, 21 April 1785; *Massachusetts Centinel*, 4 May 1785; *Continental Journal*, 5 May 1785; *Falmouth Gazette*, 7 and 28 May, 6 June, and 3 September 1785; *Independent Ledger*, 9 May 1785; *Independent Chronicle*, 12 May 1785; *Norwich Packet*, 19 May 1785; *Vermont Gazette*, 11 July 1785; *American Herald*, 22 August 1785; *American Mercury*, 29 August 1785.

40. Punctuation in the last quote in this paragraph has been modernized in order to improve readability. *Salem Gazette*, 10 and 24 May and 23 August 1785; *Boston Gazette*, 16 and 23 May 1785; *Hampshire Herald*, 24 May 1785; *New Hampshire Mercury*, 24 May 1785; *Exchange Advertiser*, 18 August 1785; *American*

176   NOTES

Herald, 22 August 1785; *United States Chronicle,* 25 August 1785; *Connecticut Courant,* 29 August 1785; *American Mercury,* 29 August 1785; *Massachusetts Spy,* 1 September 1785; *Falmouth Gazette,* 3 September 1785.

41. *Continental Journal,* 8 April and 1 September 1785; *American Journal,* 19 April 1785; *Massachusetts Spy,* 21 April and 12 May 1785; *Essex Journal,* 11 May and 8 June 1785; *Plymouth Journal,* 17 May 1785; *Falmouth Gazette,* 21 May 1785; *Salem Gazette,* 30 August 1785.

42. Silver, "Aprons Instead of Uniforms," 177–79; Duniway, *Freedom of Press in Massachusetts,* 136–37; Lee, *History of American Journalism,* 110–11; Mott, *American Journalism,* 143–44; *American Herald,* 22 August 1785; *Salem Gazette,* 23 August 1785; *American Mercury,* 29 August 1785; *Falmouth Gazette,* 3 September 1785; *Independent Chronicle,* 20 April 1786; *Massachusetts Gazette,* 15 and 24 May and 5 June 1786; *Worcester Magazine,* first week in June 1786; *Continental Journal,* 8 June and 3 August 1786.

43. Buckingham, *Specimens of Newspaper Literature,* 1:34; Lee, *History of American Journalism,* 111; *Salem Gazette,* 2 August 1785; *Falmouth Gazette,* 17 September and 19 November 1785; *Essex Journal,* 9 November 1785; *American Recorder,* 23 December 1785.

44. Shipton, *Isaiah Thomas,* 42; Mott, *American Journalism,* 143–44; Handbill, published by Isaiah Thomas to announce end of *Massachusetts Spy,* 3 April 1786; *Essex Journal,* 19 April 1786; *Massachusetts Gazette,* 24 April 1786.

45. *Worcester Magazine,* fourth week in June 1786, fourth week in July 1786, first week in October 1786, fourth week in March 1787; *Continental Journal,* 3 August 1786, 21 June 1787; *Massachusetts Gazette,* 7 August 1786, 5 January 1787; *Hampshire Herald,* 26 September 1786; *American Herald,* 9 October 1786; *Boston Gazette,* 16 October 1786; *Independent Ledger,* 16 October 1786; *Essex Journal,* 18 October and 20 December 1786, 10 January 1787; *Continental Journal,* 19 October 1786.

46. John B. Hench, "Massachusetts Printers and the Commonwealth's Newspaper Advertisement Tax of 1785," *Proceedings of the American Antiquarian Society* 87 (1977): 199–211; Duniway, *Freedom of the Press in Massachusetts,* 137; Lee, *History of American Journalism,* 112; *American Herald,* 24 March 1788; *Massachusetts Gazette,* 25 March 1788; *Worcester Magazine,* fourth week in March 1788; *Massachusetts Spy,* 3 April 1788.

47. Richard Buel, Jr., "Freedom of the Press in Revolutionary America: The Evolution of Libertarianism, 1760–1820," in *The Press and the American Revolution,* edited by Bernard Bailyn and John B. Hench (Worcester, Mass.: American Antiquarian Society, 1980), 59–98; Hench, "Newspaper in a Republic," 183–87; Bill F. Chamberlin, "Freedom of Expression in Eighteenth-Century Connecticut: Unanswered Questions," in *Newsletters to Newspapers: Eighteenth-Century Journalism,* edited by Donovan H. Bond and W. Reynolds McLeod (Morgantown: School of Journalism, West Virginia University, 1977), 255; John Adams, *The Works of John Adams,* edited by Charles Francis Adams, 10 vols. (Boston: Little, Brown and Company, 1856), 7:182; *Independent Ledger,* 16 May 1785.

48. Dwight L. Teeter, Jr., "Decent Animadversions: Notes Toward a History of Free Press Theory," in *Newsletters to Newspapers: Eighteenth-Century Journalism,* edited by Donovan H. Bond and W. Reynolds McLeod (Morgantown: School of Journalism, West Virginia University, 1977), 242–43; Don Higginbotham, *The War of American Independence: Military Attitudes, Policies, and Practice, 1763–1789* (New York: MacMillan Publishing Company, Inc., 1971), 259–60; Levy, *Emergence of a Free Press,* 173; *New London Bee,* 3 September 1800, quoted by James Morton

Smith, "Political Suppression of Seditious Criticism: A Connecticut Case Study," *The Historian* 18 (1955): 56.

Chapter 6. The Press and Political Issues: A Time of Unity, 1775–1781

1. The landmark study in agenda-setting was done at the University of North Carolina School of Journalism by Maxwell E. McCombs and Donald L. Shaw. For this study, and other examples, see Maxwell E. McCombs and Donald L. Shaw, "The Agenda-Setting Function of Mass Media," *Public Opinion Quarterly* 36 (1972): 176–87; Maxwell E. McCombs and Donald L. Shaw, "Structuring the 'Unseen Environment,'" *Journal of Communication* 26 (1976): 18–22; Donald L. Shaw and Maxwell E. McCombs, *The Emergence of American Political Issues: The Agenda-Setting Function of the Press* (St. Paul, Minn.: West Publishing Co., 1977); Jane Lange Folkerts, "William Allen White's Anti-Populist Rhetoric as an Agenda-Setting Technique," *Journalism Quarterly* 60 (1983): 28–34.

2. During the Revolutionary era, republican concepts became the dominant ideology among American leaders. Increasingly disillusioned with the British monarchy, they sought to establish republican institutions as a means of acquiring a more suitable government. The newspapers provided a means to publicize and propagate these ideas among the American people. For discussions of growing support for republican ideas during the American Revolution, see Bernard Bailyn, *The Ideological Origins of the American Revolution* (Cambridge, Mass.: The Belknap Press of Harvard University Press, 1967); Pauline Maier, *From Resistance to Revolution: Colonial Radicals and the Development of American Opposition to Britain, 1765–1776* (New York: Alfred A. Knopf, 1972); Gordon S. Wood, *The Creation of the American Republic, 1776–1787* (Chapel Hill: Published for the Institute of Early American History and Culture, Williamsburg, Virginia, by the University of North Carolina Press, 1969).

3. For a discussion of the interaction of political ideas and public opinion following the adoption of the Constitution, see Richard Buel, Jr., *Securing the Revolution: Ideology in American Politics, 1789–1815* (Ithaca, N.Y.: Cornell University Press, 1972).

4. Sidney Kobre, "The Revolutionary Colonial Press—A Social Interpretation," *Journalism Quarterly* 20 (1943): 194; Lee Nathaniel Newcomer, *The Embattled Farmers: The Massachusetts Countryside in the American Revolution* (New York: King's Crown Press, 1953), 106; George Washington, *The Writings of George Washington, 1745–1799*, edited by John C. Fitzpatrick, 39 vols. (Washington, D.C.: United States Government Printing Office, 1931–1944), 13:483.

5. Kobre, "Social Interpretation of the Colonial Press," 202; Robert A. Rutland, *Newsmongers: Journalism in the Life of the Nation, 1690–1972* (New York: The Dial Press, 1973), 49; John Tebbel, *The Compact History of the American Newspaper* (New York: Hawthorn Books, Inc., Publishers, 1963), 53–54; J. Eugene Smith, *One Hundred Years of Hartford's Courant: From Colonial Times Through the Civil War* (New Haven, Conn.: Yale University Press, 1949), 33; Florence Parker Simister, *The Fire's Center: Rhode Island in the Revolutionary Era, 1763–1790* (Providence: Rhode Island Bicentennial Foundation, 1979), 107; Washington, *Writings*, 8:17; Nathaniel Greene, *The Papers of Nathaniel Greene*, edited by Richard K. Showman, Robert E. McCarthy, and Margaret Cobb, 5 vols. to date (Chapel Hill:

Published for the Rhode Island Historical Society by the University of North Carolina Press, 1976–), 2:75; *Boston Gazette*, 23 October and 11 December 1775, 22 April 1776, 19 January 1778, 18 June 1781; *Connecticut Courant*, 19 and 26 February and 4 and 11 March 1776; *New Hampshire Gazette*, 6 January 1786; *Independent Chronicle*, 16 January 1777, 15 January 1778; *Connecticut Gazette*, 29 June 1781.

 6. *New Hampshire Gazette*, 6 July 1776.

 7. Rutland, *Newsmongers*, 49; Tebbel, *American Newspaper*, 53–54; Smith, *Hartford's Courant*, 33; *Connecticut Courant*, 22 April 1776; *Massachusetts Spy*, 10 July 1776.

 8. *New England Chronicle*, 8 June 1775; *Boston Gazette*, 23 October 1775, 19 February 1776, 11 February 1782.

 9. *Connecticut Journal*, 23 August 1775.

 10. *Connecticut Journal*, 29 April 1775; *Newport Mercury*, 12 June 1775; *Boston Gazette*, 22 January 1776, 10 December 1779; *Connecticut Courant*, 2 July 1782.

 11. *Providence Gazette*, 22 April 1775; *Essex Journal*, 26 April 1775; *Massachusetts Spy*, 10 May 1775; *Independent Chronicle*, 12 October 1780.

 12. *Newport Mercury*, 29 May 1775, 25 March 1776; *Boston Gazette*, 14 August 1775; *New England Chronicle*, 28 September 1775; *Salem Gazette*, 6 December 1781.

 13. *Providence Gazette*, 10 January 1778; *American Journal*, 15 July 1779; *Salem Gazette*, 6 December 1781.

 14. *Providence Gazette*, 25 January 1777; *Massachusetts Gazette*, 13 May 1783.

 15. The Loyalists did not always receive their just due from contemporaries or historians, primarily because they lost. In New England, the Loyalists had little impact after the British evacuated Boston in March 1776. They became the brunt of bad jokes and were people to be hated. The Loyalists did not disappear, however. They continued to support the British government from areas the British had occupied and they sought to try and find another solution to the disagreements that produced the Revolutionary War. In this effort, they failed. For a discussion of the development and impact of Loyalist ideology during the American Revolution, see Janice Potter, *The Liberty We Seek: Loyalist Ideology in Colonial New York and Massachusetts* (Cambridge, Mass.: Harvard University Press, 1983); and Janice Potter and Robert M. Calhoon, "The Character and Coherence of the Loyalist Press," in *The Press and the American Revolution*, edited by Bernard Bailyn and John B. Hench (Worcester, Mass.: American Antiquarian Society, 1980), 229–72.

 16. *Newport Mercury*, 19 June 1775; Josiah Bartlett, *The Papers of Josiah Bartlett*, edited by Frank C. Mevers (Hanover, N.H.: University Press of New England for the New Hampshire Historical Society, 1979), 158.

 17. *New England Chronicle*, Fall 1975; *Connecticut Courant*, 8 April 1776.

 18. *Continental Journal*, 19 June 1783.

 19. *Essex Gazette*, 25 April 1775; *Essex Journal*, 26 April 1775; *Newport Mercury*, 8 May 1775; *Massachusetts Spy*, 23 January 1777; *American Journal*, 16 December 1779.

 20. Rutland, *Newsmongers*, 48–49; Charles Royster, *A Revolutionary People at War: The Continental Army and American Character, 1775–1783* (Chapel Hill: Published for the Institute of Early American History and Culture, Williamsburg, Virginia, by the University of North Carolina Press, 1979), 255–60; *Independent Chronicle*, 10 July 1777; *American Journal*, 16 December 1779; *Independent Ledger*, 24 August 1782.

 21. *Providence Gazette*, 29 March 1777; *New Hampshire Gazette*, 30 July 1781.

 22. Charles Royster, " 'The Nature of Treason': Revolutionary Virtue and

American Reactions to Benedict Arnold," *William and Mary Quarterly* 36 (1979): 163–93; *Boston Gazette*, 6 (supplement) and 13 November 1780; *American Journal*, 13 November 1780, 15 August 1781; *New Hampshire Gazette*, 20 August 1781; *Continental Journal*, 20 December 1781.

23. *New Hampshire Gazette*, 14 October 1780; *Massachusetts Spy*, 2 November 1780, 15 February, 13 September, and 25 October 1781; *Connecticut Courant*, 7 November 1780, 5 May 1782; *American Journal*, 13 November 1780; *Norwich Packet*, 21 November 1780, 7 June 1781; *Providence Gazette*, 29 November and 6 December 1780; *Vermont Gazette*, 9 July 1781; *Continental Journal*, 9 May 1782.

24. *Massachusetts Spy*, 28 June 1776, 25 October 1781; *Connecticut Gazette*, 5 and 12 December 1777, 30 January, 6 February, and 6 March 1778; *Connecticut Journal*, 24 December 1777, 7 January, 4 March, and 15 April 1778; *Norwich Packet*, 5 January 1778; *Connecticut Courant*, 24 February and 7 April 1778; *American Journal*, 13 May 1779, 12 July 1780; *Boston Evening Post*, 6 November 1779; *Providence Gazette*, 6 October 1781; *Boston Gazette*, 9 June 1783.

25. Richard Buel, Jr., *Dear Liberty: Connecticut's Mobilization for the Revolutionary War* (Middletown, Conn.: Wesleyan University Press, 1980), 86, 146, 257–58, 267–69; *New Hampshire Gazette*, 21 January 1777; *Boston Gazette*, 28 April 1777; *Norwich Packet*, 23 February 1778; Petition of the Tradesmen to the Merchants of Boston, 8 November 1779, Smith-Carter Family Papers, Massachusetts Historical Society, Boston, Mass.

26. Buel, *Dear Liberty*, 85, 146, 167–69; *Norwich Packet*, 30 June 1777; *Boston Gazette*, 12 January 1778, 15 May 1779, 24 December 1781; *Continental Journal*, 15 January 1778; *Independent Chronicle*, 12 March 1778, 7 May, 24 June, and 9 September 1779; *Connecticut Courant*, 4 August 1778, 13 April 1779, 17 and 31 July 1781; *Massachusetts Spy*, 8 July 1779; *Providence Gazette*, 21 August 1779; *American Journal*, 19 April 1780.

27. *New Hampshire Gazette*, 13 July 1776, 11 March 1785; *Independent Chronicle*, 2 January 1777, Summer, 16 December 1784; *Boston Gazette*, 2 June and 25 August 1777; *Connecticut Journal*, 15 March 1780, 22 December 1784; *Independent Ledger*, 29 August 1782; *Massachusetts Spy*, 1 August 1782; *Massachusetts Centinel*, 26 June, 10 July, and 9 October 1784; *New Haven Gazette*, 1 July 1784; *Exeter Chronicle*, 23 September 1784.

28. *Providence Gazette*, 17 May 1777; *Independent Chronicle*, 28 May 1778.

Chapter 7. The Press and Political Issues: Division between the States, 1782–1786

1. Ronald F. Banks, *Maine Becomes a State: The Movement to Separate Maine from Massachusetts, 1785–1820* (Middletown, Conn.: Wesleyan University Press for the Maine Historical Society, 1970), 10–25; *Falmouth Gazette*, 23 July, 20 August, 3 September, and 10 December 1785, 2 February 1786; *Cumberland Gazette*, 8 June 1787.

2. Charles E. Clark, *Maine: A Bicentennial History* (New York: W. W. Norton & Company, Inc., for the American Association for State and Local History, 1977), 75–76; Van Beck Hall, *Politics Without Parties: Massachusetts, 1780–1791* (Pittsburgh: University of Pittsburgh Press, 1972), 173–78; *Massachusetts Spy*, 30 June 1785; *Falmouth Gazette*, 2 July and 17 September 1785; *Salem Mercury*, 18 September 1787.

3. Charles T. Morrissey, *Vermont: A Bicentennial History* (New York: W. W.

Norton & Company, Inc., for the American Association for State and Local History, 1981), 88–100; Chilton Williamson, *Vermont in Quandary, 1763–1825* (Montpelier: Vermont Historical Society, 1949), 7–8, 112–13; *New Hampshire Gazette*, 8 December 1781; *Vermont Gazette*, 10 July, 14 August, 11 September, and 20 and 27 November 1783, 3 and 10 April and 12 July 1784, 22 May and 20 November 1786; *Vermont Journal*, 11 September 1783, 24 March, 14 and 28 April, and 30 November 1784.

4. *Vermont Gazette*, 26 June, 17 July, and 11 December 1783, 12 July 1784, 11 July 1785; *Massachusetts Centinel*, 29 December 1784; *Hampshire Herald*, 4 January 1785.

5. Jere Daniell, *Experiment in Republicanism: New Hampshire Politics and the American Revolution, 1741–1794* (Cambridge, Mass.: Harvard University Press, 1970), 124–25, 184–204; *New Hampshire Gazette*, 23 April and 22 September 1781, 25 May and 10 November 1782, 11 January, 29 March, 5 April, 5 July, 9 and 23 August, and 15 November 1783, 17 January, 7 February, and 27 March 1784, 22 July 1785, 18 March 1786; *New Hampshire Mercury*, 21 December 1785, 15 February 1786.

6. *New Hampshire Gazette*, 23 April and 29 September 1781, 2 March, 25 May, 20 July, and 10 and 24 August 1782, 7 June and 6 September 1783, 6 and 20 March 1784; *New Hampshire Mercury*, 22 March 1785.

7. *New Hampshire Gazette*, 25 January, 9 August, 6 September, and 15 November 1783, 27 March 1784; *New Hampshire Mercury*, 15 February and 24 May 1786.

8. David M. Roth, *Connecticut: A Bicentennial History* (New York: W. W. Norton & Company, Inc., for the American Association for State and Local History, 1979), 81–84; Richard Buel, Jr., *Dear Liberty: Connecticut's Mobilization for the Revolutionary War* (Middletown, Conn.: Wesleyan University Press, 1980), 172–79, 200, 211, 279–81, 297–314; Larry R. Gerlach, "Connecticut and Commutation, 1778–1784," *The Connecticut Historical Society Bulletin* 33 (1968): 51–58; Richard Buel, Jr., "Time: Friend or Foe of the Revolution?," in *Reconsiderations on the Revolutionary War: Selected Essays*, edited by Don Higginbotham (Westport, Conn.: Greenwood Press, 1978), 124–43; J. Eugene Smith, *One Hundred Years of Hartford's Courant: From Colonial Times Through the Civil War* (New Haven, Conn.: Yale University Press, 1949), 59–62; Christopher Collier, *Roger Sherman's Connecticut: Yankee Politics and the American Revolution* (Middletown, Conn.: Wesleyan University Press, 1971), 210–19.

9. On 10 March 1783 two unsigned petitions circulated among the officers at Newburgh. The first called for a meeting to discuss how to obtain satisfaction from Congress. The other declared that the officers' patience was at an end, and they would be justified in taking action. This "conspiracy" was defused by Washington's refusal to support it and his public condemnation of any plans against Congress or the Confederation. For more information concerning the Newburgh Conspiracy, see Richard H. Kohn, "The Inside History of the Newburgh Conspiracy: America and the Coup d'Etat," *William and Mary Quarterly* 27 (1970): 187–220.

10. E. James Ferguson, *The Power of the Purse: A History of American Public Finance, 1776–1790* (Chapel Hill: University of North Carolina Press, 1961), 155–67.

11. *Connecticut Gazette*, 9 May and 5 September 1783, 2 and 9 April 1784; *Connecticut Courant*, 3 and 24 June, 5 August, and 7 and 14 October 1783, 13 and 27 January and 23 March 1784; *American Mercury*, 6 December 1784.

12. *Connecticut Courant*, 13 May and 28 October 1783; Gordon S. Wood, *The*

Creation of the American Republic, 1776–1787 (Chapel Hill: Published for the Institute of Early American History and Culture, Williamsburg, Virginia, by the University of North Carolina Press, 1969), 488.

13. *Connecticut Courant*, 29 July, 12 August, 2, 9, 23, and 30 September, and 4 November 1783, 13 January, 3 February, 9 and 30 March, 6 April, and 5 May 1784; *Connecticut Gazette*, 2 and 9 April 1784; *Middlesex Gazette*, 20 March 1786; Smith, *Hartford's Courant*, 59.

14. *Connecticut Courant*, 25 November and 30 December 1783, 6 and 13 January and 13 April 1784.

15. *Connecticut Courant*, 13 January, 10 February, and 13 April 1784.

16. *Connecticut Courant*, 28 October 1783, 6 January 1784; Gerlach, "Connecticut and Commutation," 57.

17. Irvin H. Polishook, *Rhode Island and the Union, 1774–1795* (Evanston, Ill.: Northwestern University Press, 1969), 46–109.

18. Edmund C. Burnett, *The Continental Congress* (New York: The MacMillan Company, 1941), 480–81; Merrill Jensen, *The New Nation: A History of the United States during the Confederation, 1781–1789* (New York: Alfred A. Knopf, 1958), 58; Ferguson, *Power of the Purse*, 146; *Providence Gazette*, 23 February 1782.

19. Polishook, *Rhode Island and the Union*, 68–69; *Providence Gazette*, 25 January and 8 February 1783, 29 April 1786.

20. *Providence Gazette*, 19 January, 9 and 23 March, and 13 April 1782; *Newport Mercury*, 11 May 1782, 26 June 1784.

21. *Providence Gazette*, 16 and 30 March, 20 April, 20 July, 17 August, 21 September, and 19 October 1782, 11 October 1783, 29 April 1786; *Newport Mercury*, 11 May 1782, 26 June 1784.

22. *Providence Gazette*, 26 January, 23 and 30 March, 13 April, 3 August, 19 and 26 October, 2 November, and 28 December 1782, 11 January, 5 April, and 3 and 10 May 1783, 23 April 1785, 29 April 1786; *United States Chronicle*, 29 December 1785.

23. E. James Ferguson, "State Assumption of the Federal Debt during the Confederation," *Mississippi Valley Historical Review* 38 (1951): 413–14; *Providence Gazette*, 22 February 1783; *Connecticut Courant*, 6 April 1784; *United States Chronicle*, 8 July 1784.

24. *Providence Gazette*, 21 and 28 December 1782, 4, 11, and 18 January, and 1 February 1783; *United States Chronicle*, 4 and 11 January 1783.

25. *Providence Gazette*, 24 August and 21 September 1782, 15 February, 12 April, and 30 August 1783; *Newport Mercury*, 28 December 1782, 4 January 1783.

26. Polishook, *Rhode Island and the Union*, 53–80; *United States Chronicle*, 10 March 1785.

27. Polishook, *Rhode Island and the Union*, 110–20, 150–55; William G. McLoughlin, *Rhode Island: A Bicentennial History* (New York: W. W. Norton & Company, Inc., for the American Association for State and Local History, 1978), 100; *Providence Gazette*, 26 February 1785, 4 March, 20 May, 29 July, and 25 November 1786, 14 April 1787; *Newport Mercury*, 5 February and 12 March 1785, 7 and 21 August 1786, 10 April 1787, 15 May 1788, 8 January 1789; *United States Chronicle*, 3 March, 4 August, and 22 September 1785, 23 February, 2 and 16 March, 18 May, 1 and 22 June, 20 and 27 July, and 10 and 24 August 1786, 12 April 1787, 13 March 1788.

28. Polishook, *Rhode Island and the Union*, 118–19; Irvin H. Polishook, "Peter Edes's Report of the Proceedings of the Rhode Island General Assembly, 1787–1790," *Rhode Island History* 25 (1966): 33–42; *Providence Gazette*, 26 February 1785,

20 May, 29 July, and 25 November 1786; *United States Chronicle,* 3 March 1785, 23 February, 2 and 16 March, 18 May, 1 and 22 June, 20 and 27 July, and 24 August 1786; *Newport Mercury,* 12 March 1785, 21 August 1786; *Newport Herald,* 10 April 1787, 15 May 1788, 8 January 1789.

29. *United States Chronicle,* 22 September 1785, 23 February, 2 March, 27 July, and 10 August 1786, 12 April 1787, 13 March 1788; *Newport Mercury,* 7 and 21 August 1786.

30. Polishook, *Rhode Island and the Union,* 155–90; McLoughlin, *Rhode Island,* 100–6.

31. Richard D. Brown, *Massachusetts: A Bicentennial History* (New York: W. W. Norton & Company, Inc., for the Association for State and Local History, 1978), 102–28; Hall, *Politics Without Parties,* 94–184; John Bixler Hench, "The Newspaper in a Republic: Boston's *Centinel* and *Chronicle,* 1784–1801" (Ph.D. dissertation, Clark University, 1979), 147–50.

32. *Salem Gazette,* 21 August 1783; *Massachusetts Spy,* 30 December 1784; *Independent Ledger,* 31 October 1785.

33. *Massachusetts Centinel,* 7 May 1785; *Independent Chronicle,* 18 August 1785; *Independent Ledger,* 31 October 1785.

34. *Hampshire Herald,* 21 December 1784; *Massachusetts Centinel,* 9 April 1785; *Independent Chronicle,* 14 April 1785.

35. *Exchange Advertiser,* 8 April 1785.

36. *Continental Journal,* 18 April 1785; *Independent Ledger,* 10 October 1785; *Independent Chronicle,* 23 November 1786; *Boston Gazette,* 27 November 1786.

37. Charles Warren, "Samuel Adams and the Sans Souci Club in 1785," *Proceedings of the Massachusetts Historical Society* 60 (1927): 318–44; *Massachusetts Centinel,* 15, 22, 26, and 29 January, 12 and 19 February, and 2 March 1785; *American Herald,* 24 January and 7 February 1785; *Independent Chronicle,* 27 January and 18 August 1785; *Exchange Advertiser,* 17 and 24 February and 3 March 1785.

38. *Massachusetts Centinel,* 19 and 26 January and 16 February 1785; *Independent Chronicle,* 20 January 1785; *American Herald,* 14 February 1785; *Exchange Advertiser,* 24 February and 10 March 1785.

39. *Exchange Advertiser,* 24 February 1785.

40. *Massachusetts Spy,* 30 December 1784, 19 May and 28 July 1785; *Boston Gazette,* 17 January and 25 July 1785, 31 July 1786; *Essex Journal,* 30 March 1785; *Massachusetts Centinel,* 24 August 1785; *Independent Chronicle,* 23 November 1786.

41. *Massachusetts Spy,* 16 February 1786; *Independent Chronicle,* 27 July and 19 October 1786, 28 June 1787; *American Recorder,* 6 October 1786; *Worcester Magazine,* fourth week in August 1786.

42. Buel, *Dear Liberty,* 288–90; Rutland, *Newsmongers,* 55–56; Collier, *Roger Sherman's Connecticut,* 224–25; Simister, *The Fire's Center,* 231; Williamson, *Vermont in Quandary,* 112, 168–71; Daniell, *Experiment in Republicanism,* 196–99; Robert E. Brown, *Middle-Class Democracy and the Revolution in Massachusetts, 1691–1780* (Ithaca, N.Y.: Cornell University Press for the American Historical Association, 1955), 114–23, 184; Polishook, *Rhode Island and the Union,* 178; E. P. Walton, ed., *Records of the Governor and Council of the State of Vermont,* 8 vols. (Montpelier: J. & J. M. Poland, 1873–1880), 3:302–7, 366; *Massachusetts Gazette,* Summer of 1782, 22 June 1784; *Hampshire Herald,* 2 November 1784, 19 September 1786; *Worcester Magazine,* fourth week in September 1786, third week in December 1786; *Freeman's Oracle,* 26 September 1786; *Norwich Packet,* 5 October 1786; *Boston Gazette,* 23 October and 25 December 1786; *Vermont Journal,* 6 November 1786; *Independent Chronicle,* 24 May 1787.

There are numerous studies dealing with Shays's Rebellion. Among the best are Hall, *Politics without Parties*; Robert Taylor, *Western Massachusetts in the Revolution* (Providence, R.I.: Brown University Press, 1954); and David P. Szatmary, *Shays' Rebellion: The Making of an Agrarian Insurrection* (Amherst: University of Massachusetts, 1980).

43. *Massachusetts Gazette*, 25 August 1786, 5 October 1787; *Independent Chronicle*, 9 March and 15 and 29 June 1786, 18 January, 29 March, and 4 October 1787, 31 July 1788.

44. *Massachusetts Gazette*, 25 August 1786; *American Mercury*, 4 September 1786; *New Hampshire Mercury*, 6 September 1786; *Providence Gazette*, 9 September 1786; *Worcester Magazine*, third week in September 1786, fourth week in September 1786, fifth week in November 1786; *United States Chronicle*, 14 June 1787.

45. *Hampshire Gazette*, 6, 13, and 20 September, 4, 11, 18, and 25 October, 1, 8, 15, and 22 November, and 13 December 1786, 7 and 21 February and 14, 21, and 28 March 1787.

46. *Norwich Packet*, 2 November 1786; *Freeman's Oracle*, 31 March 1787; *Worcester Magazine*, first week of January 1787, first week of April 1787.

Chapter 8. The Press and Political Issues: Return to Common National Concerns, 1787–1789

1. Robert A. Rutland, *Newsmongers: Journalism in the Life of the Nation, 1690–1972* (New York: The Dial Press, 1973), 57; Irvin H. Polishook, "Peter Edes's Report of the Proceedings of the Rhode Island General Assembly, 1787–1790," *Rhode Island History* 25 (1966): 39; *American Herald*, 6 August and 1 October 1787.

2. *Massachusetts Centinel*, 4 April and 30 June 1787; *Connecticut Courant*, 28 May, 25 June, and 10 December 1787; *Independent Chronicle*, 9 August 1787; *Providence Gazette*, 11 August 1787.

3. Victor Rosewater, "The Constitutional Convention in the Colonial Press," *Journalism Quarterly* 14 (1937): 364–66; Jim Allee Hart, *The Developing Views on the News: Editorial Syndrome, 1500–1800* (Carbondale: Southern Illinois University Press, 1970), 169, 170, 171, 173; Willard Grosvenor Bleyer, *Main Currents in the History of American Journalism* (Boston: Houghton Mifflin Company, 1927), 102, 104; Frank Luther Mott, *American Journalism: A History of Newspapers in the United States Through 250 Years, 1690 to 1940* (New York: The MacMillan Company, 1962 [1941]), 131–32; Sidney Kobre, *Development of American Journalism* (Dubuque, Ia.: William C. Brown Company, Publishers, 1969), 106; Edwin Emery, *The Press and America: An Interpretative History of the Mass Media* (Englewood Cliffs, N.J.: Prentice-Hall, Inc., 1972 [1954]), 101; George Henry Payne, *History of Journalism in the United States* (New York: D. Appleton and Company, 1920), 146; Rutland, *Newsmongers*, 57–58; *New Hampshire Recorder*, 21 August 1787; *American Herald*, Fall 1787; *Salem Mercury*, Fall 1787; *Worcester Magazine*, December 1787, January 1788; *Hampshire Gazette*, 5 December 1787; *Newport Mercury*, 1788.

For a discussion of the circulation of *The Federalist Papers* outside of New York City, see Elaine F. Crane, "Publius in the Provinces: Where Was *The Federalist* Reprinted Outside New York City?" *William and Mary Quarterly* 21 (1964): 589–92.

4. *Massachusetts Centinel*, 13 June 1783; *New Hampshire Gazette*, 19 May 1787; *Providence Gazette*, 16 June 1787; *Middlesex Gazette*, 21 July 1788; Merrill Jensen, ed., *Ratification of the Constitution by the States: Delaware, New Jersey, Georgia, and Connecticut* (Madison: State Historical Society of Wisconsin, vol. 3 of *The Documentary History of the Ratification of the Constitution*, 1978), 471.

5. *Hampshire Gazette*, 10 October 1787; *Massachusetts Centinel*, 17 November 1787; *Connecticut Courant*, 16 July and 12 November 1787; *Independent Chronicle*, 19 July 1787; *American Herald*, 6 August and 30 September 1787; *United States Chronicle*, 27 September 1787; *American Mercury*, 8 October 1787; *New Hampshire Recorder*, 23 October 1787; *Boston Gazette*, 15 November 1787; *Newport Herald*, 3 July 1788.

"The Landholder" wrote thirteen essays that appeared simultaneously in the *Connecticut Courant* and the *American Mercury* between 5 November and 31 December 1787, and 3 and 24 March 1788. These essays circulated widely. All were reprinted in Connecticut an Rhode Island, seven in New Hampshire, and six in Massachusetts.

6. *Providence Gazette*, 24 February, 10 and 24 March, 7 July 1781.

7. John Bard McNulty, *Older than the Nation: The Story of the Hartford Courant* (Stonington, Conn.: The Pequot Press, Inc., 1964), 27; *Independent Chronicle*, 18 April 1782, 24 July 1783, 15 February 1787; *Exchange Advertiser*, 2 June 1785; *New Hampshire Spy*, 3 April 1787; John P. Kaminski and Gaspare J. Saladino, eds., *Commentaries on the Constitution, Public and Private*, vol. 1 (Madison: State Historical Society of Wisconsin, vol. 13 of *The Documentary History of the Ratification of the Constitution*, 1981), 76.

8. *American Mercury*, 6 September 1784, 11 September 1786; *Connecticut Courant*, 7 September 1784, 24 July 1786, 5 February, 19 March, and 6 August 1787; *Providence Gazette*, 11 September 1784; *Vermont Gazette*, 13 September 1784; *Boston Evening Post*, 13 September 1784; *Hampshire Herald*, 16 November 1784; *Exchange Advertiser*, 2 June 1785; *Independent Chronicle*, 9, 23, and 30 March, 7 and 20 April, 11, 18, and 25 May, and 1, 8, 15, and 22 June 1786; *New Hampshire Mercury*, 16 August 1786; *Worcester Magazine*, third week in May, third week in June 1786; *Boston Gazette*, 19 June 1786; *Independent Ledger*, 7 August 1786; *Freeman's Oracle*, 29 August and 5 September 1786; *Connecticut Gazette*, 8 September 1786; *New Hampshire Spy*, 6 February 1787; *Massachusetts Centinel*, 13 June 1787; *Norwich Packet*, 5 July 1787; Jensen, *Ratification of the Constitution*, 484.

9. *Independent Chronicle*, 2 June 1785; *New Hampshire Mercury*, 7 June 1785; *American Herald*, 9 March 1786; *Massachusetts Spy*, 9 March 1786; *Connecticut Gazette*, 21 April 1786; *Connecticut Courant*, 6 November 1786; *Providence Gazette*, 2 December 1786, 16 June 1787; *Continental Journal*, 3 January 1787; *Massachusetts Centinel*, 12 April 1788.

10. *Connecticut Gazette*, 28 April 1786; *Exchange Advertiser*, 22 June 1786; *Providence Gazette*, 30 December 1786; *New Hampshire Recorder*, 28 August 1787; Jensen, *Ratification of the Constitution*, 322, 402, 482; Kaminski and Saladino, *Commentaries on the Constitution*, 97, 148; Speech of Joel Barlow, 4 July 1787, excerpts recorded by Reverend Lemuel G. Olmstead, Joel Barlow Papers, American Antiquarian Society, Worcester, Mass.

Debates among historians concerning the efficacy of the Articles of Confederation has centered around the work of John Fiske. In 1898, he published *The Critical Period in American History*, in which he stated that the 1780s were the most critical era in American history because the Articles of Confederation were a bad form of government. Although Merrill Jensen questioned Fiske's conclusions in 1958 (*The New Nation: A History of the United States during the Confederation, 1781–1789*), most journalism historians have accepted Fiske's ideas. For examples, see Kobre, *Development of American Journalism*, 104; Mott, *American Journalism*, 118–19; Bleyer, *Main Currents*, 102; Payne, *History of Journalism*, 135–37; Frederic Hudson, *Journalism in the United States from 1690 to 1872* (New York: Harper &

Brothers, Publishers, 1873), 143–44; Hart, *The Developing Views on the News*, 168–69; Robert W. Jones, *Journalism in the United States* (New York: E. P. Dutton & Company, Inc., 1947), 149.

11. *New Hampshire Gazette*, 16 November 1787; *Massachusetts Centinel*, 1 December 1787.

12. *Massachusetts Centinel*, 10 November 1787, 9 January, 29 September, and 1 November 1788; *Boston Gazette*, 10 December 1787, 14 January 1788; *Connecticut Courant*, 31 December 1787; *Independent Chronicle*, 10 January and 5 June 1788.

13. *Independent Chronicle*, 4 October 1787; *Essex Journal*, 10 October 1787; *Boston Gazette*, 15 October 1787; *Massachusetts Centinel*, 20 October 1787, 7 May 1788; *Connecticut Gazette*, 26 October 1787; *Salem Mercury*, 30 October 1787; *American Mercury*, 31 December 1787; *Cumberland Gazette*, 24 January 1788; *New Hampshire Recorder*, 25 March 1788; Kaminski and Saladino, *Commentaries on the Constitution*, 563.

14. *Norwich Packet*, 2 November 1786; *Providence Gazette*, 4 November 1786; *New Hampshire Gazette*, 13 October 1787; *Connecticut Gazette*, 2 November 1787; *New Hampshire Mercury*, 1 November 1787; *Boston Gazette*, 12 November 1787; *American Mercury*, 21 January 1788; *Freeman's Oracle*, 13 December 1788.

15. *Independent Chronicle*, 8 and 22 November 1787; *Freeman's Journal*, 11 November 1787; *Providence Gazette*, 24 November and 8 December 1787, 29 March 1788; *Boston Gazette*, 3 December 1787; *American Herald*, 7 January 1788; *Freeman's Oracle*, 8 February 1788; *Newport Mercury*, 17 March 1788.

16. Practically all the Antifederalist pieces appeared in the *Independent Gazetteer* (Philadelphia), the *Freeman's Journal* (Philadelphia), the *Pennsylvania Evening Herald* (Philadelphia), the *New York Journal*, the *American Herald* (Boston), and the *Virginia Independent Chronicle* (Richmond). Although only a dozen papers were Antifederalist sheets, these publications stretched from Maine (Thomas B. Wait's *Cumberland Gazette*) to North Carolina.

Rutland, *Newsmongers*, 59, 62–63; Jackson Turner Main, *The Antifederalists: Critics of the Constitution, 1781–1788* (Chapel Hill: Published for the Institute of Early American History and Culture, Williamsburg, Virginia, by the University of North Carolina Press, 1961), 250–51; Robert A. Rutland, *The Ordeal of the Constitution: The Antifederalists and the Ratification Struggle of 1787–1788* (Norman: University of Oklahoma Press, 1965), 37–38, 72–74, 135, 138, 267.

17. John Bixler Hench, "The Newspaper in a Republic: Boston's *Centinel* and *Chronicle*, 1784–1801" (Ph.D. dissertation, Clark University, 1979), 157; *Freeman's Oracle*, 18 January 1787; *American Herald*, 15 October and 17 December 1787, 21 August 1788; *Boston Gazette*, 3 December 1787; *Providence Gazette*, 29 December 1787, 12 January 1788; *Newport Herald*, 2 October 1788; *New Hampshire Recorder*, 6 January 1789.

18. J. Eugene Smith, *One Hundred Years of Hartford's Courant: From Colonial Times Through the Civil War* (New Haven, Conn.: Yale University Press, 1949), 63–66; Judith Maxen Katz, "Connecticut Newspapers and the Constitution, 1786–1788," *The Connecticut Historical Society Bulletin* 30 (1965): 41; *Connecticut Courant*, 10 and 24 December 1787; *American Mercury*, 24 December 1787; *Independent Chronicle*, 3 January 1788.

19. Rutland, *Newsmongers*, 64–65; Main, *The Antifederalists*, 249–50; Rutland, *Ordeal of the Constitution*, 128–34; *Independent Chronicle*, 21 February 1788.

20. Christopher Collier, *Roger Sherman's Connecticut: Yankee Politics and the American Revolution* (Middletown, Conn.: Wesleyan University Press, 1971), 223; *New Haven Gazette, and Connecticut Magazine*, 8 February 1787; *Freeman's Oracle*, 29

February 1787, 8 November 1788; *Salem Mercury,* 7 August 1787; *Connecticut Courant,* 22 October 1787, 30 June 1788; *Boston Gazette,* 22 October 1787; *Hampshire Chronicle,* 25 December 1787, 9 July 1788; *New Hampshire Spy,* 8 and 11 January 1788; *Massachusetts Gazette,* 29 January 1788; *Norwich Packet,* 13 March 1788; *Connecticut Journal,* 9 July 1788.

21. *Massachusetts Centinel,* 9 January 1788.

22. Kaminski and Saladino, *Commentaries on the Constitution,* xxxvii; *Newport Herald,* 27 September 1787, 14 February 1788; *Connecticut Courant,* 26 November and 31 December 1787; *Independent Chronicle,* 10 January to 13 March 1788; *Boston Gazette,* 11 February, 12 May, 9 and 23 June, and 7 July 1788; *Essex Journal,* 13 February 1788; *Salem Mercury,* 10 June 1788; *Cumberland Gazette,* 26 June 1788; *New Hampshire Spy,* 24 June and 22 July 1788; *New Hampshire Gazette,* 26 June 1788; *Newport Mercury,* 30 June 1788; *Massachusetts Spy,* 10 July 1788.

23. Irvin H. Polishook, *Rhode Island and the Union, 1774–1795* (Evanston, Ill.: Northwestern University Press, 1969), 173, 195–96, 208, 211; *Newport Herald,* 12 April 1787, 26 March 1789; *United States Chronicle,* 1 November 1787; *Salem Mercury,* 15 January 1788; *Massachusetts Centinel,* 26 April and 20 August 1788; *Providence Gazette,* 4 and 23 August 1788; *New Hampshire Spy,* 26 August 1788; *Norwich Packet,* 8 October 1789; *Connecticut Journal,* 9 December 1789; *Connecticut Gazette,* 11 December 1789; *Newport Mercury,* 23 December 1789.

24. *Herald of Freedom,* 28 April 1789.

25. *Massachusetts Centinel,* 19 January 1788; *Connecticut Courant,* 3 March 1788; *New Haven Gazette, and Connecticut Magazine,* 19 June 1788; *American Mercury,* 14 July 1788; *Salem Mercury,* 3 March 1789.

Chapter 9. The Role of the Newspaper during the Revolutionary Era

1. Number of printers and newspapers based on summary of material gleaned from Clarence S. Brigham, ed., *History and Bibliography of American Newspapers, 1690–1820,* 2 vols. (Worcester, Mass.: American Antiquarian Society, 1947); Estate Inventory of Roger Storrs, 1820, Estate Inventory of Barzillai Hudson, 1823, Hartford Probate Records, Connecticut State Library, Hartford, Conn.

2. *New Hampshire Gazette,* 25 May 1776; *Providence Gazette,* 15 February 1783; *Independent Ledger,* 16 May 1785; *Plymouth Journal,* 17 May 1785; *Massachusetts Gazette,* 1 January 1788.

3. *American Herald,* 17 December 1787; *Providence Gazette,* 29 December 1787, 12 January 1788.

For discussions of the partisan newspaper press of the 1790s, see Donald H. Stewart, *The Opposition Press of the Federalist Period* (Albany: State University of New York Press, 1969); Sidney Kobre, *Development of American Journalism* (Dubuque, Ia.: William C. Brown Company, Publishers, 1969), 103–41; Jim Allee Hart, *The Developing Views on the News: Editorial Syndrome, 1500–1800* (Carbondale: Southern Illinois University Press, 1970), 178–96; Bernard A. Weisberger, *The American Newspaperman* (Chicago: The University of Chicago Press, 1961), 33–63; Edwin Emery, *The Press and America: An Interpretative History of the Mass Media* (Englewood Cliffs, N.J.: Prentice-Hall, Inc., 1972 [1954]), 99–127; Robert A. Rutland, *Newsmongers: Journalism in the Life of the Nation, 1690–1972* (New York: The Dial Press, 1973), 54–81; Willard Grosvenor Bleyer, *Main Currents in the History of American Journalism* (Boston: Houghton Mifflin Company, 1927), 100–

29; Frank Luther Mott, *American Journalism: A History of Newspapers in the United States Through 250 Years, 1690 to 1940* (New York: The MacMillan Company, 1962 [1941]), 113–64.

4. Arthur M. Schlesinger, *Prelude to Independence: The Newspaper War on Britain, 1764–1776* (New York: Alfred A. Knopf, 1958), 45–46; Philip Davidson, *Propaganda and the American Revolution, 1763–1783* (Chapel Hill: University of North Carolina Press, 1941), 225; Carl Bridenbaugh, *Cities in Revolt: Urban Life in America, 1743–1776* (New York: Alfred A. Knopf, 1955), 393; Sidney I. Pomerantz, "The Patriot Newspaper and the American Revolution," in *The Era of the American Revolution,* edited by Richard B. Morris (New York: Harper & Row, Publishers, 1965 [1939]), 331; Weisberger, *American Newspaperman,* 26–27; John Adams, *Diary and Autobiography of John Adams,* edited by Lyman H. Butterfield, 4 vols. (Cambridge, Mass.: Belknap Press of the Harvard University Press, 1961), 2:112, 4:156; Paul H. Smith, ed., *Letters of Delegates to Congress, 1774–1789,* 15 vols. to date (Washington, D.C.: Library of Congress, 1976–), 5:520; Frank Moore, ed., *The Diary of the American Revolution, 1775–1781* (New York: Washington Square Press, 1967), 518; *Providence Gazette,* 2 February 1782; *Massachusetts Centinel,* 19 January and 4 May 1785; *Salem Gazette,* 19 April and 23 August 1785; *Continental Journal,* 5 May 1785; *Independent Ledger,* 9 May 1785; *Norwich Packet,* 19 May 1785; *American Herald,* 22 August 1785; *American Mercury,* 29 August 1785; *Falmouth Gazette,* 3 September 1785; *Boston Gazette,* 16 October 1786.

5. Irvin H. Polishook, "Peter Edes's Report of the Proceedings of the Rhode Island General Assembly, 1787–1790," *Rhode Island History* 25 (1966): 39; Rutland, *Newsmongers,* 57.

6. Thomas Jefferson, *The Papers of Thomas Jefferson,* edited by Julian P. Boyd *et al.,* 24 vols. to date (Princeton, N.J.: Princeton University Press, 1950–), 11:47; *Worcester Magazine,* third week in May 1786.

7. The phrase "the 'second estate' " is from Flora Lewis, "Balancing Success, Independence: A Difficult Task for Fourth Estate," *Raleigh News and Observer,* 27 February 1985.

8. Gordon S. Wood, "The Democratization of Mind in the American Revolution," in *Leadership in the American Revolution,* edited by Don Higginbotham, Library of Congress Symposia on the American Revolution (Washington, D.C.: Library of Congress, 1974), 63–90.

9. Ambrose Serle, in charge of the Tory press in New York during the Revolution, described newspapers as "this popular engine" in a letter to Lord Dartmouth in 1776. Reproduced in Benjamin F. Stevens, *Facsimiles of Manuscripts in European Archives Relating to America, 1773–1783.* 24 vols. (London: Malby & Sons, 1889–1895), 24:2046.

Appendix 1: Content Survey

1. David J. Russo, "The Origins of Local News in the United States Country Press, 1840s–1870s," *Journalism Monographs* 65 (1980), and Donald L. Shaw, "At the Crossroads: Change and Continuity in American Press News, 1820–1860," Paper delivered at the 1981 Association for Education in Journalism Southeastern Regional Colloquium, Gainesville, Fl.

Bibliography

Primary Sources

NEWSPAPERS

The surviving newspapers for the period provided the major primary sources for this study. A complete list of them, as well as their printers and years of publication, is included in Appendix 2.

MANUSCRIPTS

American Antiquarian Society. Worcester, Massachusetts.
  Isaiah Thomas Papers.
  Joel Barlow Papers.
  New London, Connecticut, Tax Lists.
  Printers' File.
  Salisbury Family Papers.
  Worcester, Massachusetts, Collection.
  Worcester County, Massachusetts, Collection.
Connecticut Historical Society. Hartford, Connecticut.
  Harlow, Thompson R. "Connecticut's Contribution to Printing." An Article Prepared for the 500th Anniversary of Printing, November 1940.
  Brown, Ralph A. "The New Hampshire Press, 1775–1789." Typed Manuscript, 1954.
  Jeremiah Wadsworth Papers.
  Joseph Trumbull Papers.
  MS 73425. Isaiah Thomas to Samuel Avery, 12 November 1783.
Connecticut State Library. Hartford, Connecticut.
  Probate Records of Hartford, New Haven, New London, and Norwich.
Essex Institute. Salem, Massachusetts.
  John Mycall Letters.
Maine Historical Society. Portland, Maine.
  Andrew Hawes Collection: Titcomb Family Papers.
Massachusetts Historical Society. Boston, Massachusetts.
  Boston Printers Collection.
  Peter Edes. "Diary, June 19 to October 3, 1775."
  Smith-Carter Papers.
  Thomas B. Wait Letters.

William Cheever. "A Journal—Commencing May 19, 1775."
William Livingston Papers.
New York Historical Society. New York, New York.
Isaiah Thomas Letters.
Sterling Library, Yale University. New Haven, Connecticut.
Baldwin Family Papers.

PUBLISHED PRIMARY SOURCES

Adams, John. *Diary and Autobiography of John Adams.* Edited by Lyman H. Butterfield. 4 vols. Cambridge, Mass.: Belknap Press of the Harvard University Press, 1961.

———. *Papers of John Adams.* Edited by Robert J. Taylor, Gregg L. Lunt, and Celeste Walker. 8 vols. to date. Cambridge, Mass.: Belknap Press of Harvard University Press, 1977–.

———. *The Works of John Adams.* Edited by Charles Francis Adams. 10 vols. Boston: Little, Brown and Company, 1856.

Bartlett, John Russell, ed. *Records of the Colony of Rhode Island and Providence Plantations, 1636–1792.* 10 vols. Providence: State Printer, 1856–1865.

Bartlett, Josiah. *The Papers of Josiah Bartlett.* Edited by Frank C. Mevers. Hanover, N.H.: University Press of New England for the New Hampshire Historical Society, 1979.

Batchelor, Albert Stillman, ed. *Early State Papers of New Hampshire, 1784–1790.* Vols. 20–21 of Nathaniel Bouton *et al.*, eds. *State Papers of New Hampshire.* 40 vols. Nashua and elsewhere: State Printer, 1870–1895.

Baxter, James Phinney *et al.*, eds. *Documentary History of the State of Maine.* 24 vols. Portland: State Printer, 1869–1916.

Bouton, Nathaniel *et al.*, eds. *State Papers of New Hampshire.* 40 vols. Nashua and elsewhere: State Printer, 1870–1895.

Burnett, Edmund C., ed. *Letters of Members of the Continental Congress, 1774–1789.* 8 vols. Washington, D.C.: Carnegie Institution of Washington, 1921–1936.

Finlay, Hugh. *Journal Kept by Hugh Finlay, Surveyor of the Post Roads on the Continent of North America, during His Survey of the Post Offices between Falmouth and Casco Bay in the Province of Massachusetts and Savannah in Georgia, begun the 13th September 1773 and ended 26th June 1774.* Brooklyn, N.Y.: Frank H. Norton, 1867.

Ford, Worthington C. *et al.*, eds. *Journals of the Continental Congress, 1774–1789.* 34 vols. Washington, D.C.: United States Government Printing Office, 1904–1937.

General Assembly of New Hampshire. *The Laws of the State of New-Hampshire.* Portsmouth: John Melcher, 1792.

General Court of Massachusetts. *The Perpetual Laws of the Commonwealth of Massachusetts, 1780–1788.* Worcester: Isaiah Thomas, 1788.

Greene, Nathaniel. *The Papers of General Nathaniel Greene.* Edited by Richard K. Showman, Robert E. McCarthy, and Margaret Cobb. 5 vols. to date. Chapel Hill: Published for the Rhode Island Historical Society by the University of North Carolina Press, 1976–.

Hammond, Isaac, ed. *Documents Relating to Towns in New Hampshire.* Vol. 11 of

Nathaniel Bouton et al., eds. State Papers of New Hampshire. 40 vols. Nashua and elsewhere: State Printer, 1870–1895.

————. Rolls of the Soldiers in the Revolutionary War. Vols. 14–17 of Nathaniel Bouton et al., eds. State Papers of New Hampshire. 40 vols. Nashua and elsewhere: State Printer, 1870–1895.

Hoadley, Charles J., and Leonard W. Labaree, eds. The Public Records of the State of Connecticut. 6 vols. Hartford: State Printer, 1894–1945.

Hoadley, Charles J., and James H. Trumbull, eds. The Public Records of the Colony of Connecticut. 15 vols. Hartford: State Printer, 1850–1890.

Jefferson, Thomas. The Papers of Thomas Jefferson. Edited by Julian P. Boyd et al. 24 vols. to date. Princeton, N.J.: Princeton University Press, 1950–.

Jensen, Merrill, ed. Ratification of the Constitution by the States: Delaware, New Jersey, Georgia, and Connecticut. Madison: State Historical Society of Wisconsin. Vol. 3 of The Documentary History of the Ratification of the Constitution, 1978.

Kaminski, John P., and Gaspare J. Saladino, eds. Commentaries on the Constitution, Public and Private. Vol. 1. Madison: State Historical Society of Wisconsin. Vol. 13 of The Documentary History of the Ratification of the Constitution, 1981.

Lincoln, William, ed. The Journals of Each Provincial Congress of Massachusetts in 1774 and 1775. Boston: Dutton & Wentworth, State Printers, 1838.

Moore, Frank, ed. The Diary of the American Revolution, 1775–1781. New York: Washington Square Press, 1967.

National Archives. Papers of the Continental Congress, 1774–1789. Microfilm—204 Rolls. Washington, D.C.: National Archives, National Archives and Records Service, General Services Administration, 1958–1959.

Record Commissioners of Boston. Reports of the Record Commissioners of Boston— Town Records. 39 vols. Boston: City Printer, 1876–1909.

Smith, Paul H., ed. Letters of Delegates to Congress, 1774–1789. 15 vols. to date. Washington, D.C.: Library of Congress, 1976–.

Soule, Allen, ed. State Papers of Vermont. 16 vols. Montpelier, Vt.: Secretary of State, 1964–1968.

Spooner, Thomas, ed. Records of William Spooner of Plymouth, Massachusetts. Cincinnati: Press of F. W. Freeman, 1883.

Stevens, Benjamin F., ed. Facsimiles of Manuscripts in European Archives Relating to America, 1773–1783. 24 vols. London: Malby & Sons, 1889–1895.

Thorpe, Francis Newton, ed. The Federal and State Constitutions. 7 vols. Washington, D.C.: United States Government Printing Office, 1909.

U.S. Bureau of the Census. Historical Statistics of the United States, Colonial Times to 1970. 2 vols. Washington, D.C.: United States Department of Commerce, Bureau of the Census, 1975.

Walton, E. P., ed. Records of the Governor and Council of the State of Vermont. 8 vols. Montpelier, Vt.: J. & J. M. Poland, 1873–1880.

Washington, George. The Writings of George Washington, 1745–1799. Edited by John C. Fitzpatrick. 39 vols. Washington, D.C.: United States Government Printing Office, 1931–1944.

Secondary Sources

MONOGRAPHS

Bailyn, Bernard. *The Ideological Origins of the American Revolution.* Cambridge, Mass.: The Belknap Press of Harvard University Press, 1967.

Banks, Ronald F. *Maine Becomes a State: The Movement to Separate Maine from Massachusetts, 1785–1820.* Middletown, Conn.: Wesleyan University Press for the Maine Historical Society, 1970.

Barnes, Timothy M. "The Loyalist Press in the American Revolution, 1765–1781." Ph.D. dissertation, University of New Mexico, 1970.

Bleyer, Willard Grosvenor. *Main Currents in the History of American Journalism.* Boston: Houghton Mifflin Company, 1927.

Boorstin, Daniel J. *The Americans: The Colonial Experience.* New York: Random House, Inc., 1958.

Bridenbaugh, Carl. *Cities in Revolt: Urban Life in America, 1743–1776.* New York. Alfred A. Knopf, 1955.

———. *The Colonial Craftsman.* Chicago: University of Chicago Press, 1950.

———. *Mitre and Sceptre: Transatlantic Faiths, Ideas, Personalities, and Politics, 1689–1775.* New York: Oxford University Press, 1962.

Brigham, Clarence S., ed. *History and Bibliography of American Newspapers, 1690–1820.* 2 vols. Worcester, Mass.: American Antiquarian Society, 1947.

———. *Journals and Journeymen: A Contribution to the History of Early American Newspapers.* Philadelphia: University of Pennsylvania Press, 1950.

Brown, Richard D. *Massachusetts: A Bicentennial History.* New York: W. W. Norton & Company, Inc., for the Association for State and Local History, 1978.

Brown, Robert E. *Middle-Class Democracy and the Revolution in Massachusetts, 1691–1780.* Ithaca, N.Y.: Cornell University Press for the American Historical Association, 1955.

Buckingham, Joseph T. *Specimens of Newspaper Literature.* 2 vols. Boston: Charles C. Little and James Brown, 1850.

Buel, Richard, Jr. *Dear Liberty: Connecticut's Mobilization for the Revolutionary War.* Middletown, Conn.: Wesleyan University Press, 1980.

———. *Securing the Revolution: Ideology in American Politics, 1789–1815.* Ithaca, N.Y.: Cornell University Press, 1972.

Burnett, Edmund C. *The Continental Congress.* New York: The MacMillan Company, 1941.

Burrage, Henry S. *History of the Baptists in Maine.* Portland, Me.: Marks Printing House, Printers, 1904.

Chafee, Zechariah, Jr. *Free Speech in the United States.* Cambridge, Mass.: Harvard University Press, 1941.

Clark, Charles E. *Maine: A Bicentennial History.* New York: W. W. Norton & Company, Inc., for the American Association for State and Local History, 1977.

Collier, Christopher. *Roger Sherman's Connecticut: Yankee Politics and the American Revolution.* Middletown, Conn.: Wesleyan University Press, 1971.

Cranfield, G. A. *The Development of the Provincial Newspaper, 1700–1760.* Oxford: Clarendon Press, 1962.

Cutler, Charles L. *Connecticut's Revolutionary Press.* Chester, Conn.: Pequot Press, 1975.

Daniell, Jere. *Colonial New Hampshire: A History.* Millwood, N.Y.: KTO Press, 1981.

———. *Experiment in Republicanism: New Hampshire Politics and the American Revolution, 1741–1794.* Cambridge, Mass.: Harvard University Press, 1970.

Davidson, Philip. *Propaganda and the American Revolution, 1763–1783.* Chapel Hill: University of North Carolina Press, 1941.

Dexter, Franklin B. *Biographical Sketches of the Graduates of Yale College with Annals of the College History.* 6 vols. New York: H. Holt and Company, 1885–1912.

Duniway, Clyde Augustus. *The Development of Freedom of the Press in Massachusetts.* Cambridge, Mass.: Harvard University Press, 1906.

Emery, Edwin. *The Press and America: An Interpretative History of the Mass Media.* Englewood Cliffs, N.J.: Prentice-Hall, Inc., 1972 (1954).

Ferguson, E. James. *The Power of the Purse: A History of American Public Finance, 1776–1790.* Chapel Hill: University of North Carolina Press, 1961.

Fiske, John. *The Critical Period of American History.* Boston: Houghton Mifflin and Company, 1888.

Fitzpatrick, John C. *The Spirit of the Revolution.* Boston: Houghton Mifflin Company, 1924.

Franklin, Benjamin, V, ed. *Boston Printers, Publishers, and Booksellers, 1640–1800.* Boston: G. K. Hall & Company, 1980.

Greene, Evarts B., and Virginia D. Harrington. *American Population Before the Federal Census of 1790.* New York: Columbia University Press, 1932.

Griffin, Joseph. *History of the Press in Maine.* Brunswick, Me.: The Press, 1872.

Hall, Van Beck. *Politics Without Parties: Massachusetts, 1780–1791.* Pittsburgh: University of Pittsburgh Press, 1972.

Hamilton, Milton W. *The Country Printer: New York State, 1785–1830.* Port Washington, Long Island, N.Y.: Ira J. Friedman, Inc., 1964 (1936).

Hart, Jim Allee. *The Developing Views on the News: Editorial Syndrome, 1500–1800.* Carbondale: Southern Illinois University Press, 1970.

Hench, John Bixler. "The Newspaper in a Republic: Boston's *Centinel* and *Chronicle,* 1784–1801." Ph.D. dissertation, Clark University, 1979.

Higginbotham, Don. *The War of American Independence: Military Attitudes, Policies, and Practice, 1763–1789.* New York: MacMillan Publishing Company, Inc., 1971.

History of the Connecticut Valley in Massachusetts. 2 vols. Philadelphia: L. H. Everts, 1879.

Howe, Gilman Bigelow. *Genealogy of the Bigelow Family in America.* Worcester, Mass.: C. Hamilton, 1890.

Hudson, Frederic. *Journalism in the United States from 1690 to 1872.* New York: Harper & Brothers, Publishers, 1873.

Jensen, Merrill. *The New Nation: A History of the United States during the Confederation, 1781–1789.* New York: Alfred A. Knopf, 1958.

Jones, Robert W. *Journalism in the United States.* New York: E. P. Dutton & Company, Inc., 1947.

Kerber, Linda K. *Women of the Republic: Intellect and Ideology in Revolutionary*

America. Chapel Hill: Published for the Institute of Early American History and Culture, Williamsburg, Virginia, by the University of North Carolina Press, 1980.

Kidder, Robert Wilson. "The Contribution of Daniel Fowle to New Hampshire Printing, 1756–1787." Ph.D. dissertation, University of Illinois, 1960.

Kobre, Sidney. *Development of American Journalism.* Dubuque, Ia.: William C. Brown Company, Publishers, 1969.

Lawhorne, Clifton O. *Defamation and Public Officials: The Evolving Law of Libel.* Carbondale: Southern Illinois University Press, 1971.

Lee, James Melvin. *History of American Journalism.* Garden City, N.Y.: The Garden City Publishing Company, Inc., 1923 (1917).

Levy, Leonard W. *Emergence of a Free Press.* New York: Oxford University Press, 1985.

Lockridge, Kenneth A. *Literacy in Colonial New England: An Enquiry into the Social Context of Literacy in the Early Modern West.* New York: W. W. Norton & Company, Inc., 1974.

Lunt, Thomas S. *A History of the Lunt Family in America.* Salem, Mass.: The Salem Press Company, 1914.

McLoughlin, William G. *Rhode Island: A Bicentennial History.* New York: W. W. Norton & Company, Inc., for the American Association for State and Local History, 1978.

McMurtrie, Douglas C. *The Beginnings of the American Newspaper.* Chicago: The Black Cat Press, 1935.

McNulty, John Bard. *Older than the Nation: The Story of the Hartford Courant.* Stonington, Conn.: The Pequot Press, Inc., 1964.

Maier, Pauline. *From Resistance to Revolution: Colonial Radicals and the Development of American Opposition to Britain, 1765–1776.* New York: Alfred A. Knopf, 1972.

Main, Jackson Turner. *The Antifederalists: Critics of the Constitution, 1781–1788.* Chapel Hill: Published for the Institute of Early American History and Culture, Williamsburg, Virginia, by the University of North Carolina Press, 1961.

———. *The Social Structure of Revolutionary America.* Princeton, N.J.: Princeton University Press, 1965.

Meder, Marylouise Dunham. "Timothy Green III, Connecticut Printer, 1737–1796: His Life and Times." Ph.D. dissertation, University of Michigan, 1964.

Morrisey, Charles T. *Vermont: A Bicentennial History.* New York: W. W. Norton & Company, Inc., for the American Association for State and Local History, 1981.

Morse, Jarvis Means. *Connecticut Newspapers in the Eighteenth Century.* New Haven, Conn.: Published for the Tercentenary Commission of the State of Connecticut by the Yale University Press, 1935.

Mott, Frank Luther. *American Journalism: A History of Newspapers in the United States Through 250 Years, 1690 to 1940.* New York: The MacMillan Company, 1962 (1941).

Newcomer, Lee Nathaniel. *The Embattled Farmers: The Massachusetts Countryside in the American Revolution.* New York: King's Crown Press, 1953.

Norton, Mary Beth. *Liberty's Daughters: The Revolutionary Experience of American Women, 1750–1800.* Boston: Little, Brown and Company, 1980.

Oswald, John Clyde. *Printing in the Americas.* New York: The Gregg Publishing Company, 1937.

Payne, George Henry. *History of Journalism in the United States.* New York: D. Appleton and Company, 1920.

Polishook, Irvin H. *Rhode Island and the Union, 1774–1795.* Evanston, Ill.: Northwestern University Press, 1969.

Potter, Janice. *The Liberty We Seek: Loyalist Ideology in Colonial New York and Massachusetts.* Cambridge, Mass.: Harvard University Press, 1983.

Roth, David M. *Connecticut: A Bicentennial History.* New York: W. W. Norton & Company, Inc., for the American Association for State and Local History, 1979.

Royster, Charles. *A Revolutionary People at War: The Continental Army and American Character, 1775–1783.* Chapel Hill: Published for the Institute of Early American History and Culture, Williamsburg, Virginia, by the University of North Carolina Press, 1979.

Rutland, Robert A. *Newsmongers: Journalism in the Life of the Nation, 1690–1972.* New York: The Dial Press, 1973.

———. *The Ordeal of the Constitution: The Antifederalists and the Ratification Struggle of 1787–1788.* Norman: University of Oklahoma Press, 1965.

Schlesinger, Arthur M. *Prelude to Independence: The Newspaper War on Britain, 1764–1776.* New York: Alfred A. Knopf, 1958.

Schuyler, Livingston R. *The Liberty of the Press in the American Colonies Before the Revolutionary War.* New York: Thomas Whittaker, 1905.

Scott, Donald M. *From Office to Profession: The New England Ministry.* Philadelphia: University of Pennsylvania Press, 1978.

Shaw, Donald L., and Maxwell E. McCombs. *The Emergence of American Political Issues: The Agenda-Setting Function of the Press.* St. Paul, Minn.: West Publishing Company, 1977.

Shipton, Clifford K. *Isaiah Thomas: Printer, Patriot, and Philanthropist, 1749–1831.* Rochester, N.Y.: The Printing House of Leo Hart, 1948.

———, ed. *Sibley's Harvard Graduates: Biographical Sketches of Those Who Attended Harvard College.* 17 vols. Cambridge, Mass.: Harvard University Press, 1933–1975.

Silver, Rollo G. *The American Printer, 1787–1825.* Charlottesville: University Press of Virginia, 1967.

———. *Typefounding in America, 1787–1825.* Charlottesville: University Press of Virginia, 1965.

Simister, Florence Parker. *The Fire's Center: Rhode Island in the Revolutionary Era, 1763–1790.* Providence: Rhode Island Bicentennial Foundation, 1979.

Smith, J. Eugene. *One Hundred Years of Hartford's Courant: From Colonial Times Through the Civil War.* New Haven, Conn.: Yale University Press, 1949.

Spargo, John. *Anthony Haswell: Printer—Patriot—Ballader.* Rutland, Vt.: The Tuttle Company, 1925.

Stewart, Donald H. *The Opposition Press of the Federalist Period.* Albany: State University of New York Press, 1969.

Streeter, Gilbert L. *An Account of the Newspapers and Other Periodicals Published in Salem, from 1768 to 1865.* Salem, Mass.: William Ives and George W. Pease, Printers, 1856.

Szatmary, David P. *Shays' Rebellion: The Making of an Agrarian Insurrection.* Amherst: University of Massachusetts Press, 1980.

Taylor, Robert. *Western Massachusetts in the Revolution*. Providence, R.I.: Brown University Press, 1954.

Tebbel, John. *The Compact History of the American Newspaper*. New York: Hawthorn Books, Inc., Publishers, 1963.

Thomas, Isaiah. *The History of Printing in America*. Worcester, Mass.: Isaiah Thomas, Jr., 1810; reprint ed. edited by Marcus A. McCorison, Barre, Mass.: Imprint Society, 1970.

Weeks, Lyman Horace. *A History of Paper-Manufacturing in the United States, 1690–1916*. New York: The Lockwood Trade Journal Company, 1916.

Weisberger, Bernard A. *The American Newspaperman*. Chicago: University of Chicago Press, 1961.

Wetherell, Charles Wheeler. "Brokers of the Word: An Essay in the Social History of the Early American Press, 1639–1783." Ph.D. dissertation, University of New Hampshire, 1980.

Williamson, Chilton. *Vermont In Quandary, 1763–1825*. Montpelier: Vermont Historical Society, 1949.

Wood, Gordon S. *The Creation of the American Republic, 1776–1787*. Chapel Hill: Published for the Institute of Early American History and Culture, Williamsburg, Virginia, by the University of North Carolina Press, 1969.

Wroth, Lawrence C. *Abel Buell of Connecticut: Silversmith, Type Founder, & Engraver*. Middletown, Conn.: Wesleyan University Press, 1958.

———. *The Colonial Printer*. Portland, Me.: The Southworth-Anthoensen Press, 1938.

Wyman, Thomas B. *The Genealogies and Estates of Charlestown, Massachusetts*. 2 vols. Boston: D. Clapp and Son, 1879.

ARTICLES

Bates, Albert Carlos. "Fighting the Revolution with Printer's Ink in Connecticut: The Official Printing of that Colony from Lexington to the Declaration." *Papers of the New Haven Colony Historical Society* 9 (1918): 129–60.

———. "Thomas Green." *Papers of the New Haven Colony Historical Society* 8 (1914): 289–309.

———. "Some Notes on Early Connecticut Printing." *Papers of the Bibliographical Society of America* 27 (1933): 1–11.

Botein, Stephen. " 'Meer Mechanicks' and an Open Press: The Business and Political Strategies of Colonial American Printers." *Perspectives in American History* 9 (1975): 127–225.

———. "Printers and the American Revolution." In *The Press and the American Revolution*, edited by Bernard Bailyn and John B. Hench, 11–58. Worcester, Mass.: American Antiquarian Society, 1980.

Brown, Ralph Adams. "New Hampshire Editors Win the War: A Study in Revolutionary Press Propaganda." *New England Quarterly* 12 (1939): 35–51.

Brown, Richard D. "From Cohesion to Competition." In *Printing and Society in Early America*, edited by William L. Joyce, David D. Hall, Richard D. Brown, and John B. Hench, 303. Worcester, Mass.: American Antiquarian Society, 1983.

Buel, Richard, Jr. "Freedom of the Press in Revolutionary America: The Evolution of Libertarianism, 1760–1820." In *The Press and the American Revolution*, edited by Bernard Bailyn and John B. Hench, 59–98. Worcester, Mass.: American Antiquarian Society, 1980.

———. "Time: Friend or Foe of the Revolution?" In *Reconsiderations on the Revolutionary War: Selected Essays*, edited by Don Higginbotham, 124–43. Westport, Conn.: Greenwood Press, 1978.

Chamberlin, Bill F. "Freedom of Expression in Eighteenth-Century Connecticut: Unanswered Questions." In *Newsletters to Newspapers: Eighteenth-Century Journalism*, edited by Donovan H. Bond and W. Reynolds McLeod, 247–62. Morgantown: School of Journalism, West Virginia University, 1977.

Crane, Elaine F. "Publius in the Provinces: Where Was *The Federalist* Reprinted Outside New York City?" *William and Mary Quarterly* 21 (1964): 589–92.

Dawes, Norman H. "Titles as Symbols of Prestige in Seventeenth-Century New England." *William and Mary Quarterly* 6 (1949): 69–83.

"Early Paper Mills in Massachusetts and New England." *Massachusetts Magazine* 10 (1917): 179–83.

Eberhard, Wallace. "Press and Post Office in Eighteenth-Century America: Origins of a Public Policy." In *Newsletters to Newspapers: Eighteenth-Century Journalism*, edited by Donovan H. Bond and W. Reynolds McLeod, 145–54. Morgantown: School of Journalism, West Virginia University, 1977.

Edgett, Edward Frances. "Edes, Benjamin." *Dictionary of American Biography*. 10 vols. New York: Charles Scribner's Sons, 1927–1936, vol. 3(pt. 2): 17–18.

Fassett, Frederick G., Jr. "Maine's First Newspaper." In *A History of Maine: A Collection of Readings on the History of Maine, 1600–1976*, 4th ed., edited by Ronald F. Banks, 154–60. Dubuque, Ia.: Kendall/Hunt Publishing Company, 1976 [1969].

Ferguson, E. James. "State Assumption of the Federal Debt during the Confederation." *Mississippi Valley Historical Review* 38 (1951): 403–24.

Folkerts, Jean Lange. "William Allen White's Anti-Populist Rhetoric as an Agenda-Setting Technique." *Journalism Quarterly* 60 (1983): 28–34.

Gerlach, Larry R. "Connecticut and Commutation, 1778–1784." *The Connecticut Historical Society Bulletin* 33 (1968): 51–58.

Graffagnino, J. Kevin. " 'We Have Long Been Wishing For a Good Printer in This Vicinity': The State of Vermont, the First East Union and the Dresden Press, 1778–1779." *Vermont History* 47 (1979): 21–36.

Greene, Jack P. "Review of *Mitre and Sceptre*." *William and Mary Quarterly* 20 (1963): 597–602.

Hench, John B. "Massachusetts Printers and the Commonwealth's Newspaper Advertisement Tax of 1785." *Proceedings of the American Antiquarian Society* 87 (1977): 199–211.

Henry, Susan. "Work, Widowhood and War: Hannah Bunce Watson, Connecticut Printer." *The Connecticut Historical Society Bulletin* 48 (1983): 25–39.

Holmes, Oliver M. "Shall Stagecoaches Carry the Mail?—A Debate of the Confederation Period." *William and Mary Quarterly* 20 (1963): 555–73.

Jacobsen, Edna L. "Southwick, Solomon." *Dictionary of American Biography*. 10 vols. New York: Charles Scribner's Sons, 1927–1936, vol. 9(pt. 1):413–14.

Katz, Judith Maxen. "Connecticut Newspapers and the Constitution, 1786–1788." *The Connecticut Historical Society Bulletin* 30 (1965): 33–44.

Kiessel, William C. "The Green Family: A Dynasty of Printers." *New England Historical and Genealogical Register* 104 (1950): 81–93.

Kobre, Sidney. "The Revolutionary Colonial Press—A Social Interpretation." *Journalism Quarterly* 20 (1943): 193–204.

Kohn, Richard H. "The Inside History of the Newburgh Conspiracy: America and the Coup d'Etat." *William and Mary Quarterly* 27 (1970): 187–220.

Kulikoff, Alan. "The Progress of Inequality in Revolutionary Boston." *William and Mary Quarterly* 28 (1971): 375–412.

Levy, Leonard W. "Did the Zenger Case Really Matter? Freedom of the Press in Colonial New York." *William and Mary Quarterly* 17 (1960): 38–43.

Lewis, Flora. "Balancing Success, Independence: A Difficult Task for Fourth Estate." *Raleigh News and Observer,* 27 February 1985.

McCombs, Maxwell E., and Donald L. Shaw. "The Agenda-Setting Function of Mass Media." *Public Opinion Quarterly* 36 (1972): 176–87.

———. "Structuring the 'Unseen Environment.'" *Journal of Communication* 26 (1976): 18–22.

McCorison, Marcus A. "Vermont Papermaking, 1784–1820." *Vermont History* 31 (1963): 209–45.

Marsh, Philip M. "Maine's First Newspaper Editor: Thomas Wait." *New England Quarterly* 28 (1955): 519–34.

Miller, Frank W. "The *New Hampshire Gazette.*" *New England Historical and Genealogical Register* 26 (1872): 132–40.

Moody, Robert Earle, and Charles Christopher Crittenden. "The Letter-Book of Mills & Hicks." *North Carolina Historical Review* 14 (1937): 39–83.

Murrin, John M. "The Legal Transformation: The Bench and Bar of Eighteenth-Century Massachusetts." In *Colonial America: Essays in Politics and Social Development,* 3rd ed., edited by Stanley N. Katz and John M. Murrin, 540–71. New York: Alfred A. Knopf, 1983.

Nichols, Charles L. "Fowle, Daniel." *Dictionary of American Biography.* 10 vols. New York: Charles Scribner's Sons, 1927–1936, vol. 3(pt. 2): 560–61.

Nordell, Philip Gardiner. "Vermont's Early Lotteries." *Vermont History* 35 (1967): 35–71.

North, S. N. D. "The Newspaper and Periodical Press." *Tenth Census of the United States, 1880.* vol. 8. Washington, D.C.: United States Government Printing Office, 1884.

Polishook, Irvin H. "Peter Edes's Report of the Proceedings of the Rhode Island General Assembly, 1787–1790." *Rhode Island History* 25 (1966): 33–42.

Pomerantz, Sidney I. "The Patriot Newspaper and the American Revolution." In *The Era of the American Revolution,* 2nd ed., edited by Richard B. Morris, 305–31. New York: Harper & Row, Publishers, 1965 [1939].

Potter, Janice and Calhoon, Robert M., "The Character and Coherence of the Loyalist Press." In *The Press and the American Revolution,* edited by Bernard Bailyn and John B. Hench, 229–72. Worcester, Mass.: American Antiquarian Society, 1980.

Quimby, Ian M. G. "Introduction: Some Observations on the Craftsman in Early America." In *The Craftsman in Early America,* edited by Ian M. G. Quimby, 3–16. New York: W. W. Norton and Company for the Henry Francis du Pont Winterthur Museum, 1984.

Robertson, Marion. "The Loyalist Printers: James and Alexander Robertson." *Nova Scotia Historical Review* 3 (1983): 83–93.

Rosewater, Victor. "The Constitutional Convention in the Colonial Press." *Journalism Quarterly* 14 (1937): 364–66.

Royster, Charles. " 'The Nature of Treason': Revolutionary Virtue and American Reactions to Benedict Arnold." *William and Mary Quarterly* 36 (1979): 163–93.

Russo, David J. "The Origins of Local News in the United States Country Press, 1840s–1870s." *Journalism Monographs* 65 (1980).

Schlereth, Thomas J. "Artisans and Craftsmen: A Historical Perspective." In *The Craftsman in Early America*, edited by Ian M. G. Quimby, 34–61. New York: W. W. Norton and Company for the Henry du Pont Winterthur Museum, 1984.

Scott, Frank W. "Russell, Benjamin." *Dictionary of American Biography*. 10 vols. New York: Charles Scribner's Sons, 1927–1936, vol. 8(pt. 2): 238–40.

Shaw, Donald L. "At the Crossroads: Change and Continuity in American Press News, 1820–1860." Paper delivered at the 1981 Association for Education in Journalism Southeastern Regional Colloquium, Gainesville, Florida.

Shaw, Donald L., and Stephen W. Brauer. "Press Freedom and War Constraints: Case Testing Siebert's Proposition II." *Journalism Quarterly* 46 (1969): 243–54.

Silver, Rollo G. "Abstracts from the Wills and Estates of Boston Printers, 1800–1825." *Studies in Bibliography* 7 (1955): 212–18.

———. "Aprons Instead of Uniforms: The Practice of Printing, 1776–1787." *Proceedings of the American Antiquarian Society* 87 (1977): 111–94.

———. "Benjamin Edes, Trumpeter of Sedition." *Papers of the Bibliographical Society of America* 47 (1953): 248–68.

———. "Government Printing in Massachusetts: 1751–1801." *Studies in Bibliography* 16 (1963): 161–200.

Smith, James Morton. "Political Suppression of Seditious Criticism: A Connecticut Case Study." *The Historian* 18 (1955): 41–56.

Spargo, John. "Early Vermont Printers and Printing." *Proceedings of the Vermont Historical Society* 10 (1942): 214–21.

Spaulding, E. Wilder. "The *Connecticut Courant*, a Representative Newspaper in the Eighteenth Century." In *Selected Readings in the History of American Journalism*, edited by Edwin H. Ford, 81–91. Minneapolis: University of Minnesota, 1939.

Stewart, J. J. "Early Journalism in Nova Scotia." *Nova Scotia Historical Society Collections* 6 (1888): 118–20.

Syrett, David. "Town-Meeting Politics in Massachusetts, 1776–1786." *William and Mary Quarterly* 21 (1964): 352–66.

Tanselle, G. Thomas. "Some Statistics on American Printing, 1764–1783." In *The Press and the American Revolution*, edited by Bernard Bailyn and John B. Hench, 315–64. Worcester, Mass.: American Antiquarian Society, 1980.

Teeter, Dwight L., Jr. "Decent Animadversions: Notes Toward A History of Free Press Theory." In *Newsletters to Newspapers: Eighteenth-Century Journalism*, edited by Donovan H. Bond and W. Reynolds McLeod, 237–46. Morgantown: School of Journalism, West Virginia University, 1977.

———. "Press Freedom and the Public Printing: Pennsylvania, 1775–1783." *Journalism Quarterly* 45 (1968): 445–51.

Waite, Emma Forbes. "Benjamin Dearborn: Teacher, Inventor, Philanthropist." *Old Time New England* 42 (1951): 44–47.

Warren, Charles. "Samuel Adams and the Sans Souci Club in 1785." *Proceedings of the Massachusetts Historical Society* 60 (1927): 318–44.

Weissbuch, Ted N. "A Chapter in Vermont's Revolutionary War Finance." *Vermont History* 29 (1961): 3–12.

Whiting, William. "Paper Making in New England." In *The New England States*, 3 vols., edited by William T. Davis, 3:303–33. Boston: D. H. Hurd, & Company, 1897.

Williams, Samuel C. "George Roulstone, Father of the Tennessee Press." *The East Tennessee Historical Society's Publications* 17 (1945): 51–60.

Wood, Gordon S. "The Democratization of Mind in the American Revolution." In *Leadership in the American Revolution,* edited by Don Higginbotham, 63–90. Library of Congress Symposia on the American Revolution. Washington, D.C.: Library of Congress, 1974.

Wroth, Lawrence C. "The First Press in Providence." *Proceedings of the American Antiquarian Society* 51 (1941): 351–83.

Yodelis, Mary Ann. "Who Paid the Piper? Publishing Economics in Boston, 1763–1775." *Journalism Monographs* 38 (1975).

Index